MOTO MV
AGUSTA

MARIO COLOMBO   ROBERTO PATRIGNANI

MOTO MV AGUSTA

a history of the marque
from the birth to the renaissance
with a complete catalogue of both production
and racing models

GIORGIO NADA EDITORE

Giorgio Nada Editore s.r.l.

Editorial coordination
Antonio Maffeis

English translation
Alasdair McEwen
Neil Davenport (updating)

Graphics and layout
Guido Regazzoni
Ufficio grafico Giorgio Nada Editore
(cover and updating)

Photographic material
Bonetti-Photo MIX
Giorgio Boschetti
Cagiva Archive
Mario Colombo
The "MV Agusta" Museum
B.R. Nicholls
Tim Parker
Roberto Patrignani
Terreni
Franco Zagari (photographers E. Scipi and F. Zagari)

Acknowledgements
The authors and the publisher wish to thank all those who made significant contribution to the production of this book: Guido Boracchi, Lucio Castelli, Carlo Donchi, Ubaldo Elli, Fortunato Libanori, Arturo Magni, Ruggero Mazza, Brizio Pignacca, Mario Rossi, Enrico Sironi, Bruno Taglioretti, Carlo Ubbiali.

The catalogue of Giorgio Nada Editore publications is available at the following address:
Giorgio Nada Editore, via Claudio Treves 15/17,
20090 Vimodrone (MI) - Italy
Tel. ++39/2/27301126 - Fax ++39/2/27301454

CONTENTS

Preface

Ten years ago Edizioni della Libreria dell'Automobile published the first edition of this history of MV Agusta by Mario Colombo and Roberto Patrignani. Subsequently, in 1991, with Edizioni della Libreria dell'Automobile having in the meantime been transformed into the current Giorgio Nada Editore, a second edition was printed to satisfy the great demand from enthusiasts wishing to see the history and sporting triumphs of their favourite marque celebrated in precious images and authoritative text. This reprint added little new to the legend that been created in the aftermath of MV Agusta Corse's liquidation in 1986, an episode which seemed to have put a definitive full stop to the industrial, sporting and cultural activities of a unique marque and to have consigned it to the memories of enthusiasts throughout the world. And yet the great wheel of history has taken a highly unexpected turn that has led to an MV renaissance.

With the publication of this revised and corrected edition of Colombo and Patrignani's book we are, in fact, paying tribute to a legend that is about rise from the ashes. This latest edition finds space for the heir to the MV Agustas of old, the MV Agusta F4 that on the occasion of its presentation in the September of this year not only lent strength and new vigour to the MV legend, but with its technological and stylistic features is aiming to set the agenda for the future development of the motorcycle industry.

The merit for this epic operation lies with Cagiva and the indefatigable Castiglioni brothers. In the spring of 1992 the Varese-based company acquired the celebrated marque from the heirs of Agusta family. A tradition was revived with the intention of taking it a long way in the years to come. In fact, on the evening of the 15th of September this year, Claudio Castiglioni unveiled the MV F4 and immediately afterwards took the new-born machine to the Milan Motorcycle Show where it received enthusiastic and unanimous approval. Today, then, tracing the history of MV Agusta is not simply a matter of paying tribute to a motorcycling legend of the highest order, but also of bring to the attention of the biking public at large the newfound currency of a symbol of Italian creativity known and appreciated throughout the world.

On the international scene MV is probably unique in that it was an enterprise born to reconvert to peacetime production an aircraft factory and that, with its period of prosperity having drawn to a close, not only survived in the face of business logic but actually increased in fame as the commercial side became ever less profitable. What profits were being made were of a spiritual nature as the firm had been transformed into the hobby and perhaps even the life's work of its founder, Count Domenico Agusta. No other manufacturer was so completely dominated by the will of a single man upon whom everything and everyone depended. It was Count Domenico who decided which models were to be built, who dictated their technical and aesthetic characteristics, who established production and sales schedules, who recruited collaborators, who effectively ran the racing programme, who chose the riders and who determined the targets to be reached. A paternal dictator figure it might be said, one who today would be somewhat out of place and who would not easily adapt to modern business methods, but, for all his defects, the only man capable of achieving results in the highly specialised world of racing in which wasting time over interminable discussions, no matter how democratic they may have been, would have meant the difference between success and failure. The MV company, and in particular its competition record, was inseparably bound up with the name of Count Domenico Agusta; and it was no coincidence that the company virtually passed away along with its patron. On the death of the count, MV sank into the decline shared by other companies; a series of board meetings, demands for profitability, economic difficulties to be overcome by pruning the dead wood and the rescuing but suffocating embrace of the state with its cold and impersonal bureaucracy that cared nothing for the glories of the past and the honour to be defended. Of the MV firm all that remained were the enthusiasts' memories and the small museum organised with loving care by the former, those who contributed with their enthusiasm, labour and sacrifices to the company's success. This was the state of affairs up until 1997, the year in which in "miraculous" circumstance the powerful MV roar was heard once again.

Giorgio Nada

PART ONE

INDUSTRY AND SPORT

The technology
The races
The riders

MV IS BORN

Believe it or not the first MV was a... Vespa. It first saw the light in the dark days of the last few months of World War II, when an inevitable defeat was staring the Italians in the face and the more far-sighted among them had already realized that it was time to start thinking about how to replace the enormous but plainly doomed structure that was wartime industrial production.

At that time the MV marque still lay in the future: what did exist on the other hand was the "Costruzioni Aeronautiche Giovanni Agusta", a firm that built aeroplanes in a place called Cascina Costa di Verghera, which is not far from Milan, between Gallarate and Malpensa to be precise. The founder of this concern was a Sicilian aristocrat called Count Giovanni Agusta who had been an authentic pioneer of aviation and one of the very first Italians to follow the trail blazed by the Wright brothers: his first plane dates from 1907, before Blériot's celebrated Channel crossing therefore and before Chavez's sublime but tragic conquest of the Alps.

When the first World War broke out Giovanni Agusta enrolled in the Primo Battaglione Aviatori (First Aviation Battalion), a unit that had its headquarters in Malpensa. As soon as the war was over, he set up his first factory in the same place and promptly began producing aeroplanes on an industrial scale.

Giovanni Agusta died suddenly in 1927, aged only 48. He left control of the works, a well established concern by then, in the hands of his widow, the Countess Giuseppina, and his eldest son, Domenico. The latter was a young man blessed with a blend of his father's entrepreneurial spirit and leadership skills allied to passionate enthusiasm. He was to play a major role in the subsequent rise of the MV marque.

Domenico Agusta began manufacturing motorcycles as a response to the exigencies of the moment, but he soon found that this lucrative activity allowed him to indulge in the passions of his youth once more: these could be summed up as motorcycles, mechanical engineering and motorsport. His commitment to sport was enormous and he poured vast sums of money into this activity in a determined attempt to establish the predominance of his marque over its competitors. Nor should we neglect his purely aesthetic instincts, which took concrete form in the styling concepts he occasionally obliged his associates to accept, even when the designs were distinctly heterodox and somewhat less than convincing.

And so, MV maintained its presence – as well as its winning ways – on circuits everywhere, while continuing to churn out a steady stream of new models, even when sales slumped almost to vanishing point at the end of the Fifties. This drop in sales was due to the general crisis that assailed the motorcycle market on the one hand, and – it's useless to deny it – because of some rather unsuccessful creations on the other. To persist in this policy of constant renewal was to fly in the face of all industrial and economic logic, but this merely underlines the fact that Count Domenico's enthusiasm had completely gained the upper hand over any considerations he may have had regarding mere profit. MV had become the hobby of a man who, although he had re-established the family fortunes in the world of aviation, nevertheless seemed to get more satisfaction from his activities in the motorcycle industry. This was all partly due to the cold and dehumanized nature of the modern aircraft industry, which had quite lost the adventurous glamour of the pioneering days and those "daring young men in their flying machines". Fortunately, that same glamour remained more or less intact in the world of motorcycle racing where, despite everything, the machine was yet to overwhelm the man, and where there was still room not only for courage but also for skill, improvisational ability, intelligence and, for want of a better word, soul. But all this is "jumping the gun", and we ought to return to that unexpected Vespa. The year was 1943, the situation was worsening daily despite the optimistic noises being made by the propaganda machine and it was necessary to find a timely outlet for the production capacities of the aircraft factories. The motorcycle seemed like a solution: when the war finally finished people were sure to have more need than ever before of a reliable means of transport, also because personnel cuts and industrial decentralization had led to the birth of that characteristic modern figure, the commuter. But public transport systems were virtually non-existent while motor cars had been swallowed up by the furnace of the war. And who could afford a car anyway? That left the bicycle, it's true, but this means of transport, such a wonderful device from a sporting point of view, is a lot less wonderful when you have to pump the pedals for miles and miles every day up hill and down dale, burdened

Celebrating a win, a scene which was to be repeated many times in the history of MV, the racing marque par excellence. This is a symbolic picture because it portrays both constructors and riders, the architects of so many victories. From the left, Count Domenico Agusta and his brother Mario, with Carlo Ubbiali and Umberto Masetti.

with the shopping or maybe just tired after a hard day, or sleepy after a bad night.

The motorcycle was liable to interest a lot of people therefore: but not the roaring monster it had been up to then, good only for reckless youths or the ultra-sporty; what was needed was a simple little machine whose modest appearance and performance could inspire the uninitiated with sufficient confidence to swing themselves into the saddle and have a go.

By the August of 1943 the de-sign of the engine was already complete and work had be-gun on the construction of the foundry models. The pro-pulsion unit was a very simple affair, as indeed was the whole motorcycle: a 98 cm^3 two-stroke single with three ports, geared primary drive, wet clutch and unit construc-tion 2-speed gearbox. No flights of fancy here to con-fuse potential clients, but tried and tested design aimed at inspiring confidence and ensuring a long lifetime of honest service without fre-quent visits to the garage.

After the eighth of Septem-ber the Germans occupied the factory and so all the drawings and models of the new bike were hidden in the houses of trusted engineers and factory hands. About half way through 1944, the military presence having be-come a little less suffocating, everything was brought back to the factory and work be-gan again at such a spanking rate that the engine coughed into life for the first time only a few months later.

However the difficulties were by no means over, and major obstacles presented them-selves owing to the quasi total shortage of materials and components, especially elec-trical parts and tyres. Fly-wheel magnetos were scraped up from here and there, while tyres were acquired from a little works in Cassano Mag-nago, which was run by em-ployees of the large tyre man-ufacturing concerns. These "factories" were usually es-tablished in the basements of their owners' houses, in a sort of no man's land between part-time work and the black market.

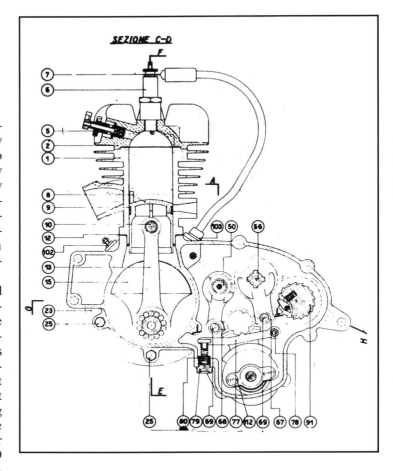

SEZIONE C-D

However the factory managed to carry on in a fairly regular fashion, so much so that on the 12th of February 1945 a limited company known as Meccanica Verghera was set up for the twin purpose of bringing the motorcycle project to a conclusion and launching it on the market.

Finally the war finished and the moment came to introduce the new product to the public. And so, in the autumn of 1945 the trade papers published the official announcement and the first photographs of the new light motorcycle. It was a pleasing and well proportioned little machine with a rigid tubular frame, girder forks and 19 inch wheels. A prominent position on the petrol tank was reserved for the trade mark, which had the letters M and V within a winged cog wheel, while the little windscreen attached to the front mudguard bore the name of the model: Vespa (Wasp) 98, a jaunty, light hearted choice that seemed both auspicious and perfectly suited to the product.

What the managers at MV did not know was that the name Vespa had already been registered by another manufacturer, and so they had to give up their first choice in favour of the distinctly more humdrum "MV

The prototype of the MV engines, in a faded drawing from the period. It was an undersquare 2-stroke unit with a cylinder capacity of 98 cm³, two transfer ports and a 2-speed unit gearbox.

One of the many rustic races organized after the war. This simple, rough and ready world was the cradle of MV racing, which went on to become one of the world's legendary teams.

98". However we still have some rare and yellowing period photographs that testify to the original name and prove that the first (in a chronological sense, at least) Vespa to appear in the world of motorcycles was a product of the Verghera factory.

The commercial launch followed a few months afterwards. The first agents were Egidio Conficoni and Vincenzo Nencioni, two Tuscans who had enjoyed brilliant sporting careers, especially in trials competition. They accepted orders for the new bike in a little shop they had hastily constructed amid what

was left of Milan's piazza Fontana where, in the shadow of the city's famous cathedral, they displayed the willingness to roll up their sleeves and get down to some good honest toil that had been the hallmark of the city before the war and is the driving force that has made it the hugely prosperous place it is today.

Minor modifications had been made to the light motorcycle here and there and it was available in two versions: the Economica, which like the Vespa prototype had a rigid frame and a 2-speed gearbox; and the Turismo,

with telescopic rear suspension units and a 3-speed gearbox. The latter version proved so overwhelmingly popular with the public that before long the other variant was discontinued.

Deliveries began in the summer of 1946 and a good rhythm was soon established. At the same time MV launched an export drive and it was not long before its product was known and appreciated on the international market. Just for the record we should add that in 1946 about fifty units were produced, all export models, with Filso magneto ignition

12

rather than a flywheel system, because it had proved impossible to find a sufficient number of the latter devices. The little bike made a name for itself right away, in a fiercely competitive period in which many new marques were coming into being (although just as many disappeared almost as rapidly as they had arrived) and innovation was the order of the day. Not only did the newcomer win over utility bike buyers,

as it was meant to, it also won a following among the sporting fraternity.

Motorcycle sport had made a splendid recovery, despite the many difficulties peculiar to the immediate post-war period: obstacles regarding the issue of permits, fuel rationing, and a shortage of decent racing machines. But people's enthusiasm, which had been bottled up over years of enforced abstinence (the last race had been held

in May 1940, in Genoa), was unbounded and the desire to unload all that pent-up emotion was almost tangible.

Competitions were instantly organized for all those new machines that were springing up like mushrooms: mopeds (or better, "micromotors" as they were called at the time), light and ultra-light motorcycles, were often subdivided into classes that were based on the various models on the market, rather than the clas-

sic criteria based on engine capacity. Like the scooter competitions, for example, or those for the famous Guzzi 65s.

Given this abundance of events, most of which were organized any old how by people whose enthusiasm was only matched by their inexperience, held in an atmosphere redolent of a country fair with little or no official blessing, it is not easy today to establish the first race in which

an MV took part; but what is sure is that the first wins date from the autumn of 1946 when Vincenzo Nencioni, the brand new marque's dynamic general agent, took first place in a trials event held in La Spezia on the 6th of October. There was another win in a speed event at Valenza a week later when Mario Cornalea won and Nencioni took third place; another first place was notched up at Alessandria on the following Sunday, when Cornalea won again. Finally a team made up of the usual Nencioni and Cornalea, aided and abetted by Mario Paleari, won another trials event held at Monza on the 3rd of November.

The construction of a real racing model soon became virtually obligatory as far as MV was concerned and in fact the matter was given prompt attention. Even though it was a direct descendant of the model we have already come across, the racing MV that first saw the light at the end of 1946 could boast quite a few innovations, which gave it a very elegant look apart from anything else. That this was so was due in particular to the telescopic forks, one of the first units of its kind to be fitted as standard in Italy, and one which lent a modern touch to the entire bike. The frame was still a tubular single-loop cradle with telescopic rear suspension, but it had been shortened by 5 centimetres in order to improve handling; the straight, narrow handlebars, the rearsets and the pad on the partially faired rear mudguard combined to ensure a decidedly sporty riding position. The fuel tank had been slightly enlarged to increase the range. Minor modifications

Motor scooter racing was very popular just after the war. The photo shows Massimo Masserini and Masetti with their Lambretta Bs (53 and 51) and Carlo Ubbiali with the MV four- speeder as they wait for the off in Bergamo in 1949.

had been made to the engine in the interests of improved performance: the size of the ports and the compression ratio were different while a new 20mm horizontal carburettor was fitted. At 5400 rpm the engine supplied about 5 hp, enough to propel the bike to 95 km/h. This was nothing to get excited about in an absolute sense, but it was a pretty good result for those days. Ignition was still by flywheel magneto and the 3-speed gearbox had the same ratios as the standard models: 19.5 - 11.5 - 8:1. The light alloy wheels were shod with 2.50-19" tyres and carried lateral drum brakes. A bright shade of red was chosen for the paintwork. Telescopic forks were also fitted to the touring models and so, as the 2-speed gearbox and the unsprung frame had been discarded, production was now made up of three models, all fully sprung with 3-speed gearboxes: the Normale (Standard) had girder forks; the Lusso (De Luxe) had telescopic forks and the Sport was as described previously. In the meantime, workers were putting the final touches to the production lines at Cascina Costa and by the end of 1946 the factory was already capable of producing thirty units a day: nearly as many as all the factories in pre-war Italy rolled into one!

The 98 cm³ class, however, was doomed to make an early exit, at least from the circuit racing scene where, after the anarchic improvisation of the early days, there was a move back to the traditional half-, quarter- and one eighth-litre capacity classes. In 1948 the Italian speed championships once more had a 125 class. This had existed twenty years before but it had been killed off by the collapse of the light motorcycle market that had followed the abolition of the various fiscal and burocratic advantages that had encouraged its popularity in the first place. To tell the truth the organizations responsible for motorsport were rather sceptical about the 125 class's chances of success, as is revealed by the fact that they opened it to riders from all categories, out of the conviction that otherwise there would have been too few entries. Instead the first event, at Casale Monferrato, attracted more than fifty entrants, proof of the importance that the smaller bikes had once more acquired. The field had to be ruthlessly thinned out by means of a series of qualifying trials; but that's not all, the industry also took a direct interest, having understood the potential publicity value of such events.

And so, the lineup at Casale Monferrato included teams from the two marques that were then market leaders in that class (Morini and, naturally, MV) as well as amateurs mounted on pre-war bikes. Morini could count on battle-hardened veterans with loads of experience like Raffaele Alberti, who had set out on his long career twenty years before, on light motorcycles funnily enough (he al-

Countess Giuseppina Agusta surrounded by her sons, in a photo from the early Fifties: Corrado, the youngest, Domenico, Vincenzo, who worked in the sales division, and Mario, the coordinator of the Group.

15

so set several world records during a spell with the Guzzi works team). Franco Bertoni was the star of the MV team. He was a youngster from the Varese area who had made his sporting debut only a year before, but had given instant proof of his mettle.

The race was won by Alberti, whose long experience enabled him to snatch victory from Bertoni who had to be content with second place after a spill had cost him vital seconds. Thus a rivalry was born between the two marques that was to keep the enthusiasm of the fans at fever pitch for years to come. A short time afterwards Mondial came along to complicate matters for both rivals, but more about that later. At this point we ought to leave the world of motorsport for a while and take a brief step further back to 1947 and the Milan Motor Cycle Show, a popular showcase where the major manufacturers always displayed their latest models. A newcomer to the market, MV immediately demonstrated the vitality and drive of its managerial and design staff: a brace of new models was put on show alongside the pre-existing 98 cm³ machine, which was shown in the Nor-

male, Lusso and Sport variants: a 125 cm³ 2-stroke twin and a 4-stroke 250 single. These were two very different bikes whose very dissimilarity testified to the marque's extreme flexibility and the fact that it was not about to let mere economic considerations colour its thinking overmuch.

Effectively speaking, to launch a new bike in the 250 class, which was an economically restricted sector dominated by established names like Guzzi, Gilera and Sertum, called for a good deal of courage; and the same held good for the little twin, which

Road racing used to be extremely popular and all the major manufacturers took part, with MV scoring numerous wins. Top left, Remo Rosati aboard the 125 4-speeder at the nighttime start of the 1952 Milano-Taranto event. Above, the engine from a competition Quattro Cilindri 500 on the test bench in 1950.

16

MV also took an interest in trials competition, with brilliant results. Right, Mario Ventura – Gold Medallist at the 1952 Six Days event – with the 150.

was presented as a luxury item in a sector whose rampant growth was linked solidly to the concept of affordable utility bikes. Anyway, going against the flow, exploring all avenues, offering bold technical features was to become an MV speciality: the new marque was positively bubbling with energy. But this was only the tip of the iceberg, even more projects remained in the experimental stage and never got beyond the walls of the laboratory and the testing rooms. These included engines conceived with an eye to future applications that somehow never came into being, or built simply for the pleasure of creating a good piece of engineering. Be that as it may, all of them were unique pieces made out of the sheer desire to create, like works of art. Not much is known about this early experimental work and it would be almost impossible to attempt a reconstruction, except perhaps through the fading memories of those who were actually involved: this would certainly be true of the 500 cm³ boxer twin, for example, created in 1948-49, or the 175 cm³ 2-stroke single from the same period; or the extraordinary 125 cm³ 2-stroke from 1950 with the in-head exhaust valve, which made a few fleeting appearances in some long distance races. Other creations, on the other hand, were shown at exhibitions or trade fairs, but were not followed up commercially: in particular there were various experiments with fuel injection systems and hydraulic automatic transmissions. A wealth of ideas therefore, which made MV one of the greats not only in the field of sport but also in the realms of pure technology, thus ensuring a pre-eminent place for the marque in the history of the motorcycle. Unfortunately, a discussion of the work done on aero engines, motor car design and impromptu one-offs like the

Hovercraft (1969) is beyond the scope of this book.

The 250 however, was a traditional MV single: long-travel push rods and rockers, cast iron cylinder barrel-head assembly, magneto ignition, unit gearbox with four speeds and primary drive by gears. The frame was a single-loop tubular cradle with telescopic suspension units. Running on a compression ratio of 6:1 the engine could develop 11 hp at 4700 rpm, enough for a top speed of around 110 km/h.

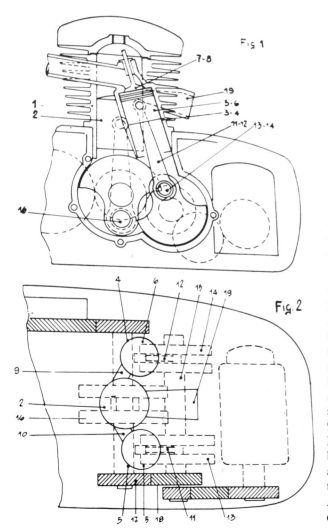

The MV team in 1958, one of the marque's best seasons. From the left, John Hartle, Fortunato Libanori, Carlo Ubbiali, Remo Venturi, Tarquinio Provini, Gilberto Milani, Tino Brambilla and John Surtees.

Truth to tell, it was not much of a success commercially, perhaps because – as we said before – the buyers of larger bikes were more attached to the older makes, and in any case MV was offering nothing particularly new with the 250. After a few years it was deleted from the catalogue without sales ever having reached appreciable levels. The 125 twin, on the other hand, was a faithful copy of the handsome and likeable lines of the 98: only the cylinders were a little out of place, perhaps because they were too small and tended to get "lost" in the structure as a whole. Apart from the twin cylinders, it also boasted another refinement for a lightweight, the 4-speed gearbox, normally reserved for 250s and above in those days. The 125 twin was acclaimed by both the critics and the public but somehow or other MV never got round to putting it on sale, limiting themselves to showing the bike at various shows and exhibitions for a while, after which it was quietly forgotten. In the years to come a similar fate was to befall many other creations produced by this enigmatic marque.

Instead, in the spring of 1948 a new 125 single, which represented the logical evolution of the firstborn 98, caught on as soon as it appeared. Clear-

An original patent held by Domenico Agusta, dating from the early Fifties: a 2-stroke engine with in-head exhaust valve whose three cylinders shared a common combustion chamber.

18

Assen 1956: the unbeatable MV team were absolute masters of the 125 event. In order, Taveri, Ubbiali (who was to win), and Libanori.

ly, a mere three years having passed since the end of the war, the market was not yet prepared for sophisticated technical features, even though demand for bikes with slightly peppier performance was beginning to grow. But most people still wanted a reasonably priced machine and in fact cheapness was still considered a winning card. The engine was a long stroker with three series of ports and two lateral transfer ports, but the piston was flat and the twin exhaust ports debouched into a single exhaust pipe. Primary drive was by gears while the gearbox offered the usual three speeds. Ignition was by fly-wheel magneto and lubrication was provided by a 14:1 petrol/oil mixture. The frame was a closed cradle made of gas welded tubing with no lugs and telescopic rear suspension; front suspension was provided by traditional girder forks, which are cheaper than telescopic units. This was the model that was to father the competition 125 that came second in the opening event of the lightweight Championship at Casale, where it was beaten by bad luck more than anything else. Obviously, the main difference between the racer and the touring version was the state of tune. The upshot of this was that the power out-put of the "over-the-counter" racer on sale to the general public was increased to 9 hp at 6800 rpm, enough for a good 115 km/h. Power per litre amounted to 72 horses therefore, anything but negligible, while the lubrication system required an 8.5:1 petroil mixture. What a difference compared to today's engines, which work away happily on a 50:1 mixture! The frame was similar to that of the touring model, but the tubing was lighter and two friction dampers had been added to the rear suspension system. The wheels were 21 inchers, the obligatory size for competition bikes, while the front brake was fitted with a small forced air intake. The MV 125 won several races in the course of 1948, ridden by both privateers and works riders, however owing to a series of unfortunate circumstances that were to dog the bike for the entire season, it failed to get the better of the rival Morinis in the Italian Championship. However the MV was to get its revenge at the end of the season and in Italy's premier speed event at that: the Grand Prix of Nations. Closely linked for many years with the legendary autodrome at Monza – out of action in the immediate post-war period as a result of war damage – the 1947 competition was held on the

19

broad avenues surrounding the Milan Trade Fair complex, while in 1948 the event migrated to the circuit at Faenza, a fast track specially built to favour the more powerful machines.

The 125s were competing for the first time in nineteen years and they produced a humdinger of a race, fought out in dashing style and rich in moments of high drama. Outstanding among the eighteen entrants were the works teams from Morini and MV, who had recruited some of the best riders around for the occasion, including a number of Guzzi and Gilera works riders who had been lent out for the day as the major outfits treated lightweight events with patrician disinterest.

Apart from Alberti, who has already been mentioned, the Morini squad included Nello Pagani, a Guzzi rider before the war who had been with Gilera for the previous couple of years; Renato Magi, a modest and courageous man with a good ten racing seasons under his belt, first with Gilera and then with MV; the young and promising Umberto Masetti; and Daniele Lambertini, who was to hang up his helmet a short time afterwards to become the "wizard" of the race shop for the Bolognese manufacturer. As well as Bertoni, the MV squad included Gianni Leoni, an ex pilot who had already notched up a number of wins in important pre-war competitions like the Circuito del Lario and the Milano-Taranto; the Scot Fergus Anderson, racer and occasional

journalist (or perhaps it was the other way round), who was shortly to become a Guzzi works rider and subsequently racing manager for that same marque; then there was the most popular of them all, Dario Ambrosini, who was to ride the Benelli 250 that same year (1948) when it returned to the racing scene after a painstaking rebuild – the various components having been begged, borrowed or stolen from here and there – at Benelli's Pesaro works, which had lost everything bar the door handles to the retreating Germans.

The Faenza race also saw the debut of a really avant-garde machine, the 4-stroke twin-cam Mondial designed by Alfonso Drusiani, a successful engineer, and built by a Milanese firm called FB, that had concentrated exclusively on motorcycle trucks until then. This was the birth of that triad, MV, Mondial, Morini, which was to animate 125 and then 250 class competition for a decade. Some of Italy's most famous riders of that period won their spurs with these teams, whose needle sharp rivalry kept the fans' enthusiasm at boiling point, a fact that was also due to the riders' habit of transferring their allegiance whenever this was convenient.

For this race, MV lined up the usual 125, which had been slightly modified, the most significant novelty being the extensive finning on the cylinder head. A group of riders shot into the lead right from the start. Strung out in line astern on the straights,

they fanned out to sweep through the bends with breathtaking abandon. The group was made up of Bertoni on the MV, Masetti, Alberti, Lambertini and Magi on Morinis, and Franceso Lama on a Mondial. It is worth adding that Lama, who had returned to racing after an eight year hiatus, had won the Italian Campionship on a blown Gilera before the war. Mechanical problems began to whittle down the field as one by one, Lambertini, Magi and Lama dropped out; then Masetti was slowed down by a spill and fell back down the rankings. Alberti and Bertoni were left locked in a neck and neck struggle, which looked much like a repeat of the opening race of the season, but this time it was Bertoni who got the better of his adversary to give MV its first win in an international class event, and a highly absorbing one at that.

The '48 season came to an end in October at the reconstructed Monza Autodrome, with a series of races held to commemorate the occasion. This time the Mondial, ridden by Nello Pagani, won the day; but the race is also memorable as it marked the debut on an MV of a young man from Bergamo called Carlo Ubbiali. Ubbiali was a relative rookie having had his first ride the year before in a minor event held in Bergamo, but he had wasted little time in making a name for himself. Of smallish build, light, determined, and gifted with a good grasp of strategy, he seemed cut out for light-

weight racing and in fact his name is linked with some of MV's greatest successes in this field. On his debut ride for MV, Ubbiali came second behind Pagani, along with team leader Bertoni: an auspicious start that was the harbinger of the triumphs to come.

In 1949, MV made radical changes in both its touring and racing models. The clientele was getting more and more demanding; people who had formerly been happy with the mere fact that they no longer had to push pedals, were now beginning to think that a little more speed would do no harm, and that it would be nice to be able to approach steep hills without nagging doubts as to the success of the enterprise or to carry a pillion passenger in some semblance of comfort. Then there was racing, where the advent of the Mondial demanded that action be taken.

And so the engine was completely changed, except for its dimensions: the light alloy head received more finning, in line with the changes made to the works bikes at the end of the preceding season; the outline of the cylinder was made more angular; while the crankcase became a longish ovoid covering a new four-speed gearbox.

The rear suspension was also modified: the old plunger springing was abandoned in favour of a pivoted fork with coil springs enclosed in cylindrical spring boxes mounted alongside the wheel, the top ends of which were attached to two large boomerang-shaped metal pressings. Two friction dampers completed the layout. There were three versions: the Turismo and the Lusso, which were slightly different in terms of tuning and finish, and the Sport with the lightened frame, 21" wheels and an engine able to supply 10.5 hp at 6700 rpm, enough to propel the bike to about 130 km/h.

That same year witnessed the development of a scooter, which also utilized the new engine with the addition of a fan for the forced air cooling system. This body was built around a pressed steel beam that ran from the steering to a point below the crankcase. Rear supension was provided by a box-section swinging arm supporting a cantilevered wheel, with cylindrical springs in tension. This scooter, which was later labelled the "B" type, developed 5 hp at 4800 rpm and could touch 80 km/h.

Scooters are utility vehicles par excellence, and would appear to be unsuited for competition, but things were different in those days. Speed events for such vehicles were very common in Italy and the various manufacturers took a fair amount of official interest because such competitions were held to have good publicity value. It was not long before MV decided to launch an attempt to break the cosy little monopoly that Vespa and Lambretta had hitherto enjoyed in this particular speciality. MV's arrival caused quite a ripple in this traditionally tranquil pond; so much so that in the first race entered by an MV scooter – an event held at the Monza Autodrome in support of a classic cycle race – there was a flurry of last minute withdrawals when the word got around that the new machine was going to race. Needless to say the MV won, with rider Romolo Ferri outdistancing the runner-up by a spanking two minute margin. Not bad for a fifty kilometre race! MV continued to take part in scooter racing over the years that followed, piling up win upon win until they

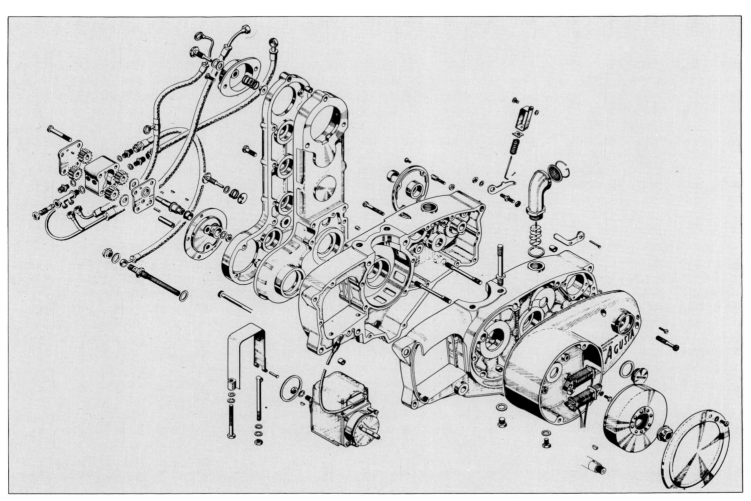

Here and on the following page, exploded drawings of the single overhead camshaft competition 125 engine. Note the timing gear, the crankshaft and the gearbox wheelwork.

21

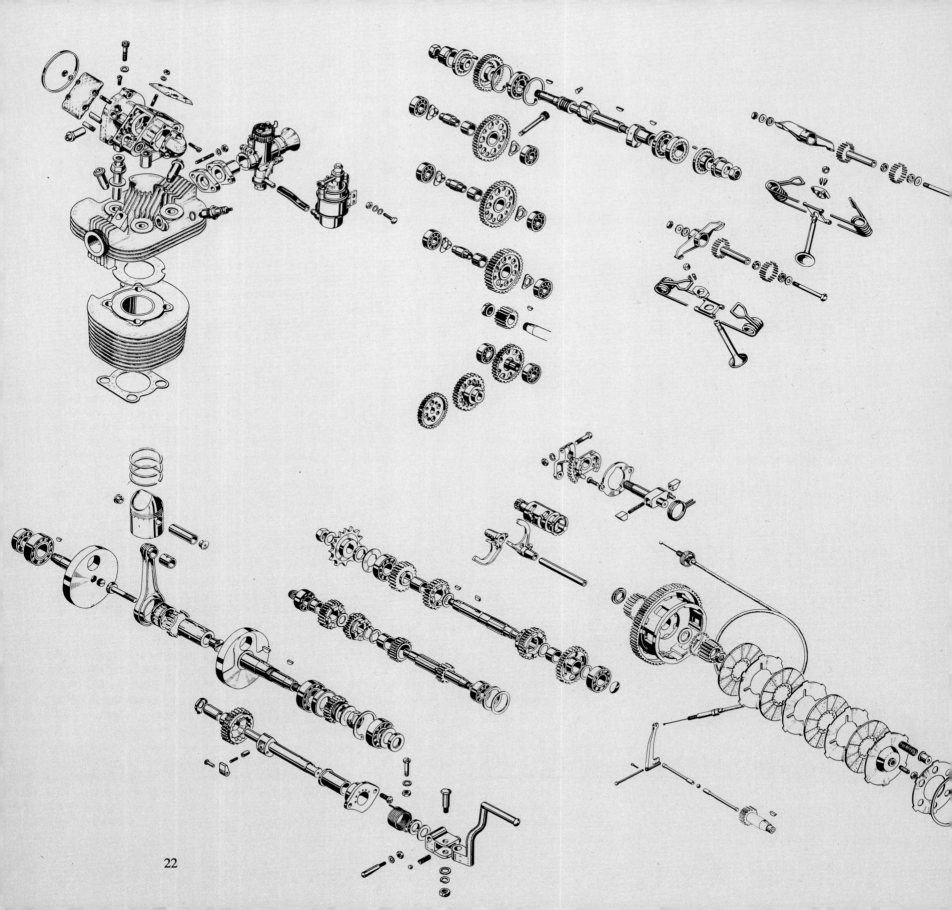

became the unchallenged master of the speciality; but it was not long before MV began to take an interest in another speciality, regularity or trials racing. For the Italians at least, the name "regolarità", so modest and unpretentious, has never done justice to this form of competition, which is incomparably the toughest on both men and machines, so much so that – in Italy as elsewhere – the sport has recently been renamed "enduro", a word that also fails to convey the full flavour but has the advantage of sounding suitably exotic and will probably win the day therefore.

Today enduro competitions are virtually all off-road events, with "special sections" that are full-blown motocross courses, but they were no cissies back in the Forties and Fifties either, given that competitors rode what amounted to slightly modified standard touring bikes. Nor had riders yet begun to concentrate entirely

on one speciality, a phenomenon that was to occur a few years later, and so it was quite common to see circuit racing stars in the line-up at trials events.

Of course MV's first ever win had been scored in a trials competition, as we have already seen, but this was the work of a private entrant. The marque made its official debut in this speciality during 1949, in time for the Six Days – then as now the most important date in the international trials calendar – an event made up of daily stages with the final rankings worked out on a team basis. A different country hosts the ISDT every year.

That year the event was scheduled to be held in Britain, winners of the title the year before. The venue was Llandrindod Wells, where a very tough course had been prepared complete with a compendious selection of classic cross-country features: grassy meadows, stony gorges, torrents, fields liberally strewn with stones made treacherously slippy by the continuous rain, and so on. It all provided a clear demonstration of natural selection and in fact only 51 entrants out of the 230 starters managed to finish.

The Italian presence amounted to 17 riders divided into three squads, with the most

representative mounts of the day: six Sertums, then considered the best Italian trials bike, three Morinis, two Guzzis, two Gileras and four MV 125s, obviously the new type with the 4-speed gearbox.

On an individual level the Italians made a worthy showing with six riders returning a clean sheet to receive the

gold medals that such a feat manifestly deserves; however the team rankings, i.e. the ones that really count, were not so rosy and the Italians came third overall. The MVs were ridden by Attolini, who had to withdraw after a fall on the second day, and speed aces Ferri, Bertoni and Ubbiali, who all finished. Berto-

23

ni, exhausted by his labours, suffered a series of bad spills during the third stage and was able to continue thanks only to the sense of altruism displayed by Ferri who, unmindful of his own position in the rankings, stopped to lend his teammate a hand and then stuck with him all the way to the finish. Ubbiali on the other hand soon got accustomed to the new environment (but of course the people from his part of Italy have cross-country racing in the blood...) and went on to win a gold medal.

The year 1950 brought a number of novelties along with it. In the 125 class, following the appearance of the overwhelming 4-stroke Mondial, Morini immediately replied with a useful chain-driven single-cam engine and MV suddenly found itself clearly outclassed. Although its brilliant lightweight had certainly showed that it was the fastest 'stroker in international competion during the previous season, the gap separating it from its 4-stroke opponents was well nigh unbridgeable. In addition that year also saw the birth of the World Championship, with the result that the number of spectators immediately be-

came much larger and so every win – and likewise every defeat – came to assume far greater importance than ever before. In those days the technology of 2-stroke engines, even though it had made giant strides since the pioneering days, was still fairly primitive and therefore – unlike the situation today – the superiority in terms of power of the 4-stroke engine was most marked. In order to stay out in front therefore it was necessary to take the plunge and adopt the technical features employed by the opposition.

From that point onwards MV's Grand Prix bikes were to have very little in common with standard production machines: they were built exclusively for racing in an attempt to create the best possible product, while no economic considerations were to hinder their development. Only at the end of the marque's existence was there any attempt to re-establish a certain connection between racing and series production. It was almost as if they had wished to round off, with this return to the roots, the career of a marque that was certainly one of the most glorious, best known and most successful the world had ever seen, even though not one of the longest lived. Towards the end of 1948 the rumour mill was already

abuzz with the idea that MV was preparing a new 4-stroke bike. This was partially due to the fact that the company had recently established contacts with some of the most illustrious motorcycle engineers of the day, like Speluzzi – a highly esteemed and even feared professor at the Milan Polytechnic – and Remor, who had left Gilera a short time before after having created the air-cooled version of the 500 cm^3 Quattro Cilindri, among other things.

The competition 125 4-stroke was seen for the first time at the Milan Trade Fair, which used to include a motorcycle show in those days, together with a genuine fireball: a 4-cylinder shaft-driven competition 500. It seems impossible, when you think of the jealous, quasi maniacal care with which MV's later racing machines were protected from prying eyes, guarded round the clock by mechanics-cum-watchdogs capable of working on the bikes without removing the heavy tarpaulins under which they were hidden; it seems impossible we were saying, that MV could regale the visitors to an exposition with two machines that certainly represented the contemporary state of the art and that still had to go through the development process into the bargain. It was a bit like saying: look, we

are a pretty capable outfit and we are so convinced of our superiority that we can even afford to reveal our secrets. Beat that, if you can! The good old days, right enough; but we should add that MV has always kept faith with its policy of the *coup de théatre*, offering a sensational innovation at every show or review in which it has taken part. Very often these novelties were never followed up in practice, as we mentioned before, but they nevertheless served to underline the vitality and inventiveness of the marque's engineering staff.

This divergence between competition technology and what could be described as touring bike production now obliges us to follow the threads of two entirely different tales. As a consequence the next chapter is devoted entirely to series production thus leaving racing fans, doubtless curious to know more about all these fabulous innovations we have been hinting at, in an agony of suspense. Well, that was the idea anyway.

The English Tourist Trophy, for many decades the most important race in the world, saw MV victorious on 34 occasions. On the facing page, a shot of the 125 race in 1956: Nello Pagani is signalling the extent of his lead to Carlo Ubbiali.

FROM GREATNESS TO DECLINE 2

Although MV had gone over to four-stroke engines for the major events, the marque kept faith with strokers for touring bike production for a few more years. Effectively speaking the enormous success of the postwar motorcycle industry was due to the appearance of cheap, simple models that were easy to ride and required little in the way of maintenance. Two-stroke machines were undoubtedly the best bet as far as the bike-starved public of the day were concerned, since, apart from the odd problem with fouled plugs, they generally provided first class service.

At that time the various marques favoured a strategy based on low prices rather than high performance in their battle to win over the customers, and all the factories were committed to keeping costs and prices down in a determined bid to carve out the largest possible share of the market: Innocenti, for example, succeeded in reducing the price of their latest Lambretta, the "C", to an incredible 125,000 lire, thanks to a new frame construction method: shortly afterwards Vespa also introduced an economical model with extremely spartan finishing. Barring a few exceptional models destined for an elite niche market that had never

quite disappeared, all of the major manufacturers were now moving downmarket. And so MV, whose products were made even more attractive by their low prices, thought of backing up their "B" scooter (the utility machine par excellence, which was later to be rebaptized the CLS 51, i.e. "the '51 version of the type C Lusso Super")

with a cheaper model known as the CGT 51 or Gran Turismo. This was to be mechanically identical to its predecessor, but with a simplified body that left the engine uncovered. The launch was scheduled for the 1950 Geneva Show and the newcomer enjoyed healthy sales right from the start. One of this scooter's most useful features

was a practical stowage compartment.
But this was not enough: another even simpler and cheaper scooter was introduced at the 1951 Milan Trade Fair. This had a single-beam tubular frame with neither partial nor full fairing; the engine, although it still had the oblong crankcase, once more had the three-

speed gearbox operated by a twistgrip control on the handlebar. It had a trailing link front fork with a swinging arm at the rear. Called the Ovunque (Everywhere) or the "O 51", it was put on sale at 141,000 lire; it looked rather like the Lambretta and all things considered it was a fairly successful machine.

A slight change in dates meant that there were two Motorcycle Shows in 1952, one in January and another in December. For the January event MV introduced a 150 cm^3 lightweight that was little more than an updated version of the 125 cm^3 trials bike the marque had sent to the Six Days event of the previous year. The 125 remained in production. The 1952 catalogue therefore included Turismo and Sport versions of the 125, plus Turismo and Sport versions of the 150, complete with telescopic forks (a cheaper model with girder forks was later added and, curiously enough, this was entered for a few trials events), as well as four scooters: the Ovunque, which had become the "Tipo 52", the economical CLS with the 125 cm^3 engine, the CGT 125 and finally the 150 cm^3 CGT Lusso.
For dyed-in-the-wool sporty types and amateur racers there was a new version of the 125 cm^3 stroker. This was the "Carter lungo" ("Long crankcase"), destined to win

fame in the less important events, where its many fine qualities and affordable price made it extremely popular with "rookies" out to make a name for themselves. In comparison with the bike from the previous year it had a new tubular duplex cradle frame with a reinforced rear section, a 4-speed gearbox, and magneto ignition, which in those days stood up to sustained high engine speeds rather better than a flywheel magneto. The crankcase had had to be lengthened in order to accommodate the new ignition system and of course this led directly to the "Long crankcase" denomination mentioned earlier.
A major innovation, destined – for better and for worse – to have anything but indifferent consequences for the motorcycle market in general and MV's commercial image in particular, was introduced at the Milan Show in December 1952. This was a 175 cm^3 4-stroke lightweight with a single chain-driven overhead camshaft, which was available in Turismo, Sport and Lusso versions.
In the post-war period the Italian motorcycle market was fairly booming (the 160,000 machines in circulation in 1939 had become almost half a million by 1949 and went on to reach 1,400,000 by the end of 1952) because the industry had finally got round to producing reliable and economical products and also because of the tax advantages enjoyed by machines with less than 125 cm^3 engine capacity,

which did not have to carry licence plates. Even though this exemption was abolished in the course of 1951, the motorcycle boom continued apace for a few more years still, but seeing that it was no longer necessary to stop at the 125 cm^3 "barrier", there was a sudden spate of models powered by 150-160 cm^3 engines (MV included, as we have seen), which could easily be produced simply by boring out existing engines. Demand for these machines grew rapidly and before long most bike manufacturers had gone even further to produce models with 175 cm^3 engines, generally agreed to represent the limit for light motorcycles in the pre-war years, when performance was far less interesting however. At virtually the same time the *Federazione Motociclistica Italiana* thought of reintroducing production bike racing, a somewhat Utopian concept that was dusted off from time to time with the laudable intention of giving privateers with limited financial resources the chance to compete. So much for theory. In practice things were never quite that simple, because every time this form of competition was revived the factories promptly produced a spate of camouflaged racing bikes at prices that only a fortunate few could afford, while thumbing the nose at those who wished to "popularize" motorcycle racing; but all things considered production racing did help improve the breed, not only in terms of pure performance but also in terms of

lightness, stability, and braking.
In 1953, however, production bikes – or rather "production-derived bikes", because some modifications were permitted – were back on the starting grid. In Italy the event that lent most lustre to this resuscitated category was the Motogiro d'Italia, a speed race split up into stages and held on roads open to traffic. This event was held for the first time in 1953 and was abolished, along with all forms of road racing, after the tragic 1957 Mille Miglia. The Motogiro was limited to bikes of up to 175 cm^3 engine capacity in a bid to keep the element of risk as low as possible and it was a success right from the start, revealing itself to be an excellent publicity vehicle for the manufacturers; but in this case too the tractable, reliable and thoroughly domesticated light motorcycles that had done so much to put Italy on wheels were converted into complex, delicate - and costly - racing machines.
The first effect of all this was the rapid decline of the heavier Italian machines. The classic "500s" that all bike fans had once longed to get their hands on were the fruit of pre-war technology and it soon became apparent that the new breed of lightweights was miles ahead as far as speed, acceleration and handling were concerned. Shortly afterwards it also became clear that the man in the street was falling steadily out of love with two-wheeled transport. Most people want-

Dustbin fairings represent a milestone in the history of the motorcycle but, although much more could have been done with them, they were decreed unsafe and consequently abolished. Here is a shot of a typical race of those days: the 350 race at the Solitude circuit in 1956. Masetti and Chadwick, both on MVs, can be seen between Dale on the Guzzi and Hobl on the DKW.

ed a docile, reliable machine to take them to and from work and they were consequently uninterested in uncomfortable highly-strung thoroughbreds, no matter how technically advanced.

Be that as it may, however, MV decided to follow the new course. Its new 175 still had a long-stroke engine with a light alloy cylinder head and barrel, flywheel magneto ignition with an external HT coil and a 4-speed unit gearbox. The open duplex cradle frame was built along the lines of the previous model,

i.e. a combination of tubular elements at the front and sheet metal pressings at the rear. The suspension was teledraulic. For the time being, the bike was offered in Turismo and Lusso versions (with a few variations in terms of finishing but both powered by an 8hp engine), as well as a Sport variant with a 9hp engine capable of exceeding 105 km/h.

The production of straight utility bikes, however, was not abandoned entirely: on the contrary, the range was increased with the addition of

a highly original bike – introduced at the Brussels Show in January 1953 – that was to set a trend and spawn a host of imitations in a very short time, both in Italy and elsewhere: the Turismo Pullman 125, a successful blend of the light motorcycle and the scooter. The designers of this new-concept machine had made considerable efforts to provide comfort, something that had been entirely lacking in previous machines because it was felt that such fripperies might damage the motorcycle's sporting image. The

Pullman had a closed frame made of fat tubes, and one rode the bike astride the saddle in the classic manner, with all the benefits – psychological and otherwise – that this bestows; in addition the medium-diameter wheels, the low saddle, and the wide running boards all combined to ensure a relaxed riding position, which enabled the rider to cover long distances without falling victim to cramp and other aches and pains.

The small 15 inch wheels were in fact the most outstanding characteristic of the new MV, because they had been shod with tyres measuring a good three and a half inches across. These tyres conferred an unusual chubby look upon the bike, which looked distinctly odd at a time when the tall, slim wheel was the mark of the sporty motorcycle.

Naturally this was dictated by reasons of practicality. Balloon tyres soak up the bumps better and therefore make a positive contribution to improved comfort.

The engine was the by then classic undersquare 125 cm^3 2-stroke unit with the long crankcase but the gearbox was still only a twistgrip-operated three-speeder, considered more than enough for this kind of bike. Final drive was via a chain mounted on the right hand side and power output was 5 hp at 4500 rpm. A fashionable look was ensured by the addition of a twin exhaust (also fitted to the Ovunque scooter), which improved performance and made for quieter running.

The engine was in-unit with the pivoted rear fork and springing was handled by two telescopic spring boxes mounted on either side of the wheel. This very simple design made it possible to keep weight and costs down so that MV could offer the bike for a more than attractive 160 thousand lire or thereabouts. Partly on account of the price and partly on account of its particular characteristics the Pullman met with an enthusiastic response from the public, who had evidently been waiting for just such a machine. But the best proof of the basic soundness and modernity of the design is provided by the fact that various manufacturers immediately rushed out a series of similar vehicles.

By the end of the 1953 season MV had become one of the most important motorcycle manufacturers in Italy. Even though Les Graham's tragic death had upset the marque's sporting plans, the year came to a close with a total bag of around ninety victories in events of all types, culminating in the conquest of the World Constructors' Championship for the 125 class. Most important of all, commercial production was growing steadily as the marque began to establish a widespread market presence. By that time Italian production had reached 20,000 units per annum, while a factory was set up in Spain, where the bikes (badged "Emevue") were produced and marketed under licence. Back in Italy the distribution network now included 250 outlets, while agencies were established in France, Switzerland, Holland, Austria, Argentina and Brazil. The results of this extremely dynamic performance, economically and otherwise, spread out to affect the entire firm; there is nothing fortuitous about the fact that, in that period, booming series production was accompanied by a major increase in avant-garde experimental work, which was seldom followed up commercially but nevertheless testifies to the inventive capacities of both management and workers alike, because only growing, economically sound companies can afford the luxury of research work that has no immediate application.

This was the case, for example, with the research involving the Badalini infinitely-variable hydraulic transmission. This work led first to the production of a 150 cm^3 2-stroke engine and then to a 175 cm^3 4-stroke unit, both of which aroused a good deal of admiration among experts and members of the public alike. The 2-stroke engine was put on display at the Milan Motorcycle Show in the November of 1953, while the 175 cm^3 engine came along the following year.

Other research involved experimental fuel injection systems for 2-stroke petrol engines, using a series-derived 125 cm^3 single-cylinder engine (it had been fitted to a 1956 Pullman model). This work can be traced back to earlier experiments (carried out in 1948) aimed at perfecting a mechanical petrol injection pump. Then there was a considerable body of work that did not concern motorcycle production at all, but outboard motors, cars and trucks and special vehicles.

But let's leave this argument for the moment and return to normal production. In 1954 the range of single knocker 175s was widened with the addition of some decidedly sporty versions like the SS (Super Sport), which had a beefed-up engine capable of developing 15 hp at 8800 rpm and a top speed in excess of 140 km/h. This instantly recognizable motorcycle was nicknamed the "Disco Volante" ("Flying Saucer") on account of the original, rounded lines of the petrol tank. In fact the nickname became so popular that even the makers eventually adopted it in preference to the bike's rather uninspiring official denomination (CSS); a phenomenon that tends to happen when particularly successful products catch the collective imagination, another famous example being the Fiat "Topolino".

The 175 "Disco Volante" was to play an important role in the history of MV, even though we have to add that its contribution was not always a positive one. Light and manageable, it retailed at 275,000 lire and was an instant hit with racing and performance bike fans who found that, in exchange for a modest sum, they could have a machine every bit as fast as any heavyweight and far superior in terms of roadholding, braking and driveability: much more fun, in other words, especially on twisty roads.

It was also an ideal machine for Sport class competition; and so it was not long before the "Flying Saucer" spawned a Sport Competizione model, with an Earles front fork, 2.75 - 19" tyres, anatomic fuel tank, magneto ignition and 5-speed gearbox. Offered as an "over-the-counter" racer, this bike was also used by works riders for the less important races, of which it won a good few.

The evolution of the MV trade mark over the years. The most significant changes were made after the death of Count Domenico Agusta.

Although the "Disco Volante" was an excellent bike for sporting purposes, it was less useful for the everyday tasks that some people insisted on trying to make it perform. Under such working conditions it was inevitably revealed as a rather fragile creature in need of much tender loving care: after all it did have a specific power of more than 85 hp per litre, as good as if not better than many contemporary Grand Prix machines, an output obtained, moreover, at engine speeds that still command respect even today. In particular, the timing chain tended to stretch, which resulted in a marked drop in performance and required frequent replacement.

Influenced by the need to dominate production bike racing, virtually all the other factories had brought out single-cam lightweights, and all these bikes suffered more or less from the same problems; as a result the motorcycle began to lose favour with the general public, who had decreed its success in the preceding years. Shortly afterwards, the compact car boom supplied that same public – who had never been fascinated by motorcycles as such

but only appreciated their cheapness – with a vehicle that was certainly slower, but more comfortable, capacious (it's not easy to pack the average Italian family onto the pillion of a Vespa), less highly strung and less prone to breaking down. And so, as 1960 approached, the decline in motorcycle sales began to bite causing many marques to go under while many others had to make drastic cutbacks. MV was among those who rode out the storm, even though its sales had fallen off considerably, and that this was so was thanks largely to the passionate support of Count Domenico, who was arguably even happy about the situation in his heart of hearts: no longer shackled by the restraints imposed by the sales department and all the problems that contact with the public inevitably involves, he could liberate his own creative imagination and aspire to satisfactions of a higher order than considerations of mere profit.

In 1954, however, there were still no clouds on the horizon, and even though a few harbingers of the hard times to come were beginning to manifest themselves abroad, the outlook for the Italian market was still rosy. And so, in full summer, and well before the usual annual appointment at the Milan Trade Fair, MV introduced a new 125 cm^3 lightweight with a 4-stroke push-rod engine, the Turismo Rapido (TR). The 4-stroke engine was making headway even in the utility bike sector for reasons that were more psychological than practical, inasmuch as they were dictated by the all-conquering fashion for sporty machines. Many people thought that 4-strokes were "real" engines, because they were fitted to cars and big bikes, whereas the common and garden stroker was good only for beginners and those without the wherewithal to procure themselves something more interesting. Those who, in their own opinion, had "arrived" were interested in machines with sufficient perceived status to promote them to a higher rank in the pecking order.

As a consequence, MV began gradually replacing its 2-stroke production with new 4-stroke models, the first of which was the TR. The engine had a square engine, unlike the traditional MV product, capable of supplying 5.6 hp at 5200 rpm, altogether a relaxing ceiling. Lubrication was by a wet sump system and ignition by flywheel magneto, while the unit gearbox was a pedal-operated 4-speeder. The frame was an open duplex cradle (made of tubing at the front and pressings at the back), with a swinging fork at the rear and telescopic forks at the front. The wheels were shod with 2.75-18" tyres. The Turismo Rapido remained in the catalogue until 1958, during which time it went through various versions. A Sport version (the RS) with a more powerful engine was also produced.

In 1955 MV entered another specific sector, that of moped production. In the immediate post-war period the "clip-on" engines mounted on common and garden bicycles had represented many people's first step towards liberation from the slavery of pedal pushing; then, a bit at a time, after it was discovered that the ordinary bicycle was poorly equipped to cope with the stresses caused by an engine, people began buying proper mopeds, i.e. two-wheeled vehicles expressly designed to house a mechanical propulsion unit, and – if they could afford to – light motorcycles or their more powerful brethren. The pedal bicycle with its micromotor soon became extinct, while the moped still possesses a share of the market to this day, thanks to its low price, simplicity and lightness, and the various fiscal advantages. It was clearly a sector that MV could not afford to neglect, and it was logical that the marque take an interest. MV's product, known simply as the Ciclomotore 50, had an electrically welded pressed steel single-beam frame, with low-slung and slightly arched lines that looked good and made for very easy handling. The trailing link front fork was also a pressed steel unit, while the rear suspension was handled by two telescopic spring boxes. The 2-stroke engine, which had a 3-speed gearbox operated by a twistgrip control, supplied 2hp at 5400 rpm, good for 50 km/h. While on the subject of speed, we should point out

that at that time there was no speed limit as far as mopeds were concerned, because the current legislation did not come into force until 1959. The selling price – 79,000 lire – was a particularly attractive one for a moped with a 3-speed gearbox and in fact it sold well, even though it did not become a major success in this most competitive sector; it remained in the catalogue until 1959 without any important modifications.

Another two interesting machines made their appearance at the end of that year. The more original of these was a 300 cm^3 4-stroke twin designed by a Roman engineer called Giannini (no relation to the Gianini who – thirty years before – had designed the OPRA, forerunner of the transverse 4-cylinder models), who was then working with MV. Giannini's twin had a 4-speed gearbox and an electric starter. The engine had cast iron cylinders tilted forward at 30 degrees and light alloy heads with special finning; the fuel supply was handled by twin-barrel carbs sharing the same float chamber, while ignition was by coil. The frame was an open duplex cradle with a swinging fork at the rear. Earles-type forks with straight legs and enclosed springs were fitted at the front.

This machine, whose avant-garde technical features aroused considerable interest among experts and members of the public alike, was not followed up commercially. A couple of years later, in 1957, a derivative was produced.

This was a Grand Prix racer with an uprated 350 cm^3 engine and aluminium cylinders tilted at 45 degrees, twin carbs, magneto ignition and a 5-speed gearbox. Another very interesting feature was the frame, which was a triangulated construction made of small diameter tubing (with detachable bottom rails). The Earles-type front forks were also made up of small-diameter tubing, while the rear suspension was a swinging fork arrangement. The bike was fitted with central drum brakes, with a four leading shoe type at the front.

The bike was subjected to exhaustive testing, almost always courtesy of Ken Kavanagh, but in the end the project was shelved in favour of the classic four-cylinder model. In effect the twin was lighter – it weighed in at 132 kilos – but the engine was unable to develop more than 47 hp at 12,000 rpm, and moreover the frame was the source of some extremely knotty roadholding problems. As a result the bike was definitively sidelined and shortly afterwards it wound up in the MV Museum, where it can still be admired to this day.

The Superpullman, on the other hand, the other newcomer introduced at the end of 1955, went into regular production. The Pullman, one of MV's most successful products, had been slightly modified but was still in production. The Superpullman was an entirely new machine, which had little in common with its predecessor except for the fact that in both cases the designers had aimed for simplicity, economy, and comfort. The frame was composed of two pressed steel shells electrically welded to form a large beam, running from the steering head to the saddle, including a central element from which the engine was cantilevered.

The engine was an undersquare 2-stroke single of new design, with a pedal-operated 4-speed gearbox. A leading link-type fork was fitted at the front, and a swinging fork at the rear. This bike had bigger wheels than the Pullman and so it had a decidedly more traditional look about it. Power output was 6 hp at 6200 rpm, enough to propel the bike to 75 km/h.

At the 1956 Milan Trade Fair MV surprised everybody with a new 250 of compact, up-to-date design. The 250 designed in 1947, although it was equipped with modern features like telescopic forks, was nevertheless a product of pre-war styling, especially as far as the engine was concerned; but this new creation, based on the 175 cm^3 single-knockers, was far more in line with the stylistic canons of the day – which tended to favour curved lines and unbroken surfaces – and it can fairly be said that this was one of the best-looking Italian bikes in production at the time. The undersquare power unit, which used a single chain-driven overhead camshaft, had a cylinder head that was slightly more rounded than those of the 175 cm^3 models. Ignition was by coil with automatic advance,

while the carburettor had the air intake in the sheltered area under the saddle; the gearbox was a four-speed unit.

The frame was made up of a large-diameter beam accompanied by two smaller tubes that formed the front downtubes of the cradle; the suspension had teledraulic forks at the front and a swinging fork at the rear. This bike weighed 116 kilos and could touch 115 km/h, thanks to the 14 hp at 5600 rpm provided by the engine: a vivacious performer without a doubt, but with the safety and reliability demanded by those who needed a hard-working bike for business or pleasure. This particular motorcycle was first introduced simply as the "Gran Turismo" model, but it was later renamed the Raid after MV held a competition in which the firm invited its agents and representatives to come up with a new name.

1957 was another good year for the motorcycle industry, but the most perspicacious experts had already glimpsed the first signs of the approaching crisis. Truth to tell this had already begun elsewhere in Europe, where economic conditions were somewhat better than in Italy: but the birth of the first really reliable Italian compact cars – first of all the Fiat 600 and, in 1957, the Nuova 500, on sale at a price that put it in competition with light motorcycles – heralded a forthcom-

ing transfer of allegiance from two wheels to four. In fact this shift came along in the space of a couple of years, and when it did it also involved the "youth market", i.e. the younger, sportier clients who were attracted by the novelty value of the car, which promised a whole new range of different pleasures that had hitherto been the exclusive preserve of the fortunate sons of well-to-do fathers.

Faced by this situation, a thrill of genuine panic ran through the motorcycle industry, and more or less all the manufacturers reacted in the same way: all superfluous costs were to be reduced to the bone (needless to say "superfluous" in this case meant involvement in motorsport, among other things) while a general move downmarket was decreed in a bid to snare all those poor unfortunates who still had to count the pennies. About ten years afterwards, under the pressure generated by the Japanese "invasion" and thanks to the renewed buying power that the public had once more come to enjoy, it was possible to relaunch the motorcycle as a leisure vehicle and a useful means of avoiding the gratuitous accusations of conformity that were often provoked by the mere possession of a motor car, but when the crisis first began to bite a cheaper product seemed the only possible lifeline.

But even in those dark days MV did not turn its back on avant-garde research: right in the middle of the slump the

firm began constructing helicopters under an American licence and this new activity ensured considerable financial security, which in turn meant that new motorcycles could be designed without any agonizing about short-term financial returns. Sporting commitments were also seen as a source of prestige and a high level vehicle for the promotion of the firm's corporate image, and not something exclusively bound up with the production of motorcycles: it was almost as if the helicopter firm had decided to sponsor a little motorbike racing, in the same way as a liquor producer might choose to sponsor a cycling team, or a domestic appliances manufacturer might back a basketball team.

The 1957 range was widened with the arrival of two economy models, the 125 Turismo Rapido Esportazione (TRE), on sale at 162 thousand lire, and the 175 Turismo Esportazione (CSTE), on sale at 199,500 lire, prices that had been made possible by cutting out the frills in order to maintain the traditional levels of quality where it mattered most. At the Milan Show that November the firm came up with a most interesting item, which the specialist press labelled the only genuine technical innovation in the whole show: this was an indirect injection system fitted to the 125, 175 and 250 cm^3 engines. The fuel arrived by gravity feed at a rotary-type pump situated under the cylinder on the left hand side of the crankcase, from where it was sent under pressure to an injector mounted on a short tube that served as a spray nozzle, mixture chamber and inlet tract. The inlet manifold had a filter over the air intake and a butterfly valve that was controlled, in synchrony with the flow rate of the pump, by the usual twistgrip.

Three fuel-injected motorcycles were placed at the disposition of the public on a test track laid out in front of the Exhibition Hall, in order to provide a practical demonstration of the efficiency and reliability of the design. For the construction of the new injection systems, which were made under licence granted by the patent holder, a German engineer named Schindele, MV established a special company, S.B.S. (an Italian acronym standing for the Schindele Patent Company), based in Cascina Costa. Research continued for some time and injection units were built for engines of up to eight cylinders and eight litres of displacement; the dimensions – the flange for the largest type was 142 mm in length and 94 mm in diameter – were decidedly moderate. But the time was not yet ripe for large-scale production of injection systems, and research in this direction was eventually abandoned.

The next Milan Trade Fair, held in the Spring of 1958 – the only show of its kind to be held in Italy that year since it had been decided to hold the Cycle and Motorcycle Show on a biennial basis – witnessed the baptism of a new

MV took an interest in motocross for a while. Here is Lucio Castelli, destined to become one of the best mechanics in the race shop, in action aboard a bike derived from a Disco Volante-type 175 single-knocker.

MV that was as interesting as it was unexpected. This was a light motorcycle that was called the Ottantatre ("Eighty-three") after its rather unusual, but rational, engine capacity. Experimentation had shown that this displacement provided enough power to transport two people at an acceptable speed in exchange for a modest rate of fuel consumption. The design was very simple: a triangulated frame made of wide-diameter tubes, which supported an overhanging 4-stroke single-cylinder pushrod engine. The suspension was teledraulic and the

wheels carried 2.50-19" tyres. Ignition was by flywheel magneto and lubrication by a wet sump system, while the gearbox was a pedal-operated three-speeder. Two versions of the Ottantatre were offered: the Normale and the Sport, which differed in finishings, performance and price.

1959 was another particularly fruitful year for MV. Galvanized by the brilliant sporting results obtained during the previous season, the marque continued to produce a rapid stream of new machines, both in the sporting and commercial divisions. At this

point we must leave the racing bikes to be dealt with in the chapters devoted to the marque's sporting activities and dedicate ourselves to a discussion of series production only, because it was precisely in this period that series production was modernized and extended thanks largely to an investment programme that saw the MV plant provided with many new workshops and much new machinery.

The Milan Trade Fair was the stage for the introduction of a new version of the 4-stroke 125, which had inherited its various denominations from

Two engines (250 and 175 cm³) equipped with the patented Schindele indirect injection system were shown at the 1957 Milan Show.

the preceding model (i.e. Rapido Extra, Rapido America, and Rapido Extra Lusso), but sported what amounted to a completely new engine. The cylinder was now fixed directly to the crankcase by a large bolted flange, in place of the old stud bolts, and the finning had also been modified. In a bid to increase strength and reliability the various bearings and shafts were all enlarged. In addition the lubrication system was now much better, thanks to the provision of a bigger sump, while a type of centrifuge for filtering the oil had been fitted to the crankshaft. More specifically, this device was composed of two little traps carved out of the edge of the left hand flywheel and in communication with the usual oilways inside the crankshaft where the lubricant is driven under pressure. Any impurities that got past the usual filter in the sump and thence to the internal oilways within the crankshaft were thrown outwards by centrifugal force to wind up in one of the two traps, from which they could be removed periodically simply by unscrewing a stopper situated beneath the sump. Performance had been improved too: the engine now supplied 7.5 hp and the bike could top 95 km/h.

Another newcomer was the 150 Sport. Its 4-stroke engine had been lifted from the 125 model and bored out – becoming oversquare in the process – to produce a little extra capacity. The 150 cm³ capacity class, which first came into being after the abolition of the various tax advantages previously enjoyed by machines of up to 125 cm³, became hot news once more in early 1959 when, after a lengthy gestation period, the Italian government issued a new version of the *Codice della Strada* (Law of the Road) in which there was a clause barring motorcycles of less than 150 cm³ engine capacity from travelling on the motorway. Obviously there was a spate of new machines in this capacity class, the MV being one of the very first.

As far as looks went, the 150 Sport was not very different from the new 125s: the most important difference, apart from the bright red and white paintwork, was the presence of a double-barrelled exhaust silencer, which was intended to reduce the decibel count without suffocating the 9.7 hp engine overmuch. This bike could get pretty close to 100 km/h and consumed about 3 litres per every 100 kilometres.

The Milan Trade Fair was also chosen for the official launch of a new 175, which had already been available for some time at MV outlets: this was the Extra Lusso with push-rod and rocker arm valve gear. A rather more tranquil engine than the overhead camshaft version – which was still in production

– but more reliable and durable, it was expected to dispel the reputation for fragility that the ultra-vivacious Disco Volante-type ohc engines had conferred upon all of MV's products. Not long afterwards the Extra Lusso was joined by the America, America Lusso, Turismo Extra Lusso and Gran Turismo versions. The Cycle and Motorcycle Show of the following autumn witnessed yet another barrage of new MVs. The new version of the 125 with the oil centrifuge was renamed the "Centomila" (Hundred thousand), because top management at MV were so sure of the goodness of the product and the efficiency of the new lubrication system that they did not hesitate to offer the bike with a year's warranty – at a time

Three fully faired racers battle it out over the Monza track in 1957. From the front, Libero Liberati on the Gilera Quattro Cilindri 500, John Surtees on an MV four, and Giuseppe Cantoni with the Gilera Saturno.

when no other manufacturer was offering more than 6 months – or alternatively a one hundred thousand kilometre guarantee. Of course the whole thing smacked somewhat of a publicity stunt, because it is no mean feat to cover such a distance on a light motorcycle, but the slogan was a successful one nonetheless.

Other novelties included a brace of scooters, a type of vehicle that MV had been ignoring for the previous few years: both machines had open coachwork, wide fixed front mudguards, headlights built into the handlebars and 3.50-10" wheels, but they had different propulsion units. The Bik had a 166 cm³ 4-stroke parallel twin engine with the cylinders tilted backwards, push-rod and rocker arm valve gear with semi-hydraulic tappets, flywheel magneto ignition and a 4-speed gearbox. This engine was a long stroker, in the classic MV tradition therefore, (46.5 × 49 × 2), and supplied 6 hp at 5000 rpm.

A classy piece of work, it was destined for a well-heeled clientele whose tastes ran more to refined engineering than brilliant performance, but it has to be said that in those days customers answering to this description were thin on the ground as far as the motorcycle trade was concerned. In fact the Bik remained at the prototype stage, one of the many MVs that stood witness to the marque's enduring inventive and technological capacities. A different fate was in store for the Chicco, first conceived as an export-only model and then sold regularly in Italy too. This was a tranquil utility bike with an honest 155 cm³ 2-stroke piston-ported flat single engine that sold pretty well. The engine was cooled by forced air and the 4-speed gearbox was a handchange unit. Maximum power output was 5.8 hp at 5200 rpm, good enough for 85 km/h.

34

Last but not least, there were two almost new arrivals in the middleweight ranks: a new version of the Raid model, with an uprated 300 cm^3 engine, and the Tevere 235. The Tevere was built along the same lines as the Raid and was, in effect, a more economical version of the latter: the principal differences lay in the finishing and the profiles of some accessories.

Following the rush of new products in the course of 1959, 1960 was a relatively tranquil year: the only newcomer was brought in to replace the Ottantatre. This was the Checca, a traditional 4-stroke ultralightweight and close relative, therefore, of the 125s and 150s dealt with earlier. It was available, for the time being at least, with two different engine capacities and three versions: the Checca GT with the 83 cm^3 engine; the Checca GT Extra with the 99 cm^3 engine and the Checca Sport GT, which had a tweaked version of the 99 cm^3 engine. As we said before, the basic design was the same as the most recent bikes in the next class up: the cylinder tilted slightly forward, push-rod and rocker arm valve gear and flywheel magneto ignition. The foot-change gearbox had only three speeds. An open duplex cradle was chosen for the frame and the wheels were 17 inchers. The standard 83 cm^3 version could touch 80 km/h, while the Sport could hit 100 km/h. 1961 was also a fairly relaxed year: apart from a new touring version – the Gran Turismo – of the 150 model, a slightly less exciting performer than the Rapido Sport version, the most salient innovation was MV's return to moped production, which had been shelved for some few years. The new road traffic legislation passed in 1959 had resulted in a few radical changes as far as mopeds were concerned. Limitations regarding engine capacity and top speeds were established but the other side of the coin was that mopeds were no longer obliged to have pedals. This was the signal for the creation of a wide variety of vehicles, from mini-scooters to mini-motorbikes, aimed at satisfying the needs of a far wider range of possible customers. The new MV, called the Liberty, belonged to the ultralightweight family: although constructed in accordance with the legal limits, this bike did not look much different from its larger stablemates: duplex cradle frame, telescopic forks and rear swinging fork. The 4-stroke engine with the abundantly finned cylinder set at a slightly forward tilt, the 3-speed unit gearbox and the oblong crankcase all combined to lend the bike a fairly imposing air, so much so that the Liberty could easily have been mistaken for a far larger model. Turismo and Sport versions of this bike were produced, which differed only in terms of finishing because performance was limited by the terms of the new legislation. These versions were later joined by the Sport S, with larger wheels, the Turismo T, the America, and the Super Sport. MV then took advantage of the generously proportioned mechanical units to prepare a new 70 cm^3 version, which was introduced at the 1965 Trade Fair. In 1962, for the first time in the history of the marque, MV failed to produce a new bike: the 1963 catalogue included the 99 cm^3 versions of the Checca, the Centomila, the 150, the Chicco scooter and the Liberty moped. This meant that the firm's range had actually been reduced, because the 83 cm^3 Checca and the 235, 250 and 300 cm^3 motorcycles had all been deleted. All this clearly indicates that the crisis had really begun to bite and all the "dead wood" (viz., all those products which had lost favour with the public) was earmarked for the axe. The epoch of the motorcycle as a cheap form of transport was about to come to an end and many manufacturers were shutting up shop. Thanks largely to Count Domenico's stubborn determination, MV stayed afloat; but it was pointless to carry on producing machines that people no longer wanted and so the cutbacks were both rational and wholly necessary.

MV returned to trials competition in 1963, with a 125 cm^3 bike derived from the Centomila. A good deal had changed in the world of trials competition in the interim: courses were now far tougher and practically all of them were off-road layouts. This had led in turn to the creation of purpose-built bikes expressly designed for this speciality, with plenty of ground clearance and reinforced suspension systems with extra travel, as well as lots of indispensable minor features that enabled the rider to extricate himself from the most difficult situations: Q.D. wheels, footrests that folded back to avoid breakages, waterproof air-filters, knobbly tyres, close gear ratios and so on. The day of the series-construction bikes, the Sertums and even the Lambrettas, was gone for ever: they had not yet got round to churning out moto-cross bikes with a headlight for appearances' sake, but that day was coming fast. The MV 125 was a well-built machine: obviously a certain period of time was required before they got it prepared the way they wanted it, but the results eventually came along, thanks in particular to the efforts of the "Gold Flames" team: Dante Mattioli, Panarari, Azzalin and Moscheni. Privateers were offered the chance to buy the 125 shortly afterwards, as we shall see.

Count Domenico had lost none of his taste for beautiful engineering in the meantime; and the Milan Show of November 1963 was the stage for a somewhat spectacular launch in honour of the Arno 160, a very handsome middleweight and a declaration of optimism that flew in the face of contemporary wisdom, which had decreed black days ahead for the motorcycle. The industry certainly needed both optimism and above all an injection of new and stimulating products: because although it is true that the ranks of utility bike buyers were destined to grow thinner, it was equally true that the motorcycle's real fans would keep faith with two wheels, providing that they were offered an up-to-date product.

The Arno's engine, a 4-stroke twin with the cylinders tilted forward at 12 degrees, was a long stroker with exactly 166.3 cm^3 of displacement; it had coil ignition and a 15 mm twin-barrel carburettor, wet sump lubrication and a 4-speed gearbox. It developed 7.5 hp at 6000 rpm and was therefore considered to be a very flexible propulsion unit, highly suited to long-distance touring and extremely durable. The frame was an open single-loop cradle. It was put on sale at a most attractive price, 246,000 lire: not much more expensive than the 150 single therefore, but with far more going for it in terms of class.

Another novelty introduced at the same Show took the form of a 2-stroke moped with pedals, which went to join the line-up alongside the more sophisticated Liberty model. The Germano, (Mallard) as the newcomer was called, had a pressed steel single-beam frame supporting a cantilevered engine and a 3-speed gearbox. Two versions were introduced: the Turismo, which had a cycle saddle and rear luggage carri-

er, and the Sport, whose wide fuel tank and long saddle gave it the look of a real light motorcycle. Needless to say such features were calculated to appeal to younger buyers. A couple of years later the Germano was radically modified when the pedals were eliminated and the engine was housed in a new tubular full duplex cradle. This was the birth of the Gran Turismo GT, Sport S and America versions.

Nothing much happened in 1964 with the only innovation, if we can put it that way, being some styling variations made to the range of 125 cm^3 lightweights. The resounding Centomila name was dropped in favour of some less presumptious initials, GT (Gran Turismo) and GTL (Gran Turismo Lusso). Modifications were made to the shape of the accessories, paintwork and chromework, but to all intents and purposes the bike was still the same biddable and robust machine as before.

Towards the end of 1965, the motorcycle market suddenly began to show signs of new life. Young people, freer and more independent than ever before — financially and otherwise – were beginning to feel a need for their own personal means of transport, something to liberate them from the shackles of public transport timetables and parental conditions. For reasons of age and limited

purchasing power the motorcycle was the obvious, almost the only, candidate. At the same time the motorcycle was rapidly acquiring an aura of "radical chic" in certain circles where the motor car, now within the financial grasp of the masses, smacked of socially unacceptable conformity. To some extent this new fashion was an echo of the American experience.

After first providing a sample of what they could do on race tracks all over the world, the Japanese launched their assault on the world market. America, of course, was a priority target and the thrust of the Japanese campaign was aimed at convincing middle class Americans that the motorcycle was no longer a means of transport favoured only by young toughs who had seen too many old Marlon Brando movies: the bike was to have a new image as a leisure vehicle tailored to suit conventional tastes. Given the fact that middle class people were accustomed to large, exclusive saloons then the motorcycle also had to be a powerful, prestigious vehicle, preferably large and expensive and certainly as unlike a moped or a modest lightweight as possible.

At that time only a few foreign manufacturers – in Germany and above all in Great Britain – were producing large, albeit somewhat dated, performance motorcycles. The Japanese industry had not yet got itself onto a firm footing in Europe and especially not in Italy, where the locals had instantly under-

stood that the winds of change were blowing and, just for once, were ready to take advantage of the situation. In November 1965 the Milan Motorcycle Show witnessed the rebirth of the Italian heavy motorcycle, finally equipped with the kind of up-to-date technical features and performance that the customers wanted. Showing an admirable sense of timing, MV unveiled a sensational bike: the 600 was a 4-cylinder double-knocker clearly derived from the marque's all-conquering racing models, which were the stuff of all true racing fans' dreams.

This bike was very much the brainchild of Conte Domenico Agusta, who was also responsible for some highly personal, but not always successful design touches, like the humpbacked fuel tank and the large rectangular headlamp, as well as the general characteristics. The most important of these was the displacement, which had been set outwith the usual sporting capacity classes precisely to prevent people racing the bike and thus creating confusion between works machines and privately entered bikes, whose results might reflect poorly on the hard-won reputation of the works team. A similar idea lay behind the decision to fit a shaft drive, planned first and foremost to lend an extra touch of refinement but also intended to discourage the privateers. Moreover the new bike was not to be sold to just anybody but to a limited clientele, directly selected by MV in a bid to ensure that this élite motorcycle (then the only four-cylinder machine in production) became the exclusive property of an equally élite group of riders.

But in the long term none of this stopped a few people from converting the bike into a racer by sleeving down the displacement to 500 cm³ or boring it out to 750 cm³; some also removed the shaft drive in favour of a chain, but in actual fact very few people were prepared to go to all this trouble.

With the exception of the long stroke prototype ($56 \times 60 \times 4 = 590$ cm³), the engine was slightly undersquare ($58 \times 56 \times 4 = 590$ cm³), and embodied several exclusive and very costly features that had been derived directly from Grand Prix racing machines. Effectively speaking all the MV fours in this and the following series were hand built, one by one, by highly specialized craftsmen using race shop methods. As a result it can fairly be said that each one of these bikes was a unique specimen that reflected the skill and the craftsmanship of the individual operative who assembled it.

The crankshaft, which also drove the cluster of timing gears for the double overhead camshafts, hung from a crank carrier that was held in place by twelve studs; the crankshaft itself was a built-up unit made up of five parts that ran on six rolling bearings. The two outer bearings were of the conventional type while the four internal ones were highly particular. The

The very interesting 146 cm³ 2-stroke lightweight with the 5-speed gearbox introduced at the 1967 Milan Show. This bike never got beyond the prototype stage.

outer race was divided into two halves, for ease of dismantling, but the surfaces in contact seemed as though they had been broken. And that's precisely the way it really was: the ball race was manufactured in one complete piece and then broken in two, so as to obtain an irregular fracture line, which nevertheless made for a highly accurate and precise fit between the two parts.

The primary drive was taken from the first crank (from the left): the propulsion unit therefore had no chains. Naturally this assembly generated rather a lot of mechanical noise, but it was extremely efficient otherwise.

Lubrication was by a wet sump system with a geared feed pump; the engine breathed through four carbu-

rettors. Ignition was by coil, fed by a battery and a 12-volt, 135-watt dynamotor, which also handled starting. But the light weight and compact dimensions that constitute the major advantages offered by dynamotors are counterbalanced by poorish electrical performance. This is due primarily to the fact that the device has to handle two opposing functions; in order to obviate this problem, at least partially, the dynamotor fitted to the MV 600 had a special transmission system based on two belts that supplied two different ratios, a lower one for the starter motor function and a higher one for the generator function.

The clutch was a wet multiplate type with five helical springs; the gearbox offered five speeds. The frame was a closed duplex cradle, with teledraulic suspension units; the wheels were shod with 3.00 - 18" tyres in front and 3.50 - 18" behind. While the rear wheel carried a normal central drum brake, the front wheel used two mechanically controlled Campagnolo discs, practically the same unit as the one the marque were testing out on their 125 Grand Prix stroker at the same time: a real first in the world of motorcycling. The sales price was fixed at 1,060,000 lire, a considerable sum (the contemporary Guzzi V7 cost about 700,000 lire), but it was good value for money given the constructional characteristics of the bike.

Even though the Quattro Cilindri was the star of the Show, it was not the only in-

novation introduced by MV on that occasion: almost as if it wished to emphasize its optimism and faith in the reviving market, the Verghera-based marque displayed two new versions of its Liberty moped: the Super Sport and America, with 2.00 - 18" wheels. MV's capacious stand also had room for an updated version of the 125 Gran Turismo Lusso, and a Scrambler version of the same bike, as well as a 250 twin that had nothing whatever to do with the Arno, even though it looked a little like a bigger version of it at first glance.

The engine was still an undersquare parallel twin with push-rods and rocker arms

An experimental version, dating from 1967, of the 250 twin with a particular frame design, and all that remains today of an original V-twin middleweight with a single chain-driven camshaft, constructed in the early Sixties.

and the cylinders tilted forward at 10 degrees, but the shape of the head and the crankcase had been altered, while the plugs were mounted in a different place. Another important change lay in the fact that the crankshaft was now supported in the centre too. Ignition was by coil and the engine was fed by two carburettors; the gearbox was a five-speed unit. The frame was an open cradle with a single downtube. With 18 hp on call, this bike could touch 140 km/h. A more successful 350 version was prepared in 1969.

Such a stream of innovations could only be followed by a period of calm and in fact MV came up with no new products for a couple of years. But the 1967 Milan Show witnessed the appearance of a little newcomer that by MV standards was highly original, even revolutionary: a 150 cm^3 rotary valve two-stroke twin. This was a product that flew in the face of all Count Domenico's fondest convictions (for he was a man with little faith in disc-valve engines), but it was technically a very interesting product just the same. All things considered, however, it was perhaps a little too far ahead of its time (because the vogue for high performance two-stroke engines still lay in the future) and so it was left at the prototype stage. Nevertheless this engine did serve as yet another demonstration of the high levels of vitality and inventiveness displayed by designers and management alike at MV.

In order to complete the portrait of this ingenious little stroker we should add that the engine was a more or less square ($45 \times 46 \times 2 = 146.3$ cm^3) parallel twin with the heavily finned cylinders tilted at 45 degrees and a five-speed gearbox. The front part of the frame was a tubular layout while the rear end was made up of the usual pressed steel elements with a cantilevered engine; the wheels were fitted with 2.75 - 18" tyres, power output was 12 hp at 8000 rpm and top speed was 125 km/h.

Everything seemed rosy in the garden at MV, therefore: production, even though the numbers involved had never been very great, was based on state of the art products while brilliant results in the sporting arena had made the company's name resound all over the world. But a cruel Destiny was preparing to turn its back on the Agusta family, and hence on the MV marque: the first blow was the sudden death of Mario Agusta, the deputy Chairman of the company, in the September of 1969. This was followed in early 1971 by the death of Domenico Agusta, the real driving force behind the company, following a massive heart attack.

The honour – and the burden – of carrying on the family business fell to the youngest of the brothers, Corradino. His was an extremely onerous inheritance, because although it may have been possible for him to equal the commitment, the capacities, and the sense of fair play whatever the stakes – be they sporting honours or a substantial contract – that his brother Domeico had always possessed, it could never have been possible for him to match the late Count's all-consuming passion for motorcycles.

Effectively speaking, even though things seemed to continue as before, something vital had gone for ever and the epic tale of the marque was about to come to an end: it had reached its apogee in the years immediately preceding the death of its principal creator and now the sun was about to set. The process was so slow it was almost imperceptible at first but the decline had begun and the company's performance began to lose some of its earlier sparkle. At the same time the aeronautical division, the pillar upon which the entire Agusta complex depended, began to creak under the weight and so it became more

The MV works during the last years in business: the assembly lines for the Ipotesi twin and its engine. In the left hand corner of the photo, a batch of engines for the Quattro Cilindri.

important than ever to keep things on a tight rein and avoid excessive spending. The fact of the matter is that the motorcycle division ran at a loss and none of Count Domenico's successors loved motorcycles enough to justify such an expensive hobby.

In any case, even though the production of mopeds and delivery tricycles had to be discontinued, ordinary motorcycle production continued much as before, for the time being. New versions were added to the range of 350 twins and the luxurious 600 four was transformed into a sporty 750. This went against Count Domenico's plans for the 600, which he had intended as a motorcycle for a refined non-sporting clientele; but the truth was that the bike had not been much of a success from a commercial point of view. The refined, non-sporting clientele had not materialized in large enough numbers while the rather sedate 600 had disappointed the sporting customers, potentially far greater in number, who wanted nothing better than to identify themselves in some way with the deeds of the national hero of the moment, Giacomo Agostini. These were the people MV now intended to cultivate, by giving them the kind of machine they had always wanted.

The first version of the 750, the Sport, appeared at the Milan Show in November 1969 and, with the exception of the engine, it did not resemble the 600 in the slightest: new forks, different mud-guards, aluminium rims, a powerful 4-LS drum on the front wheel – disc brakes had not really "arrived" yet – four separate exhaust pipes, and retouched trim had radically improved the look of the bike, which now looked quite the "café racer". And when the Supersport appeared a couple of years later with a tank like the one used on the competition Tre Cilindri and a sleek red and silver fairing it could fairly be said that the process of transforming the marque's famous competition machines into street-racers was complete.

The increase in displacement was obtained by boring out the cylinders to 65 mm, with the result that the engine acquired oversquare dimensions; power was upped to 65 hp at 7900 rpm, a figure which became 78 hp at 9000 rpm for the Supersport. The shaft drive was retained, however, despite the fact that it was not the most suitable design for strictly sporting use. A Gran Turismo version was prepared at the same time as the Supersport; this bike, which had no fairing, had cowhorn handlebars and a large dualseat and offered an intermediate performance level in comparison with the two sportsters: 69 hp at 7900 rpm.

The 750 cm^3 displacement was not just chosen because it was a "classic" capacity class, but also because the company was thinking of fielding a works bike in 750 class competition. At that time American-style endurance events, along the lines of the "Dayto-na 200 Miles", were becoming fashionable in Europe too. This kind of competition was reserved for big, production-derived machines and the regulations permitted considerable room for manoeuvre as far as modifications were concerned. From the manufacturers' point of view, such races were just what the doctor ordered because they provided good publicity at a relatively low cost.

And so the first Italian "200 Miles" race was held at Imola in the April of 1972. This was an epoch-making event accompanied by a great deal of razzmatazz – a novelty for Italy in those days – for which MV entered two 750s, to be ridden by Giacomo Agostini and Alberto Pagani, although Pagani withdrew before the start. Agostini battled on bravely, but a combination of rather poor roadholding and excessive weight made it hard for him to do much against the Ducatis (who ran out winners), and the best foreign entrants, the Nortons and the Triumphs. Then a broken valve put "Ago" and his MV multi definitively out of contention.

It was clear that the 750 required a good deal of work if it was to be employed as a serious competition bike; it needed to lose weight, chain drive had to be fitted and the chassis also needed improving. At first it seemed as if MV management might take the matter further, but then the idea of taking part in big bike competition was abandoned.

Following the death of Do-menico Agusta and the appearance of the first financial difficulties, the new management, headed by managing director Pietro Bertola, was torn by the desire to carry on a glorious motorcycling tradition on the one hand and the need to balance the books on the other.

The initial enthusiasm for production racing soon cooled, to be followed by a drastic cut back in the range of products on offer: in fact by 1974 production was limited to the Scrambler, GTEL and SEL versions of the 350 twin, with electronic ignition; and the Sport and Granturismo versions of the 750. But the same company that was cutting costs left, right, and centre went to the November '73 Milan Show with the Ipotesi (Hypothesis), a beautiful prototype embodying the best of modern motorcycling technology and styling (created in association with Giorgetto Giugiaro), which went into production not long after. This alternation of gusts of optimism followed by bouts of gloom and pessimism could not fail to have a negative influence on the market, which was upset and disoriented by these continuous changes of programme. There was life in the old dog yet, however, and in early 1975 the management came up with an ambitious growth plan involving a range of up-market products based on the Quattro Cilindri, the America version of which was introduced with an uprated 789.7 cm^3 engine, and the Ipotesi, now in production and

125
2 tempi 3 marce - 1948

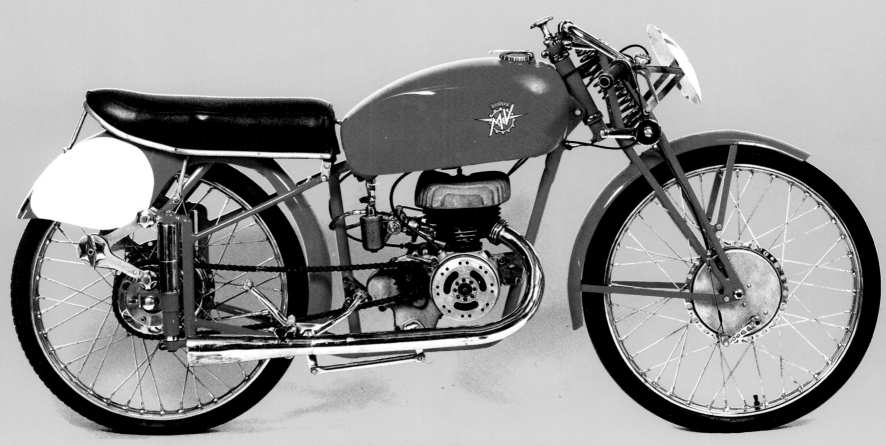

1948 model - Bruno Taglioretti's Collection

500 Turismo - 1950

1950 model - MV Museum, Gallarate

500 Turismo - 1950

1950 model - MV Museum, Gallarate

125 T E L - 1949-1954

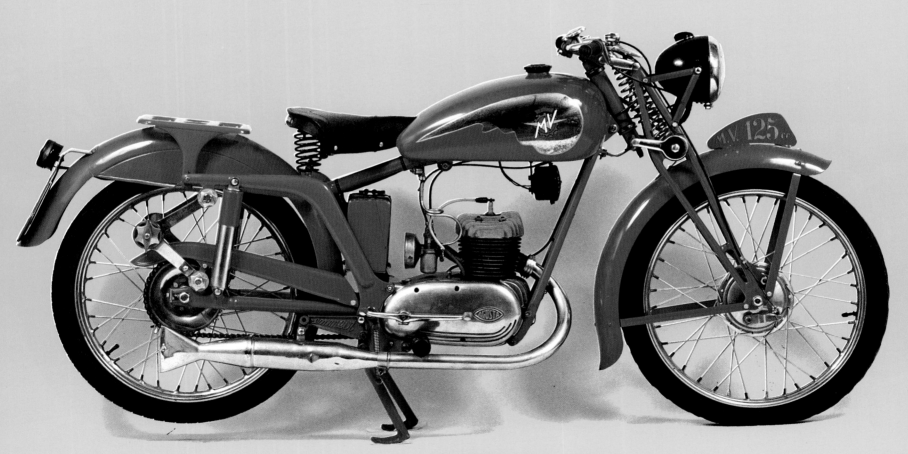

1953 model - MV Museum, Gallarate

known officially as the 350 Sport.

The America, apart from the increase in displacement and hence performance (75 hp at 8500 rpm, 220 km/h), boasted updated, angular lines, with a sculpted tank whose rear part linked up harmoniously with the side panels. A twin-disc brake with Scarab calipers was fitted to the front wheel, which retained the traditional spokes in order to conform with American homologation requirements (cast light alloy wheels were available on request): the four separate pipes ended in four chrome-plated fake megaphones.

The 350 Sport, ex Ipotesi, had a very sleek, angular look, enhanced by the shape of the horizontal top frame rails, which were curved to follow the outline of the fuel tank. The bike used light alloy spoked wheels with hydraulic disc brakes at front and rear. The push-rod engine was an oversquare unit with electronic ignition and a five-speed gearbox. A really beautiful "new" motorcycle with nothing futuristic about it, it was a perfect blend of tradition and modernity that revealed the touch of a master stylist.

Using the same basic layout, MV prepared a new 125 Sport with a single-cylinder 4-stroke push-rod engine and a five-speed gearbox. Like its larger stablemate, this bike too had squarish engine casings and bodywork and a frame with horizontal top rails. It carried spoked wheels with a disc brake on the front wheel only.

Unfortunately this pro-gramme was not destined to last much longer. The course which the Agusta concern had followed over the years was to lead to the destruction of the very motorcycle division that had kept the firm afloat not all that long before.

The Agusta family, after the loss of its senior members, was no longer able to maintain direct control over the firm's rapidly growing array of commitments; furthermore changing times and the growth of the company had eroded that special relationship with the workforce which – although it had its negative aspects – was nevertheless the best way to obtain positive results in certain highly specialized production areas. This combination of circumstances, plus the impelling necessity to cut costs made it necessary to axe all the loss-making sectors and at the same time to seek a partner able to guarantee the necessary support at managerial level. Such a partner was eventually found in the form of EFIM (a public body set up to finance the manufacturing industry), but the price was the winding up of the motorcycle division.

This decision was certainly a hard one for the Agusta family, who tried to save the motorcycle manufacturing division right to the end; a fact borne out by a long series of rumours and contradictory statements that followed one another throughout 1977. After the first rumours that the company was about to abandon the sector immediately, there was talk of continuing commercial production under the Ducati name, then owned by EFIM; then MV issued an official statement saying that the company intended merely to abandon all forms of sporting activity, period. Finally, in April, a long statement was issued:

"Following the articles that have recently appeared in the national and foreign press regarding the affairs of the MV Agusta company and with a view to dispelling any misunderstandings that could damage the company and its activities, the Board wishes to state that its sporting commitments have been suspended for the 1977 season. The Agusta Group, of which MV is a part, has nevertheless decided to continue its research programme, so as not to lose the considerable technological patrimony represented by the Grand Prix engines.

Production: autonomous motorcycle production will continue at MV according to market indications. The merger with Ducati, mentioned in the press, is not an issue at present. We intend to proceed with existing plans for a series of new vehicles intended to replace the current range. These new products, upon which the company's hopes for the future rest, should become a concrete reality by early next year."

Unfortunately the reality was a lot different, even though studies for prototypes were made: for example, there were plans for a four-cylinder 16-valve dohc engine with the cylinder block tilted at 30 degrees from the horizontal and the sump extended forwards, as on the competition Tre cilindri. It all added up to a beautiful propulsion unit that could have been built with cubic capacities ranging from 750 to 1200 cm^3, with either chain- or shaft-drive. It was thought that this engine might be displayed at the 1977 Milan Show, where MV had booked its usual stand.

But the stand was to remain empty. Right to the end, ANCMA, the constructors' association that organizes the show, hoped that MV would make an appearance: the secretary of the association sent a touching letter to Agusta in which he made a heartfelt appeal to Count Corrado's sense of tradition. But the Count had to reply that unfortunately his company had had to sacrifice sentiment, no matter how noble or profound, upon the altar of commercial exigencies and that Agusta was obliged to wind up its motorcycle manufacturing division definitively.

And so MV, despite its enormous wealth in terms of technical know-how, experience and – not least of these – of men, had to shut up shop. The bikes remained on the market for a couple more years, until stocks ran out. As supplies dwindled some machines were more and more in demand – especially the Quattro Cilindri – but in early 1980, the last unit having been sold, the curtain fell once and for all on the brief but fascinatingly intense history of the one of the most celebrated marques in the world.

THE QUEEN OF THE LIGHTWEIGHTS

From the day the little stroker howled to victory for the first time at the Valenza circuit in October 1946, to the unforgettable roar of the 350 four that Giacomo Agostini piloted to victory for the last time on the 26th of September 1976 at Mugello, exactly thirty years had passed. In the course of those thirty years MV had played, at first timidly, then with authority and finally with the strength of desperation, a major role on the world motorcycling scene. During that time MV became the world's most successful factory in the sporting arena, racking up a record number of wins that seems unbeatable in many cases: 37 World Constructors' Championships, 38 World Riders' Championships, 28 Italian Senior Championships, 7 Italian Junior Championships and an incredible "bag" of over three thousand victories overall (3,028 according to official data), of which 270 were obtained in races valid for the World Championships. The factory's most important honours include an outstanding 34 wins at the English TT; but neither should we overlook the victories in trials competition, both in the Six Days and the national championships, nor the long distance road races like the Milano-Taranto and the Motogiro d'Italia, nor in-

deed the records for the Hour and the 100 Km set by Mike Hailwood at Daytona in 1964. But although the bare-bones statistics give an idea of the importance of the phenomenon, they say little about the events that made such results possible. In the following pages we shall be dealing with these events as we leaf through the sporting history of this great Italian marque that still has large numbers of fans throughout the world. In order to give a clear picture of the technical development of the bikes, the story of MV's sporting career has been subdivided into two sections, one dedicated to the small- and medium-capacity machines, where all the models can trace their ancestry back to the dohc 125 from 1950, and another reserved for the 350 and 500 cm^3 multis, which were also closely interrelated.

The four-stroke engine fitted to the 125 competition model from 1950, the first real Grand Prix racer built by MV, had no futuristic features but was the embodiment of everything that experience had shown to be useful in the search for maximum power. It was therefore an engine with gear-driven dou-

ble overhead camshafts, hemispheric combustion chamber, inclined valves, magneto ignition and a separate lubrication system aimed at providing abundant circulation and efficient cooling of the lubricant.

In this first version, the engine was a long stroker, with the same dimensions as the two-stroke bikes: 53 x 56 mm. Cylinder barrel and head were both in light alloy, the valves had bucket-type tappets and exposed hairpin springs. The built-up crankshaft had a small ancillary external flywheel, on the left. The primary drive was by gears, with a wet clutch; the gearbox was a four-speeder. Practically speaking, the frame was still the same as the one used for the strokers, with girder forks, pivoted rear fork, springs enclosed in telescopic spring boxes and adjustable friction dampers. The newcomer made its debut at the Dutch GP at Assen. In the Italian races MV was still fielding the two-stroke bikes – including the new "Long crankcase" version – which were still highly competitive, especially in the long distance road races: in fact they won the 125 class in the prestigious Milano-Taranto endurance race, while in the 24 Hours trials event a team made up of Benzoni, Fornasari and Ventura – Ital-

y's best trials racers, who had left the Sertum team just before – carried all before them.

Assen was not to be a lucky race for MV: the two entries, ridden by Renato Magi and Franco Bertoni, despite their 13 hp at 10000 rpm, fell victim to the usual niggling tuning problems and were therefore unable to get the better of the Morinis and especially the powerful Mondial team, which had recently acquired the talented and forceful Ubbiali. No great results emerged from the Italian debut at the Monza Grand Prix of Nations either: there was plenty of power all right, but something always cropped up to ruin everything. Just for the record, Bertoni and Magi managed seventh and eighth place on the day. Throughout 1950 and '51 the results were fairly disappointing therefore, despite the factory's commitment and the use of avant-garde technical features – like the application of full or partial fairings – and it was not until 1952 that Fortune began to smile on MV. In the meantime the dohc engine had been fitted to a competition scooter, that form of racing being very popular at the time in Italy. To call this a scooter was stretching things a little, but it was in line with the letter of the regulations, which laid down that there had to be a gap of a few centimetres between the steering head and the tank, just enough to make it possible to define the machine as an "open frame" model. But to all intents and purposes this was a light motorcycle, and it was in this version that the dohc engine scored its first victory – with Franco Bertoni aboard – in Bologna.

The 1952 Circuito di Parma event witnessed the debut of the revised version of the 125, whose engine had undergone a few external modifications, the most outstanding of which was the transfer of the oil pump assembly to a point on a level with the magneto, while a great deal of work had been done in a bid to eliminate the causes of the poor roadholding that had dogged the bike up to that time. There was also a new telescopic fork, characterized by a large central teledraulic element in the place occupied by the big spring in a girder fork assembly, plus a new anatomical fuel tank with greater capacity. Power output had been upped to 15 hp at 10,800 rpm, while weight remained at the outstandingly low limit of 80 kilograms. This renewed twin-cam came second at Parma, where it was ridden by Angelo Copeta, but the best was yet to come: a good three wins in a row, at the Isle of Man TT, the Dutch GP and the Ulster GP. The rider on all three occasions was Cecil Sandford and this combination of British riding skill and Italian engineering was enough to give MV the World Championship ahead of Ubbiali and the Mondial team. This was the first of that long series of championship victories that was to make MV the most successful factory the world has ever seen.

In 1953 Ubbiali returned to Cascina Costa, a return that was to prove permanent and the beginning of a long series of wins for both rider and stable, which went on to become one of the most successful double acts in the history of the sport. On the technical front, much of '53 was spent perfecting the engine, which acquired almost another two horses, and the chassis. The rear part of the frame was fitted with two sheet metal elements to support the shock absorbers, now with exposed springs, while the oil tank was shifted to a point behind the petrol tank, thus reducing the length of the saddle. Then the steering head was covered with a small fairing that ran back to the fuel tank, to which it was attached. For the CONI Grand Prix, the inaugural event held at the Imola circuit in the April of that year, Copeta's 125 was fitted with a simplified Earles fork, which was kept on for the rest of the season, albeit with a few modifications (exposed springs rather than enclosed spring boxes). The front mudguard was extended forward almost to ground level, an "aerodynamic" feature that was enjoying a considerable vogue in those days. The wheels measured 19 inches.

The external flywheel was eliminated for the Grand Prix of Nations while the weight of its internal counterparts was increased. Strangely enough, this modification was decided upon after a bike

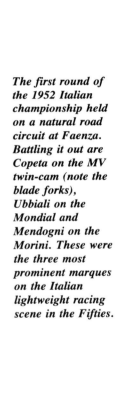

The first round of the 1952 Italian championship held on a natural road circuit at Faenza. Battling it out are Copeta on the MV twin-cam (note the blade forks), Ubbiali on the Mondial and Mendogni on the Morini. These were the three most prominent marques on the Italian lightweight racing scene in the Fifties.

had shed its external flywheel during a race without any anomalous behaviour ensuing, so much so that the rider had not even noticed!

All these modifications had resulted in a weight increase of about 6 kilos, but this handicap was more than compensated by the extra power and improved stability. Results were mixed throughout the season, a fact due partly to the eruption of the NSU team onto the sporting scene: the Germans, who had been quarantined up to then because of – presumably – their misdeeds during the war, had taken advantage of their enforced absence to prepare themselves thoroughly and their explosive return to the sporting arena had given their British and Italian rivals more than one sleepless night. For that matter, the same thing had happened in four-wheeled motorsport, where the formidable Mercedes team had shown itself to be virtually unbeatable. In the end, however, things did not turn out so badly, because MV retained the World Constructors' Championship for the 125 class. Furthermore Cascina Costa could boast the most sought-after title of all, thanks to Les Graham, who won the Isle of Man TT; Ubbiali and Copeta also racked up useful wins in Germany and Spain.

In the chapter on series production we saw that MV had prepared an overhead

44

Top left, the start of the 125 event at Faenza in 1953: Sandford (166) with the Earles forks, Ubbiali (once more with MV), Zinzani with the Morini, and Copeta. Below, a 175 race at Spoleto in 1955: note the different fairings on Ubbiali's bike (5) and Franzosi's (1). Beside them is Mendogni with the Morini.

The two shots on this page show the dustbin-type fairings used by MV for work on the fast circuits between 1954 and 1956. Above, Taveri at Assen in 1956 (his face is deformed by the wind); below, Ubbiali at Monza in '55. Visible in the photo are the oil tank and the internal part of the "tail".

camshaft 175 cm³ lightweight (for the '53 season), whose unassuming appearance hid the heart of a thoroughbred racer; but the surprises in store for racing fans did not stop here. In fact, in order to meet some of the requirements of private entrants, always on the look out for a more competitive machine, and with a particular eye to the needs of the younger riders in the junior classes, who could not race with bikes classified as Grand Prix machines – even if they had possessed the wherewithal to buy such costly items – MV marketed a splendid 125 whose frame had been lifted from the previous season's works bike and whose sohc engine – with the exception of the tim-

ing gear – had also been directly derived from a factory racing model. With the usual long-stroke dimensions and a gear-driven camshaft, this engine still had the external flywheel on the left, magneto ignition, the oil pump mounted on the magneto shaft and the four-speed gearbox. A scooter version was also prepared with the same engine, and in this case too the cycle parts used were those of the dohc model.

On sale at 580 thousand lire, the MV 125 single overhead camshaft model was an instant commercial success, which was followed up shortly afterwards by a healthy series of wins and placings both in the minor championships and the long-distance road races.

On a world championship level, the bike to beat in the 125 cm^3 class was again the NSU, which showed up looking more competitive than ever for the '54 season. At that time the NSU team was at the peak of its powers (the factory was then leading the world in terms of units produced per annum) and was backed up by a highly efficient organization.

Apart from ordering some minor mechanical changes (the most relevant modification was the adoption of a five-speed gearbox), the men at MV had put their money on aerodynamics, in particular the use of fairings that were fuller and more "scientific" than anything used up to that time.

For the first Italian outings of the season – Modena, Ferrara, Monza, all rounds in the Italian Championship – MV was still using the mini fairing from the previous season, but when the first World Championship date rolled round at the Isle of Man Ubbiali's bike appeared with a light alloy dustbin fairing fitted with two rectangular air scoops at the front. Strangely enough the new fairing was mounted around the old mini fairing to which it had been carefully joined. In the course of the season the fairing was gradually modified and improved until the Grand Prix of Nations at Monza where the bike appeared in a full fairing extended to cover the rear wheel. The old mini fairing had disappeared altogether to be replaced by an extended "dustbin" at the front,

which covered the rider's hands leaving only a small plexiglass screen in the middle. Two air scoops in the nose channelled the air towards the cylinder. The tail fairing was also made of light alloy. Sandford's mount had a slightly different fairing that belled out to cover the ends of the handlebars. The air scoops were located directly beneath the windscreen.

But the gap in power separating these machines from the NSU was considerable, and the fairings alone were not enough to bridge it. Ubbiali was able to score a brilliant second place behind Hollaus at the Isle of Man TT (where for the first time that year the small bikes had raced round the short and sinuous Clypse

circuit), but when the championship circus moved on to the faster continental circuits, Ubbiali was never able to do better than third place.

MV fielded a good six works bikes for the Monza GP. For the record these were in the hands of Ubbiali, Colombo, Copeta, Pagani, Sala and Sandford, and to the best of our knowledge no other team to this day has ever fielded a larger number of entrants in a single class; but on the other hand the NSU team withdrew out of respect for the memory of Hollaus who had lost his life during practice for that very race.

Victory went to MV on the day, thanks to Sala; but the Monza event is also memorable for the appearance of an

The privateers went over to dustbin fairings too: the photo shows Englishman Bill Webster on an MV 125 ahead of Bartos with the CZ at Assen in 1956.

experimental engine fitted with a direct injection system. The new system was mounted on Ubbiali's bike, which gave an excellent demonstration of its possibilities. Ubbiali streaked straight into the lead right from the start and only relinquished his hold on first place to teammate Sala in the final stages, following problems with a broken oil tube, and after having pushed up the lap record to 150.500 km/h.

Still in 1954 MV wound up

holding the first three places in the Italian Championship with Copeta, Sala and Ubbiali, after a hard fight against a reinvigorated Mondial team. The factory also racked up several non-championship wins abroad, where the new single overhead camshaft model was also raced.

NSU, which had been MV's most feared adversary over the previous two years, withdrew from racing at the end of 1954, but this did not mean that MV could catch up on some of that lost sleep: competition was fiercer than ever and Mondial, in particular, was emerging as a real threat. During the winter a good deal of improvements were made to the double-knocker 125, which showed up for the '55 season looking rather different.

The valves were set at a different angle just for a start and this had meant modifying the shape of the timing cover; ignition was by an 8-volt battery and coil set-up while the gearbox was now a six-speeder. As far as the cycle parts were concerned, the Earles fork had been abandoned in favour of a classic telescopic unit with enclosed springs while some slight modifications had been made to the frame; MV tried out an original structure with downtubes outboard of the engine run-

Modena 1954: Ubbiali (32) on the 203 cm³ single between Colombo (44) and Venturi with the 245 cm³ twin that had been obtained by siamesing two dohc 125 units. Left, the unusual propulsion unit.

47

ning directly from the steering head down to the pivot of the rear swinging fork, but this design was shelved almost right away. Power had increased to about 18 hp at 11000 rpm and with the dustbin fairing fitted top speed was more than 180 km/h. Modifications had also been made to the fairing: after opening the season at Naples clad in the old fairing, the bike appeared with a new version in time for the Sanremo event. The new fairing had two large air intakes and a bigger windscreen and was used alternately with the older version in the World Championship events.

Although the 1955 Italian Championship went to Mondial, the World title was an authentic triumph for MV. The Swiss rider Taveri won the Spanish GP by a large margin over Ferri on the Mondial and Ubbiali, also aboard an MV. This was followed by a real purple patch of five straight victories for Ubbiali, who showed Taveri a clean pair of heels at the ultra-fast Reims circuit and the very tough Isle of Man TT. At the Nurburgring, Ubbiali, Taveri and new boy Remo Venturi crossed the line separated by the finest of margins, while in Holland the Italian beat the Swiss by a

few metres. Finally at Monza, where it seemed that – apart from the Mondial team – a certain opposition might have materialized in the form of the DKW stroker, the all-conquering Ubbiali romped home about half a minute ahead of his teammates Venturi and Copeta. It goes without saying that Carlo Ubbiali won the 1955 World Riders' Championship; but this fortunate season should also be remembered for many other reasons: the construction of the double-knocker 175 for Sport class racing and above all MV's entry into the 250 class.

In the previous chapters on series production we spoke of the creation and popularity of Sport class racing and of the fact that this – in many ways – laudable initiative had led the various manufacturers to enrich their catalogues with some genuine Grand Prix machinery; the arrival of "Formula Two" racing, which was a much more relaxed category as far as technical restrictions went (even dohc engines were admitted), accelerated this trend. And so, in homage to the new regulations, MV homologated a new 175 that differed from the works 125 only for the presence of lights. The structure of the engine was identical, as was the con-rod assembly: the extra cubes had been obtained by increasing the bore to 63 mm leaving the stroke unchanged at 56 mm, with the result that this was an oversquare unit. The carburettor was a 25 mm instrument, as laid down by the rules, and ignition was by magneto. The lighting system was run off a small flywheel-alternator on the left. The gearbox offered five speeds, the frame was made of tubing, the wheels measured 19 inches and the weight was around 90 kilos.

In this specification the bike was used for long-distance road races and for Junior Championship events, in the hands of more or less "works" riders like Fortunato Libanori and Dante Paganelli. It was also raced in the new 175 Senior class events, ridden by the usual Masetti, Ubbiali, Venturi, and company. Dustbin fairings similar to those used with the 125 were fitted for these races.

For the first time, MV decided to enter a 250 class race at the 1955 Shell Gold Cup meeting, held at the Imola Autodrome. At that time the quarter litre class was dominated by Guzzi and NSU, but the latter – as we have already seen – had withdrawn from racing at the end of 1954 leaving Guzzi alone at the top. The Mandello marque had a very fast and robust 250 racer but it was getting a bit

Ubbiali aboard the 125 at the Isle of Man TT in 1957. As can be seen from a comparison with the photos on page 45, the fairing had been considerably redesigned.

elderly. There was room for new blood and, virtually simultaneously, the marques that were dominating the lower capacity classes, Mondial, Morini and naturally MV, thought of "invading" the next class up. And so, almost as if they were acting on the basis of some secret agreement, they did exactly that, using 125s bored out to the minimum displacement required for 250 class competition.

This provisional solution – which had been used the year before by Guzzi when that marque had decided to compete in the 350 category, until that time a strictly British preserve – produced excellent results right away, even though all three makers obviously went on to build their own 250 engines real and proper. As a matter of fact the bored-out lightweights benefitted from a series of advantages including lightness, compactness, superior manoeuverability as well as more modern design, all factors that made up for the lack of cubic capacity.

The line-up on the grid that day at Imola included a gaggle of Guzzis – works and otherwise – ridden by Enrico Lorenzetti, Romolo Ferri, Cecil Sandford, Alano Montanari, Adelmo Mandolini and Arthur Wheeler; two privately entered NSUs with Hans Baltisberger and Florian Camathias, Provini on a Mondial twin-cam, Mendogni on a Morini, also a twin-cam, Virgilio Campana on a Morini Rebello and, last but not least, Gino Franzosi

aboard the MV 203. It was instantly clear that the beefed-up Mondial, Morini and MV had a lot more pep than people had expected: in fact they were all far superior in terms of speed to the "real" 250s, which they rapidly outstripped to dominate the race with arrogant ease. Provini won on the Mondial, but the winning margin of only three seconds over Franzosi was probably more a measure of the riders' respective skills than any other consideration: in fact the third man home, the old fox Lorenzetti on the Guzzi, was a good minute behind the leaders.

Proof of the MV's enormous potential was provided by Bill Lomas's striking win at the Isle of Man TT, the hat-trick at Assen (the winner was Taveri) and Ubbiali's benefit race at Monza: the 203 went on to land MV the World Constructors' title in its first season.

The Grand Prix of Nations at Monza also witnessed the debut of a new 250 twin – obtained by simply siamesing two 125 cm³ cylinders – with a single timing cover on the right hand side and coil ignition.

The newcomer was ridden by Lomas, who came fifth, and Masetti, who took sixth place. This engine developed about 32-33 hp, more horses than the 203 could provide, but nevertheless it was never proved to be demonstrably superior either to the 203 cm³ unit or the 250 single, which as we shall see was prepared for the following season. The Bicilindrica was therefore

used only sporadically (it nevertheless managed to win the 1957 Belgian GP with John Hartle) and was eventually pensioned off definitively. The twin that appeared shortly afterwards in 1959 was to have a very different career, but we shall come to that later.

MV got off to a promising start in all the various capacity classes in 1956. During the third round of the Italian Championship, at Faenza, the factory pulled off a feat unique in the annals of motorcycle racing when it won all four races on the programme: the 125, 175, 250 and 500 cm³ events. Just to prove that this was no fluke, MV did it again at the Belgian GP, a world championship meeting, with victories in the 125, 250, 350 and 500 events. This not only demonstrated the strength of this dynamic Italian marque, able to field entries in four different capacity classes, but also the courage the Agusta brothers had shown in facing all the risks and difficulties involved in maintaining such an imposing racing division.

On the technical side, 1956 also saw – again at Faenza – the victorious debut of a new version of the middleweight single with the engine uprated to 220 cm³, and then the construction of a "real" quarter-litre machine for the World Championship. Decidedly undersquare ($72.6 \times 60 = 249$ cm³), it developed 29

hp, which became 32 by the end of the season, good enough for more than 210 km/h with an integral fairing at front and rear. As for the rest of the bike the general characteristics remained unchanged.

From a sporting point of view, the 1956 season could be summed up in one terse statistic: the 125 and 250 classes of the World and Italian Championships amount to an overall total of twenty rounds, eighteen of which were won by MV and the brilliant Ubbiali. But a few details will do no harm. At the Isle of Man TT Ubbiali had a fairly easy time of it against Sandford on the Mondial 125 and – in the 250 event – Miller on the NSU, while in Holland Ubbiali scored a great one-two beating Provini on the Mondial in the 250 race and romping home in the 125 event ahead of teammate Taveri.

The thrilling Belgian GP, the one where MV swept the board to win all four events, was enhanced by epic challenges from Lorenzetti on the Guzzi special in the 250 class and Ferri on the Gilera 125 twin, both of whom held the lead for several laps before retiring, leaving Ubbiali with a clear run to the finish ahead of teammates Taveri and Libanori to win with record averages: 168.696 km/h in the 250 event and 160.790 in the 125. In the German Grand Prix, over the difficult Solitude circuit, Ubbiali came in a few seconds behind Ferri aboard the extremely lively Gilera 125, but he made up

for that disappointment in the 250 race, where he won ahead of Taveri and Venturi: MV had swept the board again!

Ubbiali failed to score his usual double in Ulster, where the 250 race was won by Taveri (on the MV) in any case, but he roared back to form in the Monza Grand Prix of Nations meeting. During the last lap he took – and held on to –

a two second lead over Lorenzetti on the Guzzi 250 after having shadowed the latter for virtually the entire race. He repeated this feat in the 125 event, where he beat Provini and Ferri (on the Gilera) after a series of heart-stoppingly fast 190 km/h duels.

It was business as usual in the Italian Championship, with Ubbiali winning both the 125

and the 250 classes, while the Junior championship results also reflected MV's crushing superiority with the titles going to Francesco Villa (125), Augusto Baroncini (175) and Ernesto Brambilla (250). To sum up, by the end of that year MV found itself with a rich bag of wins including three World Constructors' Championships, three World Riders' Championships,

three Italian Senior Championships and three Italian Junior Championships: no one had ever won so much in a single season before!

The 1957 season opened in a promising fashion with Ubbiali's win in the Spanish GP aboard the fully faired

One for the album at the 1957 TT. Familiar faces include Nello Pagani, Vittorio Carrano (half-hidden by Pagani), Ubbiali, Colombo (holding the helmet), Bill Webster and Luigi Taveri. Giulio Cella is on the far right.

125, but MV's hegemony was about to be broken. A series of spills rendered some of the works team stars hors de combat and, to make matters worse, MV's major rivals – Mondial in particular – had come on song and were determined to stop the men from Cascina Costa from pulling off a repeat of the previous season's performance. MV's fortunes did not begin to change until the end of the season when Ubbiali won at Monza, but this was obviously small consolation in view of the previous season's results. All this made Remo Venturi's splendid win in the Motogiro d'Italia even more welcome, as he took the chequered flag aboard a 175 twin-cam ahead of a top-flight field of sports bikes composed of Benellis, Ducatis, Mondials, Morinis and Parillas. In the following chapters we shall talk at greater length about the new situation that came into being at the end of 1957 following the withdrawal of Guzzi, Moto Gilera and Mondial from racing. After the withdrawal it looked like things would be much easier for MV: but although this proved true

enough in the larger capacity classes it was a different story as far as the smaller bikes were concerned. That this was so was not so much the result of foreign competition, which was still in the future, but of two Italian adversaries that had shown themselves to be worthy of the greatest respect: Morini and Ducati.

For Morini it was a return to the limelight after a longish spell in the wilderness; Ducati on the other hand, although it had a respectable sporting tradition behind it, was a new force on the international scene, which it had invaded in force armed with

The 1957 version of the fully faired 250 at Assen with Roberto Colombo and, on the facing page, with Ubbiali at Monza. Far left, the 250 cm³ single with indirect injection seen for the first time at Modena in 1959, where it was ridden by Tino Brambilla. The photo clearly shows the pump, on the timing cover, and the injector on the induction manifold.

52

ultra-modern, highly competitive models like the "desmodromic" 125 single. But when the sums were totted up at year's end it was revealed that for the first time ever a single marque had won all the World titles – both for riders and constructors – in all four classes for solo bikes, 125, 250, 350 and 500. Needless to say the marque in question was MV Agusta, whose dream of a record clean sweep was realized when the battle for the 125 title was finally resolved in their favour. On the technical side, the 125 had been further perfected and it showed up for the sec-

ond round of the Italian Championship at Marinea Roma sporting a lowered frame with a different rear triangulation; the oil tank was forward of the saddle, the fairing had been trimmed back to leave the front wheels exposed as required by the new rules, while the front brake was also a new fitment. The engine now pumped out 20 hp at 12,500 rpm.
A programme was drawn up that called for participation, with at least two machines, in all the solo events on the World Championship, Italian Senior and Junior calendars, as well as the most important

non-title international meetings. The team was made up of Ubbiali, Provini (once his closest rival and now no longer with Mondial), Surtees, Hartle, Bandirola, Venturi, Libanori, Gilberto Milani and Tino Brambilla.
In addition MV also followed up an initiative promoted by the FIM, which had suggested that a few works bikes be lent to the most promising new riders. After a few trials held to aid selection Galliani and Vezzalini were both lent twin-cam 125s while Cantoni, winner of the FMI Singles Trophy, received a 500 four. The pecking order in the MV

team was as follows: Provini was the front runner in the 250 class and Ubbiali in the 125 class, with each man expected to support his team leader. For the first year at least, this agreement allowed these two fighting cocks to rule in the same roost and things went fairly well; the 125 class that season featured a series of knock down, drag out battles against the Ducatis of Gandossi, Spaggiari and Taveri (who had left MV), but at the end of the day the title remained with Ubbiali, who won at the Isle of Man, Holland, Germany and Ulster. Provini had an easier time of

Both pages show works and privately owned lightweights. Right, a "production-derived" 125 single-knocker with headlamp, number plate and stand.

it on his way to the World 250 Championship: the Morini threat did not materialize until the end of the season when Emilio Mendogni scored a brilliant victory at Monza with Giampiero Zubani coming in second.

Below, Ubbiali on the way to victory at Cattolica in 1958 – a mixed event for Senior and Junior riders – with the 175 "Formula Two".

After having won all four world solo titles for both riders and constructors, MV began the 1959 season determined to repeat the previous

year's exceptional performance and, naturally enough, no expense was spared. The by then classic 125 and 250 cm³ twin-cams had their engines and cycle parts retouched: the 125 engine was fitted into a neater frame, with the oil reservoir shifted to a point forward of the fuel tank where lubricant (and rider) would benefit more from the cooling airstream; the oil tank on the 250 was mounted under the saddle. In the first round of the Italian Championship, at Modena, spectators were treated to the sight of an all-new 125 with desmodromic valves, which gave a good account of itself in Provini's capable hands, and a fuel-injected 250 ridden by Tino Brambilla. These two machines were then side-

54

lined for the rest of the season, but whereas MV kept faith with the 125 twin-cam – which managed to retain the world title in the end despite the efforts of the East German MZ factory – it was decided to prepare a new twin-cylinder engine for the 250, which was to bear no resemblance to the quarter-litre unit that had been produced in 1955 by mating two 125 cm^3 engines.

Although the new 250 engine retained the characteristic "long" dimensions (53 × 56 × 2) it had the cylinders tilted forward by five degrees and – unusually for a small capacity MV engine – it had a wet sump lubrication system. The twin camshafts were driven by a gear cluster on the right; the hairpin valve springs were exposed. Power was fed to the six-speed gearbox by a geared primary drive. The cycle parts and the fairing were practically the same as those fitted to the single-cylinder model. Weight was about 115 kilos and power output was in the region of 37 hp at 13,500 rpm, good enough for more than 200 km/h.

The adversaries for the '59 season were much the same as before, with the addition of the MZ two-strokes that had reached good levels of power and reliability. But the atmosphere in the racing department was getting somewhat strained with Ubbiali, who was a cool tactician, at loggerheads with Provini, a hot-blooded character with a riding style to match. By the end of the season their differences had led to a total

breach and the matter was resolved with Provini's departure for Morini.

During the year, however, MV's two aces had had to work very hard to keep the various Ducati 125s, Morini 250 twin-cams and the MZs in their place. At the end of the day Ubbiali's supremely tactical style won the day and he wound up with both the world titles, even though it had been no walkover in either category. By the end of the quarter-litre championship season Ubbiali had

racked up two wins (Germany and Italy), while Provini also won twice (Isle of Man TT and Holland) as did Gary Hocking on the MV (Sweden and Ulster). Ubbiali's wins were particularly exciting affairs; he won in Germany by a mere three tenths of a second over Mendogni on the Morini, while at Monza a cat-like final sprint took him surging past Degner's MZ virtually on the finishing line to win by a whisker. In the 125 championship Ubbiali notched up three wins to Pro-

vini's two and a brace of victories for the MZ team.

In winding up the story of the 1959 season we should mention that a scaled-up 253 cm^3 version of the new 250 twin was prepared for 350 class racing on particularly tortuous circuits where the Quattro Cilindri had its problems. This bike was seen for the first time when Brambilla rode it at the Grand Prix of Nations, where it made an early retirement after leaving the track at the "Parabolica" bend; further bored out to

Finally, Tino Brambilla, the winner of the Junior Formula Two 175 event at Sanremo-Ospedaletti in 1956. Note the differences with Ubbiali's bike: oil tank and pump, front brake and rear suspension.

285 cm³, it won the 1960 French GP at Clermont Ferrand with Gary Hocking (ahead of Surtees), but despite this success the "Quattro" was eventually preferred.

The 1959 season had been a real triumph for MV, and everything seemed to suggest that 1960 would be a carbon copy. As a matter of fact MV continued in its winning ways in 1960 but, in the lower capacity classes at any rate, it was by no means as easy as many had predicted. This was because in these classes – which are objectively less demanding both technically and financially – several strong contenders had come to the fore all at once to re-establish the pluralism that had been brusquely interrupted by the withdrawal of several factories in 1957. As if that were not enough, some old adversaries, like MZ, had finally reached a state of tune that enabled them to give MV more than a few headaches, especially in the 125 class. As a matter of fact in the '60 season the 125 and 250 classes were much more interesting than the 500 class, even though the half-litre crown was still the one everyone wanted to win. Apart from the MZ two-strokes and the Ducatis, the 125 championship was enhanced by the arrival of the Spanish Bultaco and Montesa strokers, the Czech CZs, as well as a few Mondials that, despite the non-participation agreement, appeared in more or less official guises. The 250 class witnessed the debut of the new Ducati and Bianchi twins, the Benelli four and the Jawa twin.

But the major novelty was undoubtedly the arrival of a strong contingent of Japanese who, following their tentative first apearance at the English TT the previous year, had now embarked upon the aggressive policy of "global domination" that has produced the results we all recognize today.

Even more than the bikes, beautifully constructed and far superior to the ones seen the year before, Europeans were impressed by the imposing nature of the Japanese organization: four or five bikes per capacity class, swarms of mechanics, cold, precise and impeccable in their white gloves, the best riders obtainable, and a single-minded determination to achieve the desired results. When it came down to the nitty-gritty, however, the Suzuki Colleda 125 two-stroke twins and the Honda four-stroke 125 were still not good enough to trouble MV, even though the outstanding Honda 250, with its dohc four-cylinder engine and four valves per cylinder – a feature abandoned by the European industry in the Thirties and successfully dusted off by the Japanese nearly three decades later – got dangerously close to the MV twin, coming second behind the Italian machine at Ulster with Phillis and second again at Monza with Jim Redman.

At any rate the MV 250, with an improved frame, was still the best quarter-litre around in 1960 while the 125 was still on top of the world too. The "Desmodromic" made another fleeting appearance at Cesenatico at the beginning of the season with Taveri aboard. Unfortunately the Swiss rider "lost it" early in the race and withdrew.

The 1960 World Championship began in France, but the real opening took place at the Isle of Man TT, which boasted an imposing lineup of men and machines on the starting grid. Right from the first few metres Hocking dominated the 250 race, tenaciously opposed by Provini on the Morini; after more than 300 kilometres of hard-fought competition Hocking took the chequered flag forty seconds ahead of teammate Ubbiali and 51 seconds ahead of Provini. They were followed in by three Hondas, the first of which was almost seven minutes behind the winner.

Ubbiali got his own back in Holland, Belgium, Ulster and finally at Monza, where he had a comfortable win over Redman's Honda, as we have already mentioned, and Degner's MZ; needless to say this was enough for him to win the world title.

The 125 championship got under way at the Isle of Man TT, where Ubbiali scored a magisterial victory crossing the line a good twenty seconds ahead of teammate Hocking and third man Taveri, who has more than two

Scooter 125 C G T - 1950-1952

1952 model - MV Museum, Gallarate

125

Motore Lungo - 1950-1953

1953 model - MV Museum, Gallarate

125

Motore lungo - 1950-1953

1953 model - MV Museum, Gallarate

500

4 cilindri cardano - 1950-1953

1953 model - MV Museum, Gallarate

Tarquinio Provini during his victorious gallop through the mist and the rain at the 1958 Ulster GP. The bike is a 250 with a dolphin fairing as required by the new rules.

minutes adrift. Then came the MZs, about two and a half minutes behind the winner. Ubbiali won again in Holland, but he was beaten by the MZs of Degner and Hemplemann over the very fast Francorchamps circuit in Belgium. The Italian rider Gandossi and his MZ gave Ubbiali and Hocking a good run for their money in the Ulster GP, but the two MV riders were able to take advantage of a miscalculation to wrap up the race in MV's favour.

MZ were back in the lists for Monza, where Degner was able to stand the pace set by MV's star pair Ubbiali and Spaggiari for the entire race. On the last lap all three riders emerged from the "Parabolic" bend in a tight bunch, and it was anyone's guess who was going to win the day. But MV had worked out a strategy for this kind of situation: first Spaggiari took the outside track, on the stand side, with the German hot on his heels, then Ubbiali suddenly swerved towards the opposite side of the track, i.e. towards the pits. In this way Spaggiari succeeded in keeping Degner behind him while Ubbiali opened up enough of a lead to enable him to beat his opponents, despite the fact that Spaggiari's last lap had been the fastest of the day, at over 160 km/h.

Three's a crowd. Ubbiali on the MV followed by Spaggiari and Hailwood on Ducatis stick together in the 125 event at the '59 Assen Grand Prix.

1961 was a year of sensations. Just for a start, Count Domenico Agusta suddenly decided to withdraw his unbeaten motorcycles from competition, a decision justified by the increase in the number of races valid for the World Championship, a move that had made participation in the Grand Prix circus a frighteningly expensive hobby for a factory interested in four-stroke production. As a matter of fact, since the World Championship began in 1949 (before the war there had only been the European Championship), the number of rounds had gradually increased from six to eight, while ten were planned for 1961, including the new Argentinian Grand Prix, a race that certainly justified the "world" part of the title but one that involved a notable financial commitment.

At the same time the market was showing marked signs of recession and it became clear that racing was taking a large bite out of rapidly dwindling profits. It was therefore necessary to tighten the belt, at least for the time being, because maintaining a stable of twenty racing bikes was an expensive hobby even for a very rich man. But Count Domenico was too much of a sportsman to contemplate a total withdrawal from the track and the drastically worded January communiqué was tempered a short while afterwards in April, when the firm announced that some of the Grand Prix bikes had been sold to trusted riders,

who would race them as privateers, albeit with a certain amount of assistance from the factory. For the next few years therefore MVs were spotted at tracks everywhere bearing a conspicuous logo made up of the classic MV winged cogwheel and the word "Privat" in large letters. Another sensation was the retirement of two of the factory's most gifted riders: Carlo Ubbiali and – as we shall see – John Surtees, the undisputed king of the half-litre class. In Surtees's case the decision was determined by

the desire to open up new horizons in the world of four-wheeled motorsport (and of course the Englishman was the only man, to this day, to become world champion two and four wheels), Ubbiali on the other hand simply wished to wind up a long and eminently successful career in order to look after his private interests.

In any case, the responsibility of bearing the MV colours, or at least the "Privat" version of them, fell mainly onto the shoulders of Gary Hocking. Having skipped the first

events on that season's calendar, the "Privat" bikes showed up for Imola, where Hocking duly bagged the 500 event; this was followed by Barcellona, where Hocking won again on the 250 Bicilindrica, and then all the other World Championship events. But while the 350 and 500 fours were practically unbeatable, thus permitting Hocking to win both titles, life was getting much harder for the smaller bikes. In fact – and this was another event of capital importance – 1961 was the year in which the Japa-

nese industry exploded onto the scene with a vengeance. After having limited themselves to testing the waters for the previous seasons the Japanese were now determined to establish themselves as a major presence on the world stage, both in sporting and commercial terms.

The familiar Honda and Suzuki marques were now joined by Yamaha; but for the time being the most committed, determined and dangerous of the three was undoubtedly Honda. At that time the efforts of this dynamic Japanese marque were concentrated upon the lightweight classes, but they were already beginning to raise their sights, a fact proved by the preparation of a four-cylinder 250 bored out to 285 cm^3 for competition in the 350 class.

Starting from Hockenheim (and from Barcellona in the 125 class), all the 125 and 250 events on the calendar were won by the Honda team,

which in many cases – the Isle of Man TT, for example – achieved really sensational results, such as taking the first five places.

In some races the MV Privats accepted the challenge thrown down by Honda, but they were always foiled by breakdowns. Within the space of a few months these hitherto virtually unbeatable bikes showed that they could do little or nothing to stop their new opponents, and the same can be said for the other European marques. They should have been updated or perhaps replaced with more modern designs, but MV's new policy had no place for such plans. After the first disappointing results it was decided to concentrate on the bigger capcity classes, which seemed out of danger for the time being, and the glorious 125 and 250 twin-cams were put out to grass.

After that they were spotted here and there sporadically:

in 1964 the factory gave a 125 to Spaggiari who promptly racked up a series of first places (Modena, Cervia, Imola, Cesenatico, Vallelunga) to win the Italian Senior title, while that same year the 250 made a fleeting appearance at Modena in the hands of Mendogni, who failed to finish. It was re-exhumed in 1966 when Giacomo Agostini rode it to victory at Alicante. After that both bikes were packed off to the MV Museum, thus bringing one of the finest chapters in the factory's history to a close.

In conclusion we should add that in 1965 the factory prepared a new 125 two-stroke flat single with some decidedly advanced features: disc valve induction, and a hybrid cooling system using air for the head and water for the cylinder – which had a chromed bore and a ringless piston. Ignition was by coil, the gearbox was a seven speeder and the frame was a tubular duplex

cradle. Also worthy of mention were the box-section swinging arm and the mechanically operated 230 mm disc brake on the front wheel.

This bike made its first public appearance during practice at Cesenatico, with Walter Villa in the saddle, but it soon became clear that its state of tune still left lots to be desired and Villa, rather than withdraw, got permission to race a single, which was not even the latest model. More experimentation followed but then the bike was dumped, largely because Count Domenico was never very enthusiastic about rotary valve designs, which he considered as being on the same level as supercharged engines, i.e. not sanctioned by the rules. This 125 stroker was to be the last racing lightweight produced by MV: from then on the field was left to the Japanese, who went on to dominate it undisturbed for a long time.

60

MV'S BEST MEN

The riders that chose MV are legion: amateurs and professionals, reserves and first team regulars, nine-day wonders and established stars who left an indelible mark on the sport at its highest levels. It would be practically impossible to mention them all, while it would be an injustice not to include the best of them.

And so, by way of a little light relief after all those cold technical descriptions and ranks of arid statistics, we thought to pay tribute to some of these great riders by including this little series of potted biographies.

Franco Bertoni

MV's first star, Bertoni rode the 98s and three-speed 125s during the period immediately after the war, when he was the first man to draw public attention to the fledgling marque, albeit in low-level competition. He made his debut at Carate Brianza in 1947, obviously in a third class event, and notched up his first victory in the second event of the day, held on the tricky Arsago Seprio circuit. Bertoni's father watched the race from the pits, from where he shook a menacing fist at his son every time the latter flashed past on his Benelli 250. It seems that Bertoni Senior disapproved of Franco's flat-out style, an opinion that was not shared by MV, who offered the youngster a works ride aboard a 98. Bertoni rode the 98 to victory at Como and several other meetings.

In 1948 Bertoni and MV starred in a score of races, amassing a good number of wins (Varese, Cremona, Vigevano, Sondrio, Pisa), which culminated in a brilliant success at the Grand Prix of Nations at Faenza. After that Bertoni raced less frequently, but carried on winning none the less (even on scooters) and finished the 1950 season as Italian Champion in the 125 cm³ class. He was to compete – and win – again in 1951, after which he gradually abandoned the sport in order to devote himself to his flourishing car and motorcycle business.

Renato Magi

Renato Magi's name is tragically linked to MV's first attempt to set a world record: an attempt that took place on the 17th of April 1951 on the "Fettuccia" at Terracina (a long straight often used for such purposes) with Magi riding a fully faired 125. At a certain point, perhaps after seizing up, the bike bucked alarmingly and then fell on its side, sliding for a few hundred metres. Magi was still alive when they extracted him from the wreckage but he died shortly afterwards in hospital.

Renato Magi – born in 1913 – was one of the most romantic figures in the world of Italian motorcycling; a good man, he was sweet natured, shy, modest, and moved by an extraordinary passion for motorcycles. He began racing before the war with a Gilera, upon which he won lots of races, hillclimb events in particular. His first outings with an MV took place in 1946 and produced victories at Lomazzo and Pavia. In 1949 he was signed by Alfonso Morini who wanted him to ride his new 125 four-stroke, with which Magi notched up wins at Legnano and Genoa. He was back with MV for the following season to score a sparkling win in the very tough long-distance Milan-Taranto road race, a victory that was facilitated by the disqualification of his teammate Carlo Ubbiali. Despite his victory, Magi was in tears at the end because he was so upset over his friend Ubbiali's disqualification!

Then came the long and meticulous preparation for the record attempt – Magi was also a first class mechanic – and the fatal appointment at Terracina, which ended a career featuring few epic moments but one that had been lived with enthusiasm and a truly sporting spirit.

Carlo Ubbiali

With his nine world titles, Ubbiali is one of the all-time greats, along with Agostini, Nieto and Hailwood. He was also a truly versatile rider, as he proved when he won a gold medal at the 1949 International Six Days Trial.

Ubbiali had two spells with MV: the first came along shortly after his competition debut, a win aboard an elderly DKW 125 at the Circuito delle Mura in his home town of Bergamo in 1947; the second – and definitive – tour of duty began in 1953, after a three year spell with Mondial that had earned him the 1951 World Championship. After a bad patch in the first few years, caused by the technical superiority of the works NSUs, Ubbiali was free to express all his enormous talent and to take on all comers, teammates included, right up to his retirement from racing in 1960. Upon the conclusion of this eight-year career with MV, Ubbiali's "bag" amounted to five world 125 titles, three world 250 titles, plus three Italian 125 titles and a brace of 250 titles.

Nicknamed "la volpe" (the fox) for his cunning and "il cinesino" (the little Chinaman) for his slant eyes, Ub-

Carlo Ubbiali in 1949, the "Flying Chinaman" at the Mura circuit on the MV scooter and, 11 years later, the cold, lucid, rational stylist as the peak of his extraordinary powers.

biali was certainly one of the most feared riders on the circuit, not just because he was good, but also for his inscrutable race strategy; he was capable of remaining in contention right up to the last metre without ever revealing the exact extent of his possibilities, or the bike's for that matter. He was never one of the great crowd-pleasers, but he was a rider who guaranteed consistency and results.

A gifted mechanic and born development rider, Ubbiali was also a clear-sighted strategist in total control of his emotions. He never attempted to crush his opponents even when in a position to do so, preferring to engage them in long and extenuating duels before finishing them off with a scorching final sprint that he had planned right from the early laps, or even during practice! Ubbiali was aided in this by his brother Maurizio, who was his inseparable confidant and adviser until the latter fell ill and died in 1960. Born in Bergamo on the 24th of September 1929, Carlo Ubbiali married after retiring from racing and now lives in Bergamo with his wife and four children. He had nothing more to do with the world of motorcycling until the mid Eighties, when he was often the guest of honour at major retrospective events. Nowadays he talks willingly with friends and admirers and has a highly idiosyncratic, but nonetheless succinct and effective way of relating the events of the old days. When he was actively involved in racing, on the other hand, he

was virtually unapproachable; not out of bad nature, but because he tended to avoid any contact that might break the wall of concentration with which he protected himself.

Among the toughest opponents that Ubbiali came across during his career we find names like Haas and Hollaus (NSU), Ferri (Gilera), Provini (Mondial, Morini and MV), Degner and Fugner (MZ), Hocking, Sandford, Gandossi, Taveri and Spaggiari. Occasional rivals also included Lorenzetti, Redman and Hailwood. There were some particularly memorable duels with Degner that were only resolved after neck and neck sprints to the line, and a whole series of hard-fought battles with Provini and Hocking, the latter being a particularly dangerous adversary in the wet.

Taking into account the undoubted calibre of opponents and teammates alike, at the end of the day Ubbiali was easily MV's most reliable rider because, as we have seen, he was able to amass a record number of wins in light and middleweight competition. In 1960 Ubbiali's career reached its apotheosis when he reconquered the world 125 and 250 titles. The aftermath of this triumph brought his decision to hang up his helmet for good, despite the fact that he still had a lot left to give. In this he showed the same tactical sense that had distinguished his entire career: better to quit at the top than await the inevitable decline, or something even less pleasant.

Leslie Graham

It was this man's gifts as a development rider that contributed so much to the preparation of the 500 cm³ Quattro Cilindri. Ex RAF pilot, excellent technician, intelligent and experienced, Graham joined MV at the end of 1950 when already thirty-nine. He was born in Wallasey, England, on the 14th of September 1911.

His collection of sporting honours included victory in the first ever World Championship – in 1949 – aboard an AJS "Porcupine" 500, a third place in the 1950 championship and numerous other victories obtained by virtue of a blend of sheer riding skill with a clear grasp of tactics and an ability to get the best out of a motorcycle.

Graham was certainly the best man to aid MV in the task of ridding the "Quattro" of its many defects. The bike in question was a powerful machine but a hard one to handle as a result of the boldness of some of its technical features. Although Graham's work did not provide important results immediately, the first fruits finally appeared towards the end of 1952 when the "Quattro" took second place in the World Championship behind the Gilera-Masetti combination.

By that time it looked as if the 1953 season was going to

His experience and mechanical skills enabled Leslie Graham to ride the cantankerous Quattro Cilindri to the top in international competition.

be a very interesting one for MV, and in fact the first round, the English TT, seemed to augur well for the future: Graham himself won the 125 event, thus demonstrating that he was a versatile rider with what it takes to do well in all capacity classes. A few days later it was time for the Senior TT, held on the same circuit. Graham, hot on the heels of Norton riders Geoff Duke and Ray Amm, was going hell for leather down Bray Hill, towards the notoriously dangerous point at the bottom of the murderously long and steep slope where the road swings suddenly upwards again, an experience that must have reminded him of pulling his wartime fighter out of a steep dive. Naturally the stresses affecting the bikes on this part of the

course were truly tremendous and in this case the Earles forks fitted to the front of Graham's mount plunged straight to full bump with stunning force leaving him powerless to get the bike back under control, also because he had injured his arm quite badly during practice. Graham was killed in the ensuing fall and so this great rider left the scene before he had time to finish development work on the new MV 500, which had to wait for the arrival of John Surtees before it began to win where it really counted.

Carlo Bandirola

All instinct and impetuousness, with a crude but very spectacular riding style, the swahbuckling Carlo Bandirola was idolized by racing fans, always ready to support those

who gave it everything they had, irrespective of the final result.

Bandirola, who was born in Voghera in 1914 and died on the 26th of September 1981 in the same town, won the only major title of his long and action-packed career at 44 years of age when he took the Italian 500 class championship with an MV Quattro Cilindri after having slugged it out with the best of them for twenty years on the race tracks of Europe, where he had scored some brilliant placings and some international victories but ne'er a win in a world championship race, even though he came close on several occasions.

This is not to say that Bandirolo, with his massive physique and unfailingly genial manner, was not a champion. The truth is that he got more

satisfaction out of riding his way and he cared little or nothing about tactics and results, an attitude that he cheerfully extended to his engines, which he often bullied unmercifully.

After making his debut in a trials event in 1937 he joined Gilera, racing first with the "Eight bolt" model and then with the Saturno, with which he won several races in Italy. In 1951 he and Artesiani were signed by MV, for whom he spent eight years racing the Quattro Cilindri, which he rode to a large number of third places and two second places, both at the World Championship Montjuich circuit in Barcellona. Along with the equally tortuous Ospedaletti circuit, Montjuich was one of his favourite tracks.

Precisely because of his predilection for difficult circuits, Bandirola spent much of the latter part of his career in Spain where his efforts on the race track were used to publicize the "Emevue" marque, produced under licence in Spain. Older local fans still remember an epic duel in Barcellona between John Surtees and his Italian teammate, who was decidedly long in the tooth by that time. Surtees must have been surprised by "old man" Bandirola's powers of resistance: he did not give an inch until a sick engine finally put him out of contention.

Cecil Sandford

Englishman Cecil Sandford was the rider who brought

MV the first of their extraordinary series of world titles. Signed on in 1951 as part of MV's plan to break Mondial's stranglehold on the championship, MV's new star helped his teammates (Graham, Sala, Copeta and – sporadically – Lomas) to realize their goal with a hat-trick of victories and two third places.

With his unspectacular but undoubtedly effective style, Sandford, born in Blockley on the 21st of February 1928, was one of the many English riders who had served their time aboard singles (particularly for AJS and Velocette), as well as a man with a good knowledge of the various world championship circuits, having worked as Les Graham's reserve during his English period. Courteous but not particularly communicative, his serious features characterized by a deformity of the upper lip, Sandford was considered a valuable man by many works teams in the course of his career. He was never signed on explicitly as the star rider but, during his time with MV (and later with Mondial in 1957), his tenacity and consistency were decisive elements in successful, if somewhat surprising assaults on the world title.

Sandford stayed with MV for three seasons. They were not easy years for him because his teammate was Ubbiali, and then there was the problem of the virtually unbeatable NSU squad. Nevertheless, he did manage to come second behind NSU rider Haas in the 1953 championship, although his placings in the following season were not enough to get him in among the leaders. In 1953 he made another sortie aboard the 500 four at Monza, but could do no better than fifth place, behind the all-conquering Gileras.

Angelo Copeta

A small capacity bike specialist, Copeta served a long apprenticeship riding at all levels of competition. He became a successful scooter racer, winning first on a Lambretta and then on an MV. Attracted by his tenacity and consistency, MV engaged this little rider with the slicked back and pomaded hair à la Rudolf Valentino to serve as a reliable and competitive reserve, a role at which Copeta excelled, as he was in fact to prove on more than one occasion. As early as 1952 we find him occupying a high position in the world rankings with his MV 125; he came fifth at the Isle of Man and Assen and fourth in Germany, at the Solitude. He did even better the following season with fourth places at the TT, Germany and Monza, as well as a sparkling win in the last round of the World Championship on Barcellona's difficult Montjuich circuit, where he held off his teammate Sandford and NSU riders Hollaus and Brandt to win at a faster average than the winner of the 250 event. Relegated to the sidelines of the World Championship in 1954, Copeta shone on the Italian racing scene, where he won the national 125 title. In 1955 he was back in the thick of the World Championship

Angelo Copeta, a doughty second rider from the MV stable, who rose successfully to the first rank on many occasions.

and did well in several rounds, coming fifth at Barcellona and Reims and third at Monza. Then, after having served MV faithfully and well during his term of employment with them, Copeta hung up his helmet and dedicated himself to his moped business.

Bill Lomas

The name Bill Lomas is indissolubly connected with Moto Guzzi and their famous eight-cylinder racer. But this extraordinary English rider, a classic stylist and never-say-die competitor, was also a likeable and enthusiastic man who played an important – albeit transitory – role within the MV team, with which he came desperately close to winning the world title in 1955.

Lomas, born in Alfreton in 1928, was first approached by MV in 1952, after he had made a bit of a name for himself with the usual Velocettes and AJSs. MV offered him a ride at the Ulster GP on the 125, with which he was to come second to teammate Cecil Sandford, and the 500 four, which he rode to third place behind Cromie McCandless on the Gilera and Rod Coleman on the AJS. Perhaps MV had expected something better, at any rate the Lomas connection remained a one-off for the time being.

The matter lay in abeyance until the Isle of Man TT in 1955, when Lomas was already with Guzzi (and in fact he rewarded Guzzi's faith

Bill Lomas at Faenza in 1954, ahead of Campanelli and Paciocca on the Gilera Saturnos. The MV 500 shown here is fitted with an early dolphin-type fairing.

with a victory in the World 350 Championship that same year). He raced for MV in both the 125 and 250 events; this turned out to be a good decision for although he could manage no better than fourth in the 125 race, he scored a magisterial victory aboard the 250 handing out a riding lesson to Sandford (Guzzi) and Muller (NSU).
As luck would have it, it was Muller and NSU who were to dash MV's legitimate aspirations to winning the 250 championship. Muller's wafer-thin lead at the end of the season was due to a penalty awarded against Lomas at the Assen Grand Prix in Holland, where he was relegated to second place after having refuelled without switching off the engine, as required by the rules. Thus ended a relationship that could have produced far better results if it had lasted a little longer.

Nello Pagani

Nello Pagani was the perfect all-rounder; a fine stylist, intelligent and experienced, he raced just about everything there was to race. He rode for MV between 1953 and '55 before spending a much longer spell as racing manager, a post he held until 1960.
His best results as an MV works rider include a victory at Castelfusano, a second place at Senegallia, third places at Hockenheim and Ospedaletti and a fifth in Barcellona. But his best ride on a 500 four was beyond any doubt his fine win in an Italian championship race at

A raincoated Nello Pagani – who had been promoted to racing manager by that time – chats with Masetti and Ubbiali at the Nürburgring in 1955. The dustbin fairing fitted to the 125 racer still has the little windscreen.

Monza held in driving rain. Born in Milano on the 11th of October 1911, Nello Pagani was the first Italian rider to win a World Championship (with the 125 Mondial in 1949). After his retirement from racing he did not turn his back on the sport as so many other great champions of his era did, but haunted the circuits for many years, during which time he freely dispensed invaluable advice to his son Alberto and to a host of other young riders preparing for the tough world of Grand Prix racing. Today he still takes part in classic bike racing.

Ray Amm

Ray Amm's connection with MV was cut tragically short when this courageous rider lost his life during his first race with the 350 four, the Shell Gold Cup at Imola, which took place on the 11th of April 1955. Ray Amm, born on the 10th of December 1927 in Salisbury, in what was then Rhodesia, was widely admired for his daredevil riding skills. Thin and not very tall, Amm – who looked a little like the great Tazio Nuvolari – based his extraordinary efficiency on raw courage. He once said: "if I don't get the feeling that I'm not going to make it when I'm half way through a bend, it means I'm not pushing hard enough". He fell on a good number of occasions, but he found time to notch up a series of brilliant wins and high leaderboard placings astride Norton 350s and 500s,

despite the presence of the more powerful Italian fours. His most memorable wins include the 350 event at Monza in 1952, both the 350 and 500 events at the Isle of Man TT in 1953, and the controversial 1954 TT, interrupted owing to bad weather while Duke was refuelling his Gilera 500 in the pits.

Norton chose Amm to ride their newest and most difficult machines in the 1953 and '54 seasons. These included the models with the external flywheel, the bikes with the rather odd "half-dustbin-type" fairing, and even the "Silver Fish", a very bold design that obliged the rider to drive practically prone with rearsets like those used on modern sidecar outfits. The "Silver Fish" was built with a view to beating some world records set by Amm himself in 1953; these included the Hour at a mean speed of 215.100 km/h.

Needless to say more than one Italian marque was interested in acquiring the services of such a man and in fact MV won the race to sign him up in 1955. But this was followed right away by the fatal fall at the Rivazza bend during the twentieth lap, while Amm was hot on the heels of ex Norton teammate Ken Kavanagh on the Guzzi.

Fortunato Libanori

It can fairly be said that Libanori was a hundred percent MV man. He began his racing career on 125 and 175 single-cams in 1954, before going on to compete in several

World Championships with the MV works team. Finally, when both he – and the marque itself – retired from racing, he took up a management position with the firm's helicopter division.

Fortunato Libanori, born in Milan on the 14th of June 1934, was a stylish rider and a good loyal team member who was sure of himself without being arrogant. Count Domenico took a particular liking to him, a rare privilege but one that did not lead to any preferential treatment. On the contrary, the Count practically brought Libanori's riding career to an end – as he had already done in the case of Nello Pagani – preferring to keep these two riders as his trusted representatives rather than risk losing them in the

perilous hurly-burly of Grand Prix competition. Among other things, Libanori played an important role testing the firm's most demanding production bikes. After reaping an abundant crop of wins at a lower level, he also achieved his share of satisfactory results in World Championship competition. Among these, together with some fourth places with the 125 and the 250 in the difficult 1956 and 1957 seasons, there was an outstanding second place behind Ubbiali in the 125 event at Francorchamps in 1957.

Luigi Taveri

Although his greatest wins were with Honda (three World 125 Championships), Luigi Taveri, the diminutive

Luigi Taveri, a Swiss German whose Latin looks and name point clearly to his Italian descent, was a brilliant and much appreciated MV stalwart for several years.

but rock hard Swiss-German rider with the gentle but determined manner, was an MV works star for many years. Or rather, more than a star (a difficult role when the team includes the likes of Ubbiali and Hocking), we should say that he was a species of "supersub", a highly reliable and consistent reserve and a source of the vital strength in depth that is the life-blood of a major works team.

The all-round ability, discipline and experience that Taveri had to offer was the fruit of a long and varied apprenticeship that began in 1947 and included a good number of races both at home and abroad as a sidecar passenger. Taveri, born in Horgen on the 19th of September 1949, gained his first experience on solos astride Norton 350s and 500s, with the result that – in the early part of his career – he was considered as more of a big bike man despite the fact that his size and riding style were more suited to smaller machines.

His MV debut took place at the 1954 Grand Prix of Nations where he steered a 500 four to eighth place. Despite this modest placing his efforts were appreciated just the same and his signing was confirmed, with the proviso that he race in the smaller capacity classes the following season. Taveri stayed with MV from 1955 to 1960, with the exception of a few brief spells with Ducati and MZ. In these years he came second to Ubbiali in the '55 World 125 Championship and third in

'56 and '57. With the 250 he finished fourth in '55, second (again behind Ubbiali) in '56 and third behind Ubbiali and Hocking in 1960. His finest victories aboard a 125 were at Barcellona in '55 and Ulster in '57, while his best result in quarter-litre competition was at Assen in '55, although this last result was somewhat overshadowed by the judges' decision to relegate racewinner Bill Lomas to second place because he had refuelled with his engine running. Taveri would have scored more victories had the demands of team strategy not made it essential that he let senior teammates through.

Umberto Masetti

From a certain point of view Umberto Masetti chose the wrong moment to be born. By this we do not mean that he was unable to show off his skills as a rider, because he was a major protagonist of many's the memorable sporting exploit; we are referring to his character, his exuberant temperament and *joie de vivre*. In the early Fifties these were all attributes that were considered vaguely unsuitable for athletes, but today the same qualities would have made him a "personality", attracting hordes of fans rather than criticism and backbiting gossip.

A skillful, combative and efficient rider, albeit rather prone to lapses of form, Masetti took the first all-Italian 500 class title when he won with the Gilera in 1950, and again in 1952. The arrival of

Geoff Duke, who joined Gilera in 1953, together with problems arising from one of his frequent personal vicissitudes, combined to keep Masetti away from the circuits for a while and he made only sporadic appearances here and there.

In 1955, more out of a liking

for the man himself rather than any real tactical necessity, MV invited the gifted but wayward Masetti to join their works team. Prompted by his strong sense of self respect, Masetti made sure they did not regret the invitation.

His best ride with MV – and the source of much personal

Umberto Masetti after his sensational win at the 1955 Grand Prix of Nations at Monza.

satisfaction – was undoubtedly his win at the Grand Prix of Nations of that same year, when he and his 500 Quattro Cilindri were good enough to get the better of Armstrong and Duke on the Gileras, no less.

Masetti did not race much in 1956, but he nevertheless managed to rack up some excellent placings and wins in Italian Championship races at Faenza and Cesena, both with the 500. The following year was much the same, but this did not stop him from very nearly bringing off a stunning win in the Shell Gold Cup at Imola. He was well on the way to a comfortable victory, when the wind caught the scarf of the rider ahead and sent it flying straight into one of the MV's carburettors thus obliging Masetti to perform acrobatics in a bid to remove the offending article. Unsurprisingly, these manoeuvers caused the luckless Masetti to "drop it", with ruinous consequences.

Masetti made even fewer appearances in '58; then he went to live in Chile. He made a brief return to Italy in 1960 and MV gave him a "Quattro", which he piloted to third place at Imola. The man from Parma (where he was born on the 4th of May 1926) returned to Italy for good in 1972. Cheery, likeable and exuberant as ever, like many other stars of yesteryear Masetti is frequently seen at classic bike events, where he is always accorded an enthusiastic welcome by a public that has never forgotten him.

Remo Venturi, although overshadowed by Surtees's presence in the squad, nevertheless notched up some prestigious wins, including three Italian titles in the 500 class.

Remo Venturi

Remo Venturi is one of those riders whose career was forever being overshadowed by the presence in the same team of an outstanding champion who always ended up by queering his pitch in one way or another. This was certainly the case during his time with MV, where Surtees – unassailable in every sense of the word – showed him a clean pair of heels in the 500 class of the World Championship in both 1959 and '60. This ultra-versatile Italian rider, born in Spoleto in 1927, had to be content with becoming one of the best half-litre men his country had ever produced. Not particularly tall, with a round, good-natured

face and delicate lineaments, Venturi's ready smile and well-mannered ways did nothing to suggest that he was "tough" in any sense of the word; but he was nevertheless highly sought-after for his ability with all sizes of bikes and he rode for Mondial and MV, followed by Bianchi, Benelli and Gilera, the marque with which he ended his career in 1966.

Having made his name in lightweight road racing, Venturi was signed by MV in 1955 and until the end of the 1957 season he was used exclusively in 125 and 250 competition, obtaining high placings in the World Championships. In 1957 he won the last Motogiro d'Italia.

In 1958 Venturi was "promoted" to the bigger bikes. This was a good decision because, even though Surtees was virtually infallible, it is never a good idea to leave the top man without some form of back up. Venturi did very well in this role and until the end of the 1960 season he dutifully notched up a fine series of second places in World Championship events. He also managed to find the time to win the Italian 500 Championship on two occasions (1959 and '60). In 1960 he finally savoured the pleasures of victory at the highest level when he returned the fastest lap of the day to win the Dutch GP.

After a two-year hiatus, Venturi obtained a "Privat" 500 four, with which he won another Italian Championship and came second to Mike Hailwood at Monza.

John Surtees

When MV approached rising star Surtees towards the end of 1955, the latter had already taken the chequered flag on no less than seventy-seven occasions, mostly with Norton 350s and 500s. It was a classic case of signing the right man at the right time because, right from his debut season in 1956, Surtees rode the Quattro Cilindri to its first world title in the 500 class, beating Zeller on the BMW, Hartle on the Norton and Monneret and Armstrong on Gileras.

Born into a well to do family of motorcycle enthusiasts in Catford on the 11th of February 1934, Surtees had a high brow and clean-cut, boy-next-door looks. Far more than just another young man who could make a motorcycle go extraordinarily fast, he was also the inventor of a riding style all of his own that was to prove highly controversial and, in our view, was to form the basis of the modern style, in which the body is held at a steeper angle than the bike when negotiating the inside of a bend.

"This way – explained the man himself – you have better control of the bike as you come out of the bend, because it tends not to widen

the line so much". The results certainly proved him right because, following that first title, Surtees went on to win another six, three with the MV 350 and three with the 500, between 1958 and 1960. Of course, Surtees is also the only man ever to win the World Championship on both two and four wheels; as many will remember he won the 1954 F1 Championship at the wheel of a Ferrari.

If Surtees had any cause for regret it was most probably the sensational withdrawal of

the Guzzi and Gilera squads in 1957, which robbed him of the chance of a direct confrontation with his closest rivals. "Big John" as he was known to his fans and the sporting press, therefore had to content himself with defeating pale shadows of his former adversaries and breaking just about every record in the book on circuits throughout Europe. It is rather a pity that, perhaps bored by this "easy" success, he hung up his helmet before the Japanese really got their

John Surtees, shown at Silverstone in 1959, was the first man to win a world title with the Quattro Cilindri. Note the abbreviated fairing used for twisty circuits.

act together; because they were to set new standards in competition as Mike Hailwood, for example, was to prove. The uncharitable among us have also been known to suggest that Big John's decision might have been hastened by the presence of an aggressive up and comer like Gary Hocking in the same team, but it must be admitted that the thirst for

71

victory of a man like Surtees could hardly be slaked by a struggle to see who was top dog in the MV team. After a long spell in the world of four-wheeled motorsport, first as a driver and then as a constructor and technician, John Surtees has recently returned to his first love: now completely white haired, but still the speedy and stylish rider of old, he is an enthusiastic competitor in "revival" races for the stars and bikes of the past, which have become more and more popular in recent years.

Roberto Colombo

Born in Castenovo (Brianza) on the 5th of January 1927, Roberto Colombo's is the classic story of the privateer who, after much hard work and patience, finally gets a ride with an established

works team. In return for his contract with MV, Colombo offered all his dedication and loyalty and ultimately even his life, which he lost tragically during practice for the Belgian GP at Francorchamps, the fourth round of the 1957 World Championship.

After having raced privately-entered Mondials, NSUs and Guzzis, Colombo's name first appeared on the leaderboard at a World Championship event when he rode an MV 125 to second place at the 1954 Barcellona Grand Prix, won by Provini on a Mondial. But Colombo had to wait until 1956 before MV decided to entrust him with a works ride aboard an important bike: his brief was to back up Ubbiali in the 250 championship. He scored a good number of leaderboard placings, but his best effort was a fine second place behind his team leader in the Isle of Man TT.

In 1957 he was used in both the 125 and 250 championships. With the smaller bike he came third at Hockenheim and sixth at the Isle of Man, while at Assen his was the first MV across the line immediately behind winner Provini with the Mondial.

Roberto Colombo waits for the off at Faenza in 1956, with the MV 203 Mono.

With the 250 he racked up another second place at Hockenheim and a third in the English TT. Then came Francorchamps. With Ubbiali was out of action after a fall, Colombo suddenly found himself burdened by the team leader's responsibilities. But the Stavelot bend and the incredible slowness of the emergency services were to prove his undoing; and so any dreams of glory that this brave and modest man may have harboured died with him on the asphalt.

John Hartle

John Hartle is another of those riders whose destiny was to serve as esquire to one of the great champions of his day, in this particular case, John Surtees. Tall, with crewcut blond hair and fine features, Hartle was an excellent rider who got his first ride with MV following Colombo's tragic death in the 1957 Belgian Grand Prix. The Englishman, who had already made a name for himself on the Norton 350 and 500, upon which he had won the Ulster GP of the previous year, did not let his new team down as he won the 250 event ahead of a brace of Mondials ridden by Miller and Sandford, who went on to win the title that year.

In 1958 Hartle, born in Chapel-en-le-Frith on the 22nd of December 1933, became to all effects and purposes MV's second man in both the 350 and 500 squads.

He promptly scored a whole series of second places behind

125

Monoalbero - 1953-1956

1954 model - Bruno Taglioretti's Collection

250

Monocilindrica - 1955-1959

1957 model - MV Museum, Gallarate

500 6 cilindri - 1957-1958

1957 model - MV Museum, Gallarate

250 Bicilindrica - 1959-1966

1960 model - MV Museum, Gallarate

John Hartle, a great but unlucky English rider, at the 1959 TT with the 350 four.

front runner John Surtees. As far as the 350 class was concerned it was the same story the following year, while in the half-litre class the stable gave the second ride to Venturi more often than not. This did not prevent Hartle from shining on other occasions, which included an outstanding second place in the 350 event at the 1959 Isle of Man TT, followed by outright victory in the same race the year after accompanied by a fine second place in the 500 event. But events at the Ulster of that same year were to take an even more spectac-

ular turn. MV gave Hartle a ride in the 350 event but not in the 500: Hartle duly came second behind Surtees in the 350 race and then went on to savour what must have been an enormous personal satisfaction in the 500 event when he took the chequered flag aboard his privately-entered Norton ahead of Surtees on the MV.

After that exploit Hartle did not have much luck. He had a nasty spill at Scarborough and was laid up for a long time after. Then there was another bad fall at Imola in '64. After a spell with the ill-fated Scuderia Duke, he found himself once more in the saddle of an MV in 1968 as second stringer to Agostini

at the Isle of Man, but he was unable to start in the 350 race after falling in practice and retired with a sick engine during the first lap of the 500 event.

On the 31st of August that same year he met his death at Scarborough astride a Matchless he had ridden to second place in various World Championship events the previous year.

Gilberto Milani

For love of MV Agusta, Gilberto Milani, one of the nicest and wittiest men ever to grace the world of motorcycling, accepted what amounted to a "demotion". When the factory offered him a

works ride in 1957, Milani was already racing in top flight competition (the present Senior Championship) while MV wanted to use him in Junior class racing. "Gilba" accepted because the deal did not involve riding the 125s and 175s that he was accustomed to, but a big powerful 500 Quattro Cilindri, which had been duly modified for racing in the lower categories. A little resented by those of his peers who were left with their privately-entered singles, Milani nevertheless proceeded to do his duty by winning the three races on the programme and the Italian Championship into the bargain. There is no doubt that he would have won again the following year were it not for the fact that the Championship was annulled as it had been possible to hold only two races. Although he was only with MV for a brief spell, Milani found the time to win a few 175 races and, like the good road racer he was, to take second place in the '57 Motogiro d'Italia, won by teammate Lino Venturi.

His real ambition, however, was to compete in the World Championship, a wish that MV did not seem disposed to grant him, and so Milani eventually packed his bag. Some time afterwards he joined Aermacchi where he was to remain – first as a rider and then as racing manager – until the present day, after faithfully following the latter company through its many changes of ownership (it was bought over by Harley Davidson, who later sold out to Cagiva).

"Gilba" was born in Milan on the 13th of February 1932, but has lived in Varese for many years now, not far from the Cagiva factory, where many ex MV employees later found positions.

Terry Shepherd

It had already happened to other riders. Terry Shepherd had done so well on Nortons that he was offered a ride by MV (thanks to the good offices of John Surtees), but he never managed to reproduce his Norton form aboard the more demanding and difficult "Quattro Cilindri".

To be fair, maybe the whole matter went deeper than questions of form or riding problems as such. A man accustomed to riding his own machine in his own way without having to answer to anybody for his results, Shepherd was suddenly catapulted into the abrasive world of a major works team where riders had to shoulder special responsibilities as well as ride machinery that was distinctly hard to handle. Men thrust into such situations often suffer psychologically and the loss of form can be such that they no longer seem even a pale shadow of their former selves.

Perhaps this preamble seems rather unflattering as far as Terry Shepherd is concerned, on the contrary, our intention is solely to do justice to a rider of undoubted talent who was also a fine man, but too sensitive and perhaps even

Tarquinio Provini starred in some thrilling duels with his friend and rival Ubbiali, most of which took place when they were riding for the same team.

too simple a soul to cope with the task he had been burdened with.

Anyway, Shepherd embarked on his MV career with an unexciting fifth place at Hockenheim in '57, then he fell badly in practice for the Tourist Trophy and was out of action until late in the season, which he wound up with a sixth place in Ulster and an-

other sixth at Monza. MV did not offer him another contract for 1958.

We wanted to include Shepherd in this gallery of MV riders because he represents a case – not a rare one, unfortunately – of a rider who "fizzled out" just when it looked as if he was about to reach his peak. This was not the first time that MV had pulled this

kind of "stroke" on one of their riders. We remember the case of Ken Kavanagh, lured away from Guzzi for the '57 season and then, inexplicably, left to twiddle his thumbs on the sidelines.

Tarquinio Provini

World 125 champion on the Mondial in the 1957 season, Tarquinio Provini raced with MV for only two years, in 1958 and 1959. Provini and many other great riders of the day had suddenly found themselves high and dry when three top Italian racing teams withdrew from the sport (Mondial, Gilera and Moto Guzzi). MV's timely offer of a place in the works team alongside Ubbiali saved this fine rider from the gloomy prospect of unemployment or some temporary occupation until better times arrived. With this astute move MV also made sure that no one else could sign this dangerous adversary while the fierce rivalry between Ubbiali and new signing Provini was bound to provide plenty of free publicity.

Both Count Domenico – who predicted the sensation the signing would cause – and those who foresaw that Provini and Ubbiali would inevitably "make sparks", were proved right at the end of the day, for the two aces spent the next two years plotting each other's sporting downfall in private while maintaining a brittle impersonation of team unity in public. In fact rumour has it, as far as this particular rivalry went, that

neither man's interpretation of fair play was always entirely above reproach.

In terms of temperament, looks, and riding style, Provini – born in Roveleto di Cadeo (near Piacenza) on the 29th of May 1933 – was the exact opposite of Ubbiali, the cool calculator. In his own way Provini was a calculating type, but in an intuitive rather than mathematical way.

Provini rode with extraordinary passion and commitment, and watching him was a truly unique experience because no other rider was capable of forging that quasi mystical bond between man and machine the way he could. Then there was that extraordinary style of his, hugging the machine tightly to himself in a bid to cheat the wind as much as humanly possible. Perhaps he could best be compared to Omobono Tenni, even though the structure of bikes in Tenni's day did not make

for such a complete and successful fusion of man and machine.

Despite his undeniable gifts Provini did not win much during his time with MV. He did win the world 250 title in 1958, but the other titles at stake in those two years went to Ubbiali. Provini took the Italian 250 championship in '58 and '59 as well as wins at the Isle of Man, the Nurburgring, in Sweden and in the Coppa d'Oro meeting. These were all prestigious victories but, rather than accept the status quo at MV, Provini preferred to start from scratch with a new bike in 1960. He continued to do well with Morini and Benelli, but he did not always have the good fortune a rider of his ability deserves. And so matters continued until August 1966, when a hair-raising fall with the Benelli at the Isle of Man put paid to his racing career, but not to his connec-

tions with the world of two wheels. An extraordinary personality who deserved to win more honours than he did, Tarquinio Provini now runs his own firm – Protar – that manufactures models of the world's most famous motorcycles. He is often to be seen at period bike "revivals".

Bruno Spaggiari

A faithful Ducati man from his debut in 1954 until the end of the 1959 season, Bruno Spaggiari was invited to join the MV works squad of Ubbiali, Taveri and Hocking for the 1960 season to compete in the 125 championship.

That year he came fourth in Belgium and Ulster and second at Monza behind Ubbiali, with whom he was soon at loggerheads following the latter's controversial win in an Italian championship event at

Siracusa. Before that season came to an end Spaggiari was to notch up another two wins, at Bilbao and Madrid, before he was caught up in MV's partial withdrawal from racing (the "Privat" period). He spent the years that followed riding for Benelli and the Spanish Ducati subsidiary.

MV thought of Spaggiari again in 1964 when, prompted by the desire to prove the worth of their own dohc 125 against Francesco Villa on the Morini – then leading the Italian championship – they dusted off the old museum piece and handed it over to their ex rider. Once the national championship had been duly won, MV stuck the bike back in the Museum and Spaggiari found himself unemployed once more.

This accomplished rider, born on the 11th of January 1933 in Reggio Emilia (where he now owns a large Fiat agency), continued to enjoy a

Emilio Mendogni, who MV promoted from the smallest capacity bikes to the largest, photographed at the Solitude in 1960 aboard the 500 four.

brilliant racing career with Morini and Ducati, achieving first class results aboard 500s and 750s too. Spaggiari's engineering skills were always held in high regard, which is borne out by the fact that – long after he had retired from racing – MV turned to him when they were having tuning problems with their Grand Prix four.

Emilio Mendogni

Count Domenico Agusta always liked to "graft" new riders to his machinery to see how well the new combination might work. One of these "experiments" was Emilio Mendogni, a particularly talented rider of small capacity bikes, whom the Count wanted to try out on the big 500 four.

Born in Parma in 1933, Mendogni first made a name for himself with the Morini 125 and later with the 175 and 250. In 1960, after a good season featuring a second place at Hockenheim and a third at Monza astride the Morini 250, MV made him an offer that was as tempting as it was unexpected: at first he was to ride in the small capacity classes, then he was to join Surtees, Venturi and, occasionally, John Hartle in the 500 squad.

It has to be said that Mendogni put up an honourable show, coming third at Assen, sixth in Belgium, third in the German GP at the Solitude circuit while he also scored a rousing second place in front of a home crowd at Monza. Despite this more than cred-

itable performance, however, at season's end he decided to hang up his helmet for good. Apart from the results he was able to achieve during his brief stay with MV, Emilio Mendogni should be remembered as one of the best racers Italy produced as well as one of the most upright and intelligent men to grace the world of motorcycle racing.

Gary Hocking

The vast majority of experts agree that Gary Hocking, born in England in 1936 but brought up in Bulawayo, in what was then called Rhodesia, was one of the bravest riders ever to compete in the World Championship circus. Having left Rhodesia in 1958 with his friend and mechanic Nobby Clark – who was to become famous in the years that followed working with Mike Hailwood and other big names in the racing world – Gary and his Norton soon began to attract attention, particularly in races where the complexity of the circuit or adverse weather conditions made things even tougher; he also gave the MV fours trouble on more than one occasion. The German MZ factory, which was in the market for a rider able to tame their decidedly cantankerous 250 twin, was the first to note this combative attitude of his and

they promptly snapped him up. Hocking did the trick too, riding the MZ to victory several times.

At this point – we are now in 1960 – MV Agusta spotted the young Rhodesian, who duly signed on the dotted line. This step up certainly pleased Hocking even though, being a somewhat saturnine type, he did not let this show. In fact Hocking was a "loner" who spoke little and even then only to a few people. When, one day after practice at the Solitude, they told him that his friend Bob Brown had been killed, all he could do was utter a desperate "Why?..." before he ran off to hide his misery

Gary Hocking had a meteoric career with MV, winning two world titles with the marque. The photo shows him in action with the 500 at Mallory Park in 1961. Note the enormous rear sprocket, made necessary by the tortuous nature of the English circuit.

76

like some wounded animal. The new signing was intended to cover a dual role at MV: he was to understudy Ubbiali in the 125 and 250 championships and Surtees in the 350 class. Hocking's first win with MV came along in a 125 event at Cesenatico, where he beat Ubbiali into second place in a race made more difficult by driving rain; then he took the chequered flag in a 500 race at Siracusa, and again in the Lightweight TT, where he beat Ubbiali and Provini to the line; with the scaled-up twin he showed a clean pair of heels to a field of 350s at Clermont Ferrand and won the 350 event at Monza with the four.

In 1961 Hocking was to be the only man riding the "Privat" Quattro Cilindri, with which he scored an easy "double" winning both the 350 and 500 World Championships, but by the end of the season he had company, in the person of Mike Hailwood. This was due to the fact that Count Domenico had had second thoughts regarding at least one kind of "Privat" enterprise. The first clash on an even footing between the two took place at Monza: Hocking won the 350 race with Hailwood second, while the 500 event saw Hocking forced to retire leaving "Mike the Bike" free to take the flag.

In 1962 the two aces were together for the first part of the season only. Hocking was to win the Shell Gold Cup meeting at Imola and the Senior TT on the 500, plus a second place behind Hailwood in the Junior TT. Then a mixture of team difficulties, the death of his close friend Tom Phillis (who crashed his Honda at the TT), and a sudden longing to try his hand at car racing, combined to steer Hocking away from two-wheeled competition. But a tragic destiny was lying in wait for him on the dusty track at Durban, where he met his death that same year at the wheel of a Lotus during practice for the South African Grand Prix.

Mike Hailwood

The temptation to draw up one of those "absolute" rankings that purport to settle the vexed question as to who was the greatest of them all is admittedly all but irresistible at first sight. But, when you get to thinking about it you realize that such comparisons are impossibly unfair in any case because there are just too many differences between the various epochs: the structure of the bikes, the tyres, the roads, are only a few of the many variables that have influenced the style and the performance of the racewinners of days gone by. Neverthless, just as many would maintain (particularly those with a slight streak of romanticism) that Nuvolari was *the* racing driver, equally many would make Mike Hailwood the greatest of all on two wheels.

In effect Hailwood had everything it takes to merit such an accolade, no matter how debatable some may find the matter: he raced and won in all capacity classes, including the 125 which was certainly not ideally suited to a man of his size; he won on bikes that were notoriously difficult like the MZ 250 or the early Honda 500; he made it to the finish after falls that would have discouraged many of his peers; he had an exemplary sense of fair play; he never made a fuss about preparing the bike and – regardless of

Mike Hailwood, one of the greatest riders of all time, at Snetterton with the 500. Prompted perhaps by his height, Hailwood invented a "froglike" riding position with the knees splayed outwards. Note the differences between this fairing and the one used by Hocking.

the circuit – rode some machinery that most others would have "failed", or even refused to ride in the first place; finally, despite the effects of a bad car crash and several years without riding a racing bike, he was the only man to enjoy a victorious "comeback" – on a tough course like the Isle of Man TT to boot – a feat that had spectators and commentators alike in a frenzy of delight.

Athletic and good natured (although only with the people he liked), Hailwood – born into a wealthy Oxford family on the 2nd of April 1940 – enjoyed a more or less painless debut thanks to his father Stan's openhanded generosity, but he wasted little time in showing people that he was anything but the spoiled son of an indulgent father. He embarked on his career at seventeen years of age, in 1957, with a semi-works MV bought with a fat cheque from pater; but his golden years were the Sixties when, first with Honda, then with MV, and then Honda again, he won no less than nine world titles, including four consecutive wins on the MV 500 (from '62 to '65).

Hailwood joined MV officially towards the end of 1961. The occasion was the Grand Prix of Nations at Monza, the second last round of the World Championship, where he won the 500 event. As we have seen in the preceding pages, he became the team's star rider following Hocking's departure in '62 until the advent of Giacomo Agostini. Not that Agostini's arrival

Silvio Grassetti, a versatile and daring rider, won the 1963 Italian 500 Championship during his time with MV.

bothered him much; in fact the relationship between both men was always one of cordial respect even when Hailwood returned to Honda in 1966.

Despite his skills, Hailwood was never able to do much with the MV 350 against the more modern and efficient Hondas: he came third in the 1962 World Championship, second in '63, fourth in '64 and third in '65, a period that witnessed the total domination of the Honda-Jim Redman combination. Hailwood made up for these disappointments by winning the 500 title even though a certain lack of first class opposition led to the same kind of predictable criticism as Agostini was subjected to some years later. Salt was rubbed into these wounds when an ungenerous fate decreed that – during the one season ('63) in which he was faced by potentially dangerous antagonists in the form of the Gileras, back in racing under the Scuderia Duke banner – he was soundly beaten by Hartle and Minter, who he had perhaps underestimated; but he could plead mitigating circumstances inasmuch as he was still suffering from the after effects of a bad fall.

Although he was normally virtually unbeatable on the MV 500, Hailwood was nonetheless capable of pulling off some extraordinary feats, such as when he managed to win the 1965 TT under lashing rain, despite a fall that left the bike badly damaged with the butterfly of one carb stuck in the open position.

But perhaps the name Hailwood will remain linked to that of MV more for his feats when riding against the Italian marque than for his efforts in their favour. We are referring to the truly memorable duels between Agostini-MV and Hailwood-Honda in '66 and '67, both far more interesting than the 1965 season, when the two stars were riding for the same team.

The last time Hailwood climbed aboard an MV was in practice for the 1968 Grand Prix of Nations at Monza. Count Domenico – a great "director" as well as an enthusiastic sportsman – thought to add spice to the competition by giving a bike to Hailwood (left practically

without a ride after Honda had disbanded their works team) and thus rekindling the rivalry between the Englishman and the Italian ace. But when he was informed that the outcome of the race had already been decided in favour of his rival, "Mike the Bike" promptly spurned the MV and went to Benelli, who were more than glad to provide him with one of their 500 fours at the last minute. But Hailwood was to have little luck because, in a bid to make up for the manifest inferiority of the Benelli, he "lost it" at the Parabolic – rendered treacherous by the rain – and had to retire.

After having switched over to four wheels, with fairly satis-

factory results, Hailwood returned to his first love from time to time. In 1971, other challenge matches were arranged between he and Agostini at Silverstone and Pesaro, where he rode a Yamaha and a Benelli; finally, of course, there were the electrifying appearances at the Isle of Man in '78 and '79, which we described earlier.

In the end, as so often happens, destiny was to play a cruel trick on Mike Hailwood, and this great champion, who had faced and overcome the myriad dangers of top flight competition, was killed in a banal car crash on the 22nd of March 1981, along with his little daughter Michelle. Now he has become one of the legends of motorcycling; something that no one can ever take away from him.

Silvio Grassetti

In the course of a varied and intense career Silvio Grassetti, who raced with Benelli, Bianchi, Jawa, Morini, MZ and Yamaha, also found time for a short spell with MV. It all happened in 1963, when this skilful rider – born in Montecchio Pesarese in 1938 – went racing on a part-time basis with both Benelli and MV.

Likeable, cheerful, exuberant and a bit of a daredevil, Silvio Grassetti had a career in which periods of great form were interspersed with lacklustre moments and dramatic falls caused by an excess of determination to win. He raced all kinds of bikes,

from the Benelli 125 "Leoncino" (Lion cub) on which he began racing in 1956, to 250s, 350s and 500s. MV used him for the national championships only, where a second place behind Hailwood at Modena as well as wins at Cesenatico and Ospedaletti were enough to land him the 1963 Italian 500 championship.

The combination could have continued but, when Morini and Bianchi approached him with offers of a ride in the 250 and 350 championships respectively, Grassetti opted to give up his commitment to MV.

Giacomo Agostini

Giacomo Agostini's career can be summed up in a few bald statistics: fifteen world titles, not one serious fall in a seventeen year career. The first real mega-star in the story of the sport, he had an ability to attract the spotlight even when – after a brief and not particularly successful flirtation with four-wheeled motorsport – he returned to motorcycling as racing manager of the Yamaha-Marlboro squad.

Agostini was a good and fortunate man who attracted an incredible number of fans (including a great number of

Giacomo Agostini was an authentic idol of the crowds with an army of female admirers in particular. He brought MV and motorcycle racing to hitherto unheard-of levels of popularity.

79

women), while arousing more than his fair share of envy and criticism. The most frequent accusations laid at his door were that he was lucky (even though this is not entirely true) and that he was faced by opponents whose machinery was far inferior to his for the best part of his career.

We should like to put the record straight at this point. It is true that "Ago" was very often lucky, but everything did not always run smoothly for him: for example in 1965 he lost what would have been his first world title after a small condenser betrayed him in Japan, in the last round of the World Championship; and although it is true that there were some easy years, in the 500 class particularly, when the chips were down he showed what he was really worth against the likes of Hailwood, Pasolini, Saarinen, Read, Bergamonti and Cecotto, just to name a few. And that's not all, he also proved he could win on bikes that were completely different from "his" MV, a fact amply proved by his two world titles with the Yamaha 'strokers. Overall, from his debut in July '61 to the moment of his retirement, officially announced on the 22nd of December 1977, Agostini won on 311 occasions, including 125 World Championship events and 10 Isle of Man TTs. He also put his name on no less than eighteen Italian Championships. Can anyone reasonably claim that such an impressive number of wins is a matter of mere luck?

Born in Brescia on the 16th of June 1942 but brought up in Lovere (near Bergamo), Agostini cut his teeth on hillclimb events aboard a Morini 175 Settebello. Morini subsequently offered him a place in their works team and, having replaced Provini in '64, he began to attract a good deal of general attention. MV soon spotted this rising star and they gave him a World Championship ride as understudy to Mike Hailwood, from whom Agostini swore he learned a great deal. A compliment indeed for Agostini was not a man given to easy compliments.

The new boy did extremely well atop the massive fours of the early days, but "his" bike – arguably the machine that was tailor made for him – was the 350 cm^3 Tre Cilindri, which he was to ride to a splendid victory at the Nurburgring on its very first outing in 1965. This was followed shortly afterwards by the 500 three and "Ago" was thus provided with the weapons with which he was to carve out his own legend.

After having narrowly missed his first World Championship success in '65, Agostini was left alone to defend the MV colours in the '66 season when Hailwood signed for Honda. With the 350 he was twice runner-up to his ex teammate in 1966 and 1967, but he got his own back with a vengeance in the 500 class where both of these seasons were illuminated by a thrilling series of duels between the two rivals. In both '66 and '67 the final result was in

doubt until the last round of the season, the Grand Prix of Nations at Monza, and on both occasions the Italian champion carried the day thanks to a surprising repetition of circumstances. Hailwood, despite Honda's enormous means, arrived at the end of the season with his bike showing visible signs of wear and tear and therefore no longer able to stand the stress and strain of a protracted contest at the highest level. What's more, unlike the MV threes with their precise, user-friendly steering, the Hondas were suffering from some knotty stability problems and it was only Hailwood's raw courage that made up for this to some degree.

After Honda departed the scene in '67, the famous "easy years" began for Agostini, excepting perhaps the splendid series of clashes with Renzo Pasolini and his Benelli four, which were avidly followed by press and public alike. It was a pity that the majority of these duels took place in the Italian championships, while on the World Championship scene – despite the odd flash of brilliance here and there – the opposition was not always up to the levels set by the Agostini-MV combination.

As win followed win in an apparently endless sequence, even MV began to feel the need to restoke the fires of enthusiasm for what had become the monotony of victory and so at the end of the 1970 season they signed Bergamonti, who was to serve as

both teammate and goad to Agostini. It was war in the family right from the word go, to the delight of the fans (many of whom were perfectly prepared – even eager – to witness the humbling of an idol who had been perhaps worshipped to excess), but it was all to end tragically soon when Bergamonti lost his life in a crash at Riccione in April 1971.

The 1971 season went relatively smoothly, largely because the Finn Jarno Saarinen and his Yamaha were still little more than a cloud on the horizon, but 1972 marked the beginning of Agostini's (and MV's) "difficult years". The cloud on the horizon rapidly grew into a towering menace, while Pasolini, having left Benelli for Harley Davidson-Aermacchi, now had a new and powerful 2-stroke twin. This was the situation in the 350 class at any rate, because in the halflitre field things were still pretty much under control with Agostini able to count on Alberto Pagani, who had been called in to provide support.

It looked as if things were all set for fireworks in the '73 season and in fact the early part of the season was promising, but then came the 20th of May and tragedy struck at Monza, where both Saarinen and Pasolini were killed in a horrendous pile-up. This left MV in a commanding position, but the factory decided to sign Phil Read (a rider Agostini particularly disliked) in order to ensure that the inevitable rivalry would

Angelo Bergamonti, big-hearted and bold to the point of recklessness, enjoyed a rapid rise to success as one of his team leader Agostini's most dangerous opponents.

stimulate the development of the new four, earmarked to replace the glorious but now obsolescent Tre Cilindri. Agostini went on to win the World 350 title, but had to bow the knee to his new colleague in the 500 class, a fact that doubtless hardened his resolve to abandon MV in favour of Yamaha for the following season.

But Agostini was to return to MV after a brief stay with the Japanese squad and in 1976 he scored the Italian marque's last victories in World Championship 350 and 500 class competition, at the Dutch Grand Prix at Assen and at the Nurburgring respectively. The latter was a truly fitting venue because it was at the Nurburgring that Agostini had first come to the fore in 1965 and it was there that he made his victorious curtain call with the marque that had given him so much.

Angelo Bergamonti

The career of Angelo Bergamonti and its tragic epilogue with MV have points in common with the story of Ray Amm. Two riders out of the same mould, they were recklessly brave, never-say-die types who carried on fighting no matter how far down the field they found themselves. Both riders were likewise very quick to find their form again after even the ugliest falls. Another common feature was that both men died shortly after realizing their ambition to ride for MV. Poor Amm never even had the time to finish his first race whereas Bergamonti had a series of fine outings between 1970 and '71, plus his celebrated duel with Agostini, before he met his death at Riccione on the 4th of April 1971.

Before he joined MV, Angelo Bergamonti – born in the province of Cremona on the

81

Alberto Pagani, shown here with the 350 three, was an elegant rider who took the sport seriously. His long riding career began and ended with MV and, like his father Nello before him, he also did a spell as Racing Manager for the Verghera marque.

18th of March 1939 – already had a brilliant career behind him, first as a privateer, then as a works rider with Paton, Morini, and Aermacchi. In 1967 he was the Italian champion with the Morini 250 and the Paton 500, while he won the national 125 title in 1970 with Aermacchi.

Then, finally, the impossible dream came true. MV decided to line him up alongside Agostini for the Grand Prix of Nations of the 13th September 1970 and "Berga" came second in both the 350 and 500 events. He was to repeat this fine performance again at Imola the following Sunday and again at Ospedaletto shortly after that. When given carte blanche at Barcellona for the last round of the World Championship, he won both races in new record times.

During the winter he prepared himself scrupulously for the following season and, aware of the starring role now reserved for him, he showed a new maturity in resisting the temptation to "show off", something he had been prone to doing in the past. Born out of a desperate desire to show what he could do, this weakness had led to frustration and disappointment owing to the fact that Bergamonti's ambition was not matched by the quality of the machinery he was expected to ride.

But even though Bergamonti now had less to say, inside he was ambitious as ever, as he was to show at the beginning of the '71 season when he beat Agostini in the 350 event

at Modena and in the 500 race at Rimini. Then came the race at Riccione, where heavy rain had left the road full of treacherous puddles: a few laps after a poor start in the 350 event, Bergamonti was on the point of overhauling Agostini when his bike acquaplaned sending him flying headfirst into the granite curb. Tragically, death took him just as his dreams of glory were on the point of coming true.

Alberto Pagani

Although Alberto Pagani's career was not to be quite as illustrious as that of his father Nello, he nevertheless proved that he was very much his father's son during his time with MV.

Alberto, born in Milan on the 29th of August 1938, had all his father's undoubted "savoir faire". A first class stylist and a man who kept his emotions very much under control, he was nonetheless open and friendly. He was also one of the most gentlemanly and well educated men in the world of Italian motorcycling, being well travelled and a good linguist. When the time came to hang up his helmet he could have become the perfect racing manager had he so wished, but he chose to accept this responsibility for a short time only (he ran the MV team between '73 and '74, Phil Read's time).

Alberto Pagani's career started "with a bang" in 1956 when, thanks to the fact that

his father worked for MV, he made his debut as a works rider in the 125 class. But when MV stopped competing in the minor categories a short time afterwards, he carried on with his own bikes or machines lent to him by friends. It was with just such a bike, lent to him by his chum Bill Webster, that he took twelfth place in the 1960 Isle of Man TT. What he learned on the celebrated Manx circuit that day was to stand him in good stead.

In the years that followed he was to race mostly with Aermacchis and Lintos, achieving some good leaderboard placings and a few wins too, but he had to wait until 1971 before MV finally called him in to understudy Agostini fol-

82

lowing Bergamonti's tragic death. Pagani was certainly a more tractable character and therefore better suited for the part of junior rider, which he played with dignity and courage. In the course of the '71 and '72 seasons, his best results included wins at Monza and in Yugoslavia, plus second places at the Nurburgring, Imola, Assen, Francorchamps, Imatra and above all at the TT, all in half-litre competition. After ending the season as runner-up in the 1972 Italian and World Championships behind team leader Agostini, Pagani decided to retire from competition. He remained in the world of motorcycling for a couple more years as MV's race manager, as we have already said, before quitting the scene altogether and devoting himself to his various business interests.

Phil Read

Phil Read was already a worldbeater by the time he joined MV. When the call came from Cascina Costa in 1972, he already had no less than five World Championships under his belt with Yamaha (one with the 125, and four with the 250), plus a remarkable tally of victories and years of experience with Manx Nortons and Player-Nortons, interspersed with a spell on the Gilera four with the ill-fated Scuderia Duke in '63 and with Benelli in 1969. But what MV saw in Phil Read was more than just a matter of class. They were looking for an aggressive rid-

er who was not prepared to play second fiddle to anyone. Although this latter quality can be a headache for team managers, because it can easily spill over into disobedience (something Read himself had already proved when he flouted Yamaha team orders to "steal" the world 250 title from Bill Ivy in 1968), it is possible that MV signed Read precisely because Agostini needed shaking out of his unwonted timorousness in the face of the Japanese challenge. What's more, the new four was about to be launched and a second rider of the highest class could come in handy.

In 1972 Read competed in 350 class racing only, winning at the Sachsenring and notching up a few other good placings, but in '73 he was also used in the 500 class where, judging by the results, he had been given complete freedom of action since he went on to claim the 500 crown, while Agostini wound up back in third place behind Newcombe on the Konig.

After Agostini's sensational divorce from MV, Read – born in Luton on the 1st of January 1939 – became the marque's top rider in 1974. The new team leader limited himself to appearing exclusively in the 500 championship, which he succeeded in making his own again without

much difficulty when he won four out of the ten races on the championship programme.

Read stayed on at MV for another year, 1975; he was to contest that season honourably, within the limits allowed by the no longer unbeatable MV machinery, scoring a brace of wins in Belgium and Czechoslovakia plus two second places and other lesser placings. When the sums were totted up at year's end he had done enough to earn second place behind Agostini and his Yamaha.

If we make an exception for Agostini's fleeting return to the fold in the last days, Read's departure marks what

Phil Read at Mallory Park with the 500 four in 1975. Read was the last rider to win a world title with an MV. Combative and stubborn by nature, MV signed him to provoke rather than support Agostini, who he eventually supplanted.

was practically the end of MV Agusta's glorious strut across the World Championship stage. Polite and smiling, Read was a snappy dresser with a taste for luxury (his appearances at the circuits at the wheel of a white Rolls Royce are legendary). His sense of fair play (in private life, if not always on the track) has led some to compare him to that classic English sportsman Geoff Duke, but – unlike the Maestro who supported him in some of the earlier phases of his career – Read was always ready to bite back when his adversaries least expected it.

Gianfranco Bonera

If his impulsiveness had not got the better of him on too many occasions, Gianfranco Bonera could have become a far more successful rider. But, very often just when he should have been at his most responsible, this weakness of his caused him to "blow it" with the result that he threw away some excellent results that otherwise would have been his for the taking.

Born in Porpetto, near Udine, on the 2nd of April 1945, Bonera served his motorcycling apprenticeship in the area around Monza. A spontaneous, exuberant, likeable lad with a solid physique (he started out as a racing cyclist), he got a lot of good experience in endurance events and circuit racing before MV "adopted" him in 1974. This was a period in which the great Italian factory, bereft of Agostini since his departure for Yamaha, obviously felt a need to fill the gap by training another promising young rider, just as they had done with Agostini a few years before.

Bonera did rather well at first with the 500 and beat Agostini twice at Misano, before winning again in the Italian round of the World Championship at Imola, where he beat Lansivuori on the Yamaha and Phil Read. By season's end Bonera was the runner-up in the Italian Championship (behind Agostini) and also in the World Championship (behind team leader Phil Read).

But his excessive boldness was to betray him in 1975. Things got off to a bad start at Modena where he banged his knee so badly against a hay bale that he was laid up until the Dutch Grand Prix, where he came sixth. Then it looked as if he was going to end the season on a high note when he found himself holding a fifteen second lead over Agostini and Read at the Mugello, but on the second last lap he had a bloodcurdling crash that marked not only the end of his race but also his brief association with MV.

A short time afterwards Bonera quit racing altogether to devote himself to business activities in the world of motorcycling.

Armando Toracca

After Bonera was injured at Modena at the beginning of the 1975 season, MV needed another Italian rider to line up alongside Phil Read. They were looking for a young, reliable type and in Armando Toracca they found the man that filled the bill.

Toracca, born in Portovenere – a charming fishing village near La Spezia – on the 3rd of March 1951, had made a name for himself in the space of a few years under the guidance of Roberto Gallina, a good rider of the Sixties turned talent scout. His early experience was gained aboard the Paton 500 and the Yamaha 250, with which he won the '74 Italian championship ahead of Walter Villa with the Harley Davidson ex Aermacchi stroker. But that's not all, right up to the last race on the championship calendar at Mugello, where a breakdown knocked him out of contention during the second lap, he was also in with a theoretical chance of winning the 500 title, which was a three-cornered contest between Agostini, Bonera and himself.

The duration of his contract with MV was determined by the length of time Bonera needed to get back to race fitness, which was roughly half the season. During that time Toracca gave a good account of himself, coming fourth at Le Castellet behind Agostini, Kanaya and Read; fourth at Salzburg, behind Kanaya, Lansivuori and Read; fourth again at Imola, behind Agostini, Read and Kanaya. In addition he won the supporting event sandwiched between the two stages of the Imola "200 Miles".

Then, upon Bonera's return, Toracca's wonderful adventure came to an end. He carried on racing for a while with Japanese bikes in the 500 and 750 classes, before retiring somewhat suddenly and unexpectedly from competition.

CLOSE ENCOUNTERS
OF THE MV THREE KIND

Finally, by way of a post-script to our "portrait gallery", we thought it might be interesting to add the following road test written in 1969 by Roberto Patrignani, co-author of this volume and the only Italian journalist that Count Domenico Agusta permitted to ride the MV three when it was at the peak of its sporting career. Patrignani's impressions are reported here exactly as they were at the time of the test in an attempt to preserve all the spontaneity and freshness of the original experience, which was undoubtedly an important one for a mere mortal that, for a few fleeting moments, had known the sensations hitherto reserved strictly for those inhabiting the Olympus of motorcycling.

The chance to ride a machine that has just won the World Championship is not something that happens every day. Then, when you think that only two other riders have ever seated themselves in the saddle – men of the calibre of Hailwood and Agostini to boot – the whole idea is even more of a thrill.

Well, we were lucky enough to be offered just such a chance. The bike in question is the MV Tre Cilindri that has once more swept all before it to sew up the world titles in both the 350 and 500 classes, with the championship programme still to be completed. We showed up at the Monza autodrome bright and early on the day before MV was due to set off for Imatra and the ninth round of the World Championship. The bikes, a 500 and two 350s with some illustrious victories behind them, were to be put through their paces for the last time before being loaded onto the plane for the journey to Finland.

We were scheduled to ride the 350 that won the East German Grand Prix; it was going to Imatra as a reserve bike. It was in perfect condition, however, and could easily have been raced. There to meet us at Imola were race shop supremo Arturo Magni, his right hand man Ruggero Mazza, and mechanic Lucio Castelli, as well as Agostini of course. First the engine was warmed over and then Castelli popped in the 10 mm hard plugs, gave the chain, brakes, and tyres a quick once-over and the bike was ready.

The men from MV had the grace not to smother us with do's and don'ts: they limited themselves to telling us to push the revs up to 13,000 before swopping any cogs and reminding us that the gearbox was a seven-speeder. Nothing else. There is no spark advance to set while the two narrow barrels of the three carburettors need no primer. All that remained was to open the stopcock beneath the fuel tank and the little one that dribbles some oil over the chain when the bike is underway.

Push starting the bike is a piece of cake. There is no need to worry about compression, all you have to do is push for a few paces and then let out the clutch while applying a little pressure on the saddle with the hip so that the rear wheel gets a better grip when the engine catches; then, leaving the clutch alone, you just give a quick blip on the throttle and

Roberto Patrignani with Giacomo Agostini just before the beginning of the test in 1969. The other members of the group are Lucio Castelli (on the left) and Arturo Magni.

the three cylinders are suddenly burbling away ready to launch the machine forward as soon as they get the green light. You don't notice it at first but the effort required to keep three carbs open takes it out of even the strongest forearm. To facilitate matters Agostini has the mechanics tape a rod along the twistgrip so that, instead of a cylindrical object that could easily slip through tired fingers, he can grasp a species of triangle. Agostini also uses gloves with metal studs on the palm in a bid to protect his hands as much as possible against the fatigue caused by the hundreds of gearchanges that a tough circuit involves.

Patrignani and the 350 three on the track at Monza.

With the ratios used on "our" bike (the pinion had 19 teeth and the crown wheel 46), the 350 could touch 255-260 km/h at 13,000 rpm by the end of the two straights at Monza. This could be pushed up as far as 270 km/h on faster tracks. The first surprise when riding the three is the docility of the engine, when it is not being pushed hard that is, thanks to excellent torque characteristics that already provide a deep-chested shove at 9000 rpm, thus making it possible to hit the highest speeds in short order. There was no noticeable vibration (from this point of view the three was much better than many production bikes) and

even when you open the throttle wide from medium speed the carbs do not baulk and the engine does not miss a beat. This is one of the many masterpieces that MV's technicians have been able to produce by making certain parts in-house rather than ordering them from external specialists, or by working closely with the latter in order to create "absolutely exclusive" components: e.g. carburettors, brakes and rear suspension units.

According to Agostini, the 350 is not so docile in a race as it looks at first sight, and must be kept running at high revs if it is to give of its best: from 11,000 to 14,000 rpm in the intermediate gears, when maximum performance is called for. This makes it a particularly demanding bike in the wet and on circuits featuring very slow hairpin bends, which would explain one or two poor performances in the National Championships during the early part of the season.

Agostini also told us that the 500, even though it has an extra 15 horses, is a much less difficult bike – largely because the engine is already pulling well at 6000 rpm – and it is also more stable through the bends, a fact that is pretty baffling given that both bikes share virtually the same frame and structure.

One possible explanation

might lie in the fact that the bigger engine, having a wider powerband, is driving the rear wheel for more of the time. We found out just how important this can be at the Big Bend when, after changing down two gears (Agostini just swaps the one cog) and with an uncertain touch on the throttle, the bike began to sway nervously, something it has been known to do in the hands of the World Champion as well. But if treated correctly, the Tre Cilindri is exceptionally manageable and stable. Low, short, and very compact, it offers a riding stance that allows the rider to become as one with the machine, a feeling that makes this a wonderful bike to ride. It is also very light, weighing in at barely 116 kilos.

The seven-speed gearbox is a joy for the precision and smoothness of the meshing. And then the ratios are so close that you can hardly hear a difference in the engine note when changing gear. Agostini brakes 170 metres before the Lesmo bend and 250 metres before the Parabolic (he adds a mere 10-15 metres more when riding the 500). The brakes are so powerful that those who are not made of the stuff of champions usually apply the brakes even sooner than they would do normally, for fear that they might lock up bringing both bike and rider to grief.

THE FABULOUS MULTIS

Designed and built in five months by Pietro Remor, who came to MV from Gilera in the November of 1949, the 500 four introduced at the Milan Show of April '50 was raced for the first time by Arciso Artesiani at the Belgian Grand Prix, held on the very fast, very tough Francorchamps circuit. It arrived at the circuit on the Friday, barely in time for the qualifying trials, where its considerable potential was instantly apparent.

As a matter of fact the half-litre MV had looked very interesting right from the planning stage. The light alloy cylinders were cast in a block and tilted forward at 30 degrees while the double overhead camshafts were driven by a train of centrally located spur gears; the valves were inclined at 45 degrees and closed by coil springs, the whole assembly being enclosed in an oil bath. The five-bearing built-up crankshaft used rolling bearings as did the con-rods. The "square" power unit (54 × 54 × 4), breathed through two Dell'Ortos, while ignition was handled by a Vertex magneto with rotary magnets. Lubrication was by a wet sump system. All pretty much standard stuff when compared to Remor's previous work, and the postwar

Gilera four in particular; but one very particular feature was the transmission, which had the four-speed gearbox positioned longitudinally with the power arriving from the engine via a bevel pair and the clutch downstream of the gearbox. Another peculiarity was the gear lever, which took the form of a transversely mounted rocker pedal: upward gearchanges were effected by the pedal located on the left hand side, and downward changes by the pedal on the right hand side. The final drive was naturally by cardan shaft. The frame was a closed duplex cradle in tube and sheet steel pressings. Another area in which Ing. Remor chose to express his anticonformist

Leslie Graham with the 500 four at Faenza in 1953. The bike has an abbreviated fairing swept back towards the tank and Earles forks. Note also the extended front mudguard, an aerodynamic feature that enjoyed a certain popularity in those days.

personality was suspension engineering. His front fork was a girder-type unit with chrome-molybdenum steel blades and four torsion bars of 6 mm in diameter. The rear suspension was made up of two arms on each side united by short forgings, a structure that acted like a species of Watts linkage and permitted the final drive housing to swing along a straight line. This double swinging arm also had torsion bars, integrated with adjustable friction dampers. The 20" wheels were shod with 3" tyres in front and 3.25" covers at the rear.

The bike, which developed about 50 hp at 9500 rpm, soon showed that it was very fast with a top speed of over 200 km/h: at Francorchamps, with the benefit of a mere twenty minute run on the test bench before leaving Cascina Costa, it claimed fourth place behind the two Gilera fours ridden by Nello Pagani and Umberto Masetti, and Ted Frend on an AJS twin. But although the new MV was perfectly at home on fast tracks, the shaft drive and the suspension made it difficult to handle on twistier tracks. In fact, for the rest of the season it was unable to show what it could really do, despite the fact that it was ridden by men of the calibre of Artesiani, Guido Leoni and Armstrong. The best result was Artesiani's third place in the Monza Grand Prix of Nations, behind Duke on the Norton and Masetti on the Gilera.

During the winter the Quat-tro Cilindri was carefully redesigned in a bid to weed out its weaknesses. In addition, a Grand Turismo version was produced, which caused quite a sensation at the Milan Show of November 1950, where it made an unexpected appearance.

Even though many purists maintain that the "real" motorcycle engine has to be a single, there is no doubt that fours have always possessed a glamour all of their own, both for that aura of class that surrounds them and for the performance they can offer: power, pick-up, and elasticity. But four-cylinder machines, which were fairly popular between the wars – we are thinking of the many American models, the Zundapps and Puchs – seemed like an inconceivable luxury in the years of austerity, a luxury that only the aristocratic English Ariel marque was prepared to offer a privileged few. In any case these were almost always rather tractable engines, built for long distancce touring or for pulling a sidecar; the race-bred MV four was a different kettle of fish that promised hitherto undreamed-of pleasures.

The general layout of this motorcycle closely resembled its competition predecessor, including the shaft drive and the four-speed gearbox with the transverse pedal. A teledraulic fork had replaced the torsion bars, while the rear suspension – which still had the torsion bars – featured hydraulic shock absorbers in preference to the mechanical units used previously. A good deal of comment was aroused by the twin front headlamps, but these were dropped a short time afterwards. Last but not least, the bike was put on sale at 950,000 lire (the same price as the Harley Davidson 1200) which made the MV the second most expensive bike on the Italian market after the competition version of the Parilla 250. It should be remembered that 950 thousand lire was no mean sum in those days and could purchase two Moto Guzzi Falcones or a good seven and a half Lambrettas; but there is no reason to believe that the MV four would not have sold in Italy, or internationally for that matter. Sadly, however, this exceptional bike was never to go into production and after lingering on for a while as a showroom attraction the project was abandoned. Another fifteen years were to pass before MV – stimulated by the changing nature of the world motorcycle market – decided to dust off the idea of producing a roadgoing four.

But we digress. Meanwhile, back in the world of racing, MV was hungry for success. A powerful team was put together for the '51 championship: Artesiani, Bertoni and Magi were joined by new signings Bruno Bertacchini, an ex Guzzi works rider, the gifted and forceful Carlo Bandirola, and Felice Bena-sedo, a good solid team play-er and one of the few Italian privateers with some competition experience outside Italy; above all there was Les Graham. The first man to win the championship of the world (with his AJS 500), ex RAF officer Graham was a highly gifted rider with a long and varied experience in motorcycle racing. The Quattro Cilindri was fitted with a teledraulic fork, then the rear torsion bars were done away with and finally the engine was given four carburettors. Performance was considerably improved while manoeuverability and roadholding were much better, so much so that the three machines ridden by Artesiani, Bandirola and Graham managed to dominate the tough Ospedaletti event for several laps; but something always

Nello Pagani during a test ride at Monza in 1954. Here the four is fitted with a strange "half-dustbin" fairing. Pagani won the first round of the Italian championship with this bike.

Dickie Dale with the Quattro Cilindri at Faenza in 1954. The Earles fork is of a new lightened variety; the bike is fitted with the first type of dolphin fairing, a head-on view of which is shown on page 66.

cropped up (split fuel tanks at Ospedaletti) to throw a spanner in the works.

The first win came along at Ferrara by courtesy of Bandirola. This happened on the same day as the tragic crash that cost the lives of Raffaele Alberti and Guido Leoni in the 125 race. A short time afterwards Bertacchini had a win at Varese, but these were all races of secondary importance. In the international arena MV still had to bend the knee to the Gileras, Guzzis, and Nortons, whose single-cylinder engines were the least powerful of all, even though this shortcoming was more than compensated by their superior lightness and manageability on the one hand and the riding skills of rising star Geoff Duke on the other.

In the winter of '51-'52 the bike was subjected to some swingeing modifications. The engine became undersquare ($53 \times 56 \times 4 = 498$ cm³), which resulted in a more compact combustion chamber, and the cylinders were cast separately; a five-speed gearbox was mounted transversely, in the traditional MV manner, with the final drive chain on the right hand side. The frame was an all-tubular full duplex cradle and the rear suspension was made up of a swinging arm with teledraulic elements flanking the wheel; the wheels carried 3.00-19" tyres in front and 3.50-18" at the back, the beginning of that progressive reduction in wheel diameters that has led to the modern 16 inchers. Central drum brakes provided the stopping power. Les Graham had a hand in all of these modifications and the adoption of Earles forks following a disappointing performance at the Berne GP was also his idea. Earles forks were an English proprietary design featuring a long leading link with teledraulic springing elements. A bit on the heavy side, such forks offered good transverse rigidity and were very much in vogue on both sporting bikes and production tourers for a good ten years or so.

The new engine developed 52 hp at 10,200 rpm, pretty remarkable for those days; top speed was more than 210 km/h and the bike's handling was now much improved. For the first round of the Italian

Championship at Faenza, however, MV still fielded the shaft-driven bike, albeit with modified rear suspension. The new model made its debut at Parma on the 14th of April in the hands of Bandirola. It also featured an anatomical fuel tank with a peculiar appendage that ran forward to fair the steering head.

But the '52 season was also doomed to get off to a slow start: a series of retirements interspersed with the odd placing. This poor showing was still caused by a succession of irritating snags that conspired to foil the bike's obvious superiority as far as speed was concerned. The first proof of its real potential was provided at the Tourist Trophy, the famous and murderously tough meeting held on the Isle of Man.

The TT, a natural road circuit that was "demoted" because it was considered unsuitable – and unsafe – for modern high performance machinery, is one of the oldest races in the world. It began in 1907 and is still held today over a 60 kilometre course (which the 500s of the old days had to cover seven times) that snakes through villages, seaside resorts, and hamlets with ancient and mysterious names, and skirts the coast for a while before climbing up the slopes of the island's only mountain, Snaefell, in an endless series of bends and short straights, steep uphill stretches and dizzying descents flanked by stone walls, ditches and lamp posts. Just to add spice to this fiendish brew, it is

usually raining or foggy. A very glamorous and picturesque circuit, therefore, but also a very tough and dangerous one, the TT was for decades an unparalleled test of men and machines. As a matter of fact, the British still consider it the most important race of them all and far more important than a mere World Championship. What is beyond any doubt is that not so long ago a win over these roads conferred more fame and glory than any other victory could offer.

The Isle of Man was for many years dominated by British riders and bikes, partly because the length and difficulty of the course required in-depth knowledge that was

On the facing page, the MV four fitted with a dustbin fairing for the first time in 1955. Tito Forconi is the rider. Left, the 1956 Isle of Man TT. John Surtees is about to set off on the road to victory with the 500 four. Behind him, Nello Pagani – with the raincoat and flat cap – is about to start the stopwatch. Below, a moment from the 1955 Grand Prix of Nations, won by Masetti: Bandirola, with his unmistakable style, is leading Forconi (MV) and Geoff Duke (Gilera) at the Parabolic bend, which had been built that very year to replace the earlier cobbled bends.

not easy for foreign riders to acquire. Graham was therefore the ideal rider for this event and so MV put their faith in him and the bike with the Earles forks (but minus the small fairing around the steering head).

The Anglo-Italian combination covered the first four laps in second place, took the lead on the fifth, but finished once more in second place owing to the fact that the back tyre had worn out prematurely. Even though the usual technical hitch had appeared to deprive MV of an unqualified success, this was nevertheless a clear demonstration of the bike's undoubted qualities.

The gremlins struck again at

91

Ulster where Graham was foiled when the tread detached itself from the rear tyre, a fairly common problem in those days: the year before, for example, the Nortons had also been dogged with tyres "chunking". But finally, at the end of the season, MV's patience was rewarded with two sensational victories, on two circuits with completely different characteristics into the bargain: Monza and Montjuich. Both victories were the work of Les Graham, who humbled the gifted Masetti and his Gilera in both Monza and Barcellona

The beginning of 1953 found MV faced with a formidable array of rivals. Foremost among these was the Gilera team, made up of a cosmopolitan batch of riders led by Geoff Duke. Then came the Moto Guzzi squad armed with the new Guzzi four, followed by the updated fuel-injected BMW and the still dangerous Nortons aided and abetted by Kavanagh and the forceful Ray Amm. The set-up at MV was practically the same as the year before, even though the usual amount of development work had been carried out during the close season, with Les Graham making many useful suggestions. At that time MV racing was practically divided into two sections: one for the 125 class bikes, headed by Giulio Cella, and another for the 500s, run by Arturo Mag-

ni, the man who was to become a living symbol of the MV race shop. A model aeroplane enthusiast, Magni was a boyhood friend of Ferruccio Gilera, who was also an expert model maker. After a brief spell with Bestetti Aeronautica of Arcore, Magni joined the Gilera race shop in 1947. Three years after that he went to MV, along with Piero Remor, and he soon won lasting fame as the "wizard" of Cascina Costa.

The two sections of the racing department were also divided in a material sense, insofar as one was in Cascina Costa and the other in the Verghera works. Neither section, however, had a real "boss" in the sense that this position was reserved strictly for Count Domenico Agusta, who held sole responsibility for technical matters, research programmes, and the choice of riders. Two technical associates – Mario Montoli and Mario Rossi – saw to the development of the various ideas, especially after Remor left the firm in 1955, but only Count Domenico could issue general directives and order the construction of a particular model, be it a touring machine or racer; furthermore the Count was free to follow up his whim of the moment, intuition, or any particular idea that had taken his fancy from a technical – or even merely aesthetic – point of view.

As we said before, therefore, the Quattro Cilindri of '53 was virtually the same as the previous year's model. The only difference was that it

was no longer fitted with the small fairing around the steering head, leading us to add that the big capacity MVs of those days did rather better without the various fairings that were tried out from time to time.

MV's plans were knocked sadly askew by Les Graham's fatal accident at the Isle of Man TT. His death deprived MV of one of the best riders and development men on the contemporary scene and the repercussions of this had an adverse effect on the team's performance for the rest of the season; but nobody gave up, quite the contrary, people pulled together as much as possible in an attempt to get over this difficult moment.

It was round about then that a completely new bike first saw the light. This was the 350 four, first conceived as a means of improving the marque's rider training programme (in fact it was first seen at the TT, where it was used to tot up an enormous number of practice laps), but later earmarked for a far more important role as far as the marque's sporting commitments were concerned. Apart from any other considerations a victory or two in the 350 class, which was practically unknown in Italy at that time but very popular elsewhere – particularly in England – represented a potentially interesting publicity vehicle for the marque's products.

The first 350 engines were obtained simply by sleeving down the cylinders of a 500;

only later, given the promising results, did the firm get round to producing a purpose-built 350 engine, and even then it followed the basic design of the 500 model. The rest of the machine also closely followed the existing model. Although the newcomer was fitted with the same Earles forks as the 500 at first, by the end of the season a different fitment had made its appearance; this was a fork similar in design to the model used on the 125, with straight downtubes and less steeply raked, covered springs. The fuel tank was also slightly smaller.

The original engine developed about 42 hp at 11000 rpm, a little more than either English rivals AJS, Norton, and Velocette or the Italian Guzzi could offer. On the debit side, this bike was a good bit heavier than its competitors, because it was basically a scaled-down 500; but, we repeat, the original idea was to create no more than a reserve bike for training purposes. And in fact, even though it showed promise right from the start – Bandiroli rode it to first place in the German Grand Prix at the extremely difficult Schotten circuit – it spent the rest of the season in harness as a practice vehicle, without ever lining up on the grid for a taste of the real thing.

The year of grace 1954 seemed as if it would be just as difficult as its predecessor, and it was a period of proving and research as far as the MV four was concerned. Two young English hopefuls by the names of Dickie Dale and Bill Lomas were called in to lend a hand; but at the end of the day the most efficient of them all was still Carlo Bandirola, now in his fortieth year, who was joined in the line-up by another "old timer", Nello Pagani, now making his final appearances before taking up the role of race manager.

1954 was also the year of the dustbin fairing. Attempts to improve the performance of bikes involving these aerodynamic appendages had been made since the Thirties, but the problem had been tackled on a purely rational basis only since 1952 - '53. Partial fairings had made their appearance before that date, but then the major manufacturers adopted the so-called "dustbin" fairings, which ran right round the front wheel and, in many cases, were rounded off by a tail section. These streamlined shells made control somewhat problematic, so much so that they were abolished in 1957. But the increase in speed guaranteed by such devices was so considerable that no marque could afford not to fit them before the ban was applied for fear of being pushed off the winners' podium for good and all.

MV was reluctant to fit a fairing to the 500 because the fours, rather tall, heavy bikes, were easier to handle without streamlining; but it was unthinkable to hand such

an advantage to the opposition. Although the MVs showed up for the first round of the Italian Championships at Modena minus fairings (a race won by Bandirola), when the time came for the second championship meeting at Ferrara the bikes had been fitted with light alloy fairings that covered the steering head before running down diagonally to flank the engine, leaving the rider's arms uncovered. The streamlining was rounded off by a small steeply raked windscreen.

At Monza for the third round of the national championships, the MVs appeared clad in some distinctly unusual streamlining: this consisted of a species of half-dustbin at the front that was cut off at tyre height before running back to link up with the panelling covering the engine. Just for the record this oddly streamlined MV won the race with Nello Pagani aboard.

Dickie Dale's 350 also received new streamlining in time for the Isle of Man. This was practically a dolphin fairing and was typical of the designs used after the abolition of the full, dustbin-type fairings: more specifically, it was a small fairing (covering the steering head and the rider's arms) that ran back to link up with the side panels.

The "half-dustbin" fairing was used on several other occasions, until the Grand Prix of Nations, where Lomas's machine appeared with what the Italians called "bocca di pesce", or "fishmouth" streamlining, which was little

more than a dustbin-type construction with the nose cut away. But the last important win scored by MV that season was achieved at Barcellona's difficult Montjuich circuit, where Dale won on a 500 with no fairing at all.

As far as the bike proper was concerned, no important changes were made in the course of the year, although the usual development work was carried out. This did lead to some improvements: power output was upped to more than 60 hp, while top speed was increased to close on 230 km/h. A lot of work was put in on the Earles forks, which now had straight arms instead of curved, and Girling and Armstrong springing in place of the MV units used previously. The exhaust pipes were no longer fitted with megaphones.

The following year (1955) was also spent experimenting with various ways and means of improving the aerodynamics: first came a new version of the "fishmouth" fairing that left the hands uncovered, and then came the first real dustbin, complete with two deep scoops to channel the cooling airstream towards the cylinders. But that March, at the Naples meeting, the MVs took the field with the "half-dustbin" fairings, while at the Ospedaletti event Bandirola and Pagani rode unfaired bikes with the old drum-shaped number carriers over the steering heads. Important modifications were also made to the cycle parts: the frame was redesigned and lowered, while a

demountable cradle was incorporated in the interests of easier engine removal; after the first outings, the Earles fork was abandoned in favour of an MV-built leading link design; various rear shock absorber units were tried out (MV and Girling); the front brake was fitted with big air intakes and the fuel tank was stretched. Power output was increased to 65 hp at 11000 rpm. With his sights still firmly set on the most coveted trophy of all, the World Championship for the half-litre class, Domenico Agusta probably felt he had done his chances no harm when he signed Ray Amm, who had spent the previous seasons in a stalwart defence of Norton's now fading colours. A Rhodesian, Amm was a slim young rider of great talent who was courageous to the point of foolhardiness and, had he lived, he could have become the natural successor to Les Graham, even from the point of view of development work. When Amm arrived in Italy he took a house on Lake Maggiore and got right down to work with all the enthusiasm of a schoolboy, but the dream was to be cut tragically short when he went off the track during his first race aboard a 350 at Imola. At first it looked like a fairly banal skid but then Amm came into violent contact with a metal fence post and was killed outright.

Agusta then called in Umberto Masetti, and so the celebrated "Gilera trio" of 1950 – Bandirolo, Pagani and Masetti – found themselves reunited under the MV banner. The season had its ups and downs, but towards the end of the year things had swung in favour of Gilera and their great English rider Geoff Duke. But at Monza, the last event on the calendar, MV got a taste of long-awaited revenge after an electrifying race. Gilera were clear favourites to win and in fact Duke took the lead after MV-mounted Bandirola and Forconi had both shown briefly. But the acrobatic Masetti hung on doggedly, snapping at the heels of the Gilera riders tucked in behind the leader, in particular Armstrong, who was in second place at that point.

But a couple of laps before the finish Duke's engine began to lose power and he found himself overhauled and then overtaken by two of his pursuers, Armstrong and Masetti, just at the end of the second lap. Things were all set up for a thrilling sprint to the line, which Masetti won by a clear hundred metres over his nearest rival.

Some years later Masetti revealed that Count Domenico had been so pleased at this win that he handed his rider a bonus of one million lire, which still meant something in those days.

At the beginning of the '56 season the MVs again presented themselves with slightly modified frames and engines; power output now stood at 67 hp, good for 250 km/h when combined with a dustbin fairing. New, MV-patented brakes were fitted with a number of small air scoops to improve internal cooling. At Monza, in the second round of the Italian championships, the bikes were fitted with two tubes, one at each side, which protruded from the nose of the fairing to serve as ram air intakes for the carburettors. As far as the fairings were concerned, the previous year's models were used for the first outings; in May, however, a new type of dustbin made its appearance at Faenza. The new streamlining was devoid of the two frontal air scoops, but it did not last long. The small fairing around the steering head and petrol tank was kept on for the twistier circuits.

Although very few noticeable modifications had been made, the four nevertheless had an extremely good season that culminated with the first of a long series of World Championship victories. Most of the credit for this has to go to John Surtees, the young English rider who had been signed at the end of the preceding season and who was to emerge as the kind of ultra high class rider that had been missing at MV since Graham's and Amm's time. Surtees instantly showed the cantankerous MV four who was boss and he rode it to a great series of wins right from the word go. Then came prestigious victories at the Isle of Man, the Dutch Grand Prix, and a "double" (350 and 500) at the Belgian GP. A fall in Germany cost him a fractured foot that kept him out of the saddle for the remainder of the season, but by that time his lead in the rankings was so commanding that all he had left to do to collect the World Championship was haul himself out of his armchair and hobble along to pick up the trophy.

Again in 1956, an updated version of the 350 four made a few sporadic appearances, greeted with some pretty flattering results (first place in the Belgian Grand Prix, as we have already mentioned). The twin designed by Giannini (see the chapter on series production) was also given a try on a few occasions, and a completely original engine obtained by mating two 175 cm³ propulsion units was also spotted, but in the end MV kept faith with the "Quattro", which had showed that it was still the best of the bunch. During the following winter much hard work was done at MV in an attempt to field an even more competitive bike for the next season. The Verghera marque's opponents were preparing some formidable weapons: particularly feared was the new Guzzi Vee-8, and although still in the development phase this half-litre "monster" had already shown that it was very quick indeed.

The new MV engine was now undersquare ($52 \times 58 \times 4 = 492$ cm³), while the frame had been lowered once more. At the end of the season experimentation began on a new dustbin design, while the usual mini fairing was used for the twisty circuits. The 500 was raced – with excellent results – in the Italian Junior Championships; no aerodynamic aids were fitted to the bike, in accordance with the so-called Formula Two regulations.

Spectators watching practice before the Grand Prix of Nations were treated to the sight of an exceptional 500 with a six-cylinder engine. The basic design was the usual one: cylinders in-line and tilted at 10 degrees, double overhead camshafts driven by a centrally mounted gear cluster, magneto ignition and a wet sump. The engine was an undersquare unit capable of developing a remarkable amount of power: 75 hp at 15,000 rpm. One very important feature of this engine was the use of chrome-bore cylinders, then a real first as far as competition engines went. The gearbox was a six-speeder. The frame was a tubular duplex cradle with a triangulated rear section and a "Featherbed"-type arrangement at the steering head. The 18" wheels carried central drum brakes, with a four leading shoe type at the front and a two leading shoe fitment at the back.

Despite the strength of its forces in the field, however, the '57 season was a particularly poor one for MV, not only in the smaller capacity classes, but also in the larger ones; and for that year there was little the machines or the men of Cascina Costa could do against the overwhelming might of the Gilera team. As a result MV had to be content with second best in the various championships and Surtees's solitary victory in Holland. At the end of the 1957 season, Guzzi, Gilera, and Mondial all agreed to withdraw from circuit racing. It was a sensational decision that caused the proverbial rivers of ink to flow. The marques in question supplied a whole series of reasons to explain the decision: there was little in the way of serious foreign opposition, furthermore motorsport in general was under a cloud following the tragic pile-up during the Mille Miglia, many experts thought the dustbin fairings were too dangerous; but all these points masked a far more pertinent problem: the cost of maintaining a racing department was skyrocketing, while the market was showing the first signs of recession.

In any case, the three marques' decision left MV practically without a rival, at least in the big capacity classes, because neither the English singles (Norton, AJS, Matchless) nor the German twins (BMW) were able to worry the Italian machines. But this situation did not make MV any less competitive, nor was the marque tempted to rest on its laurels: they could still race against the clock, i.e. there were still plenty of

Top, we are at the 1956 TT and it's Surtees again, this time at the Governor's Bridge bend, one of the classic parts of the course. Left, Bandirola at Codogno. Note the petrol pumps and the stone posts at the wayside: safety precautions were somewhat sketchy in the old days!

95

track records to beat, a feat made all the more difficult by the abolition of the dustbin fairings. Despite this handicap, Surtees managed to beat records at Assen and Francorchamps (1958), while the following year he smashed the course record at the Isle of Man and the Grand Prix of Nations, bringing the record for the latter circuit up to a mean speed of almost 192 km/h.

Two other versions of dustbin fairings fitted to the MV four: below, the 1956 version was steeply raked and had a little spoiler (the photo shows Masetti at the Solitude); right, Ken Kavanagh aboard the version seen at Monza at the outset of the 1957 season.

During the '58 season MV fielded bikes with a new red and silver dolphin fairing, built in accordance with the new regulations, as well as the old mini fairing around the steering head, which ran back to link up with the fuel tank. The fours were also raced in Formula Two competition, obviously without aerodynamic aids.

The engines were updated as usual and the power output of the 500 was now hovering around the 70 hp mark, while the 350 could pump out a good 45 hp. New 4LS front brakes made in-house by MV were also fitted. Development work continued on the new six-cylinder machine, which was entered for the Grand Prix of Nations, with rider John Hartle. But the "Quattro" showed that it was still more than good enough to sort out the best of the opposition and the outcome of the World 350 and 500 Championships was virtually never in doubt, thanks again to Surtees.

The next three years, up to 1960, are rightly considered to be the golden age of MV Agusta. During that period a total of 76 Grands Prix were raced and even though MV did not compete on a few occasions the marque still won a

staggering 63 championship races, 32 with Surtees and 17 with Ubbiali. The Italian championships were also a source of considerable satisfaction for the Verghera-based marque: Carlo Bandirola, honoured by the Italian Government for his services to sport, won the '58 Italian championship, while Gilberto Milani and Tino Brambilla dominated Junior class racing. In 1959 the frame was the object of most attention, in a bid to make further improvements in both handling and roadholding. The bikes had far more power on tap than their rivals, but on the twisty circuits it was not possible to make the most of it. The new frame had detachable bottom rails only, so that the engine could be removed with ease without jeopardizing the overall rigidity of the structure, while various triangulations were tried out for the rear section, beneath the saddle and at the shock absorber mountings.

The angle of inclination of the shock absorbers was altered several times in the course of the season. Other modifications of secondary importance included a 40 litre tank fitted for the Isle of Man TT, and air intakes for the front brakes.

A great deal of work was also done on the 350, which was lightened by 20 kilos thanks to special materials supplied by the Agusta Group's aero-

es that occurred in 1961, when MV retired from competition and the Japanese marques arrived in force to take their place. MV turned its back on the lightweights and concentrated on the "Privat" 350s and 500s, which competed for several years with almost no major modifications, except for a new fairing that was tried out in '62 and then abandoned.

The most important news regarded the changes in the MV senior class team: first of all Surtees switched over to motor car racing, followed by Hocking, winner of the 1961 world 350 and 500 class titles. The vacancy they left was filled by rising star Mike Hailwood, destined to become one of the greatest motorcycle racers of all time. Local riders Remo Venturi and Silvio Grassetti were signed for

Left, Nello Pagani with the 500 six during practice for the 1957 Grand Prix of Nations. Below, Surtees and the four in action in the same race. His bike is fitted with the latest dustbin fairing.

nautical engineering division. A new version of the 350 made its appearance in 1960 with a larger sump, sleeker streamlining, and a space-frame-type rear frame. This was the bike that Gary Hocking rode to victory in the Monza Grand Prix. Again at Monza, Emilio Mendogni showed up for practice aboard a new 500 model whose frame had a triangulated rear section, but this interesting new machine remained at the prototype stage.

In the chapter dealing with the smaller capacity bikes we mentioned the big chang-

A great picture that successfully conveys all the frenetic excitement of competition. The race in question is the 1959 Junior TT: the spectators' cameras click away furiously as Arturo Magni begins refuelling Surtees's bike even before the rider has had time to dismount. Nello Pagani is timing the operation with the stopwatch while the other two mechanics Ezio Colombo and Vittorio Carrano – who may not help without infringing the rules – look on with understandable anxiety.

the races in the Italian championship. But the easy life was to last no longer than the 1961 season: in 1962 Honda got the better of MV in the 350 championship with a 339 cm^3 four (as against the 285 cm^3 of the first "scaled up" model from the year before), while in '63 Gilera made a comeback – albeit an unofficial one – using its 1957 bikes, which competed under the Scuderia Duke banner.

Even though the "threat" posed by Gilera was to prove little more than wishful thinking, because six years is a long time in motorsport, the awesome strength of the Honda organization was getting harder and harder to resist. Finally, despite Hailwood's undoubted brilliance, MV had to relinquish its claim on the 350 sceptre for the '63 season too, although the Italian marque retained the 500 crown.

In 1964 MV – still competing under the "Privat" badge – concentrated virtually all their efforts on the 500 championship, as far as the World Championship was concerned at any rate, while the 350 made only sporadic appearances – in Holland for example – where Hailwood nevertheless had to be satisfied with second place. Undeterred, Mike won all seven of the 500 class races in which he took part, meeting only occasional opposition from the Argentinian Benedicto Caldarella, who had been given an old Gilera four by the somewhat ramshackle organization set up by Gilera and the Geoff Duke stable.

Hailwood's bike raced for the whole season with practically no modifications and "Mike the Bike" used it to beat the world speed record for both the Hour and the 100 kilometres at Daytona, a remarkable achievement from a technical as well as a sporting point of view.

That year the famous Florida resort town was hosting a World Championship event for the first time and Hailwood thought he would take advantage of the ultra fast speedbowl to make an assault on the two records, then held by Gilera. But a mix-up at the shipping company meant that the attempt had to be made with the only bike that had arrived, which just happened to be the one earmarked for the race. This left the English ace and his first rate mechanic Vittorio Carrano with just enough time to make the indispensable alterations to the gear ratios. The rest of the bike was unchanged, including the dolphin fairing and the tank, which barely guaranteed the range required to complete the distance. The attempt, made on the morning of the 2nd of February, was a re-

sounding success: the 100 kilometres were covered in 25' 44" 74/100, corresponding to an average speed of 233.047 km/h (the old Gilera record was 26' 28" 1/100, or 226.671 km/h), while at the end of the Hour it emerged that Mike had covered 233.081 kilometres, against the 227.519 racked up by the Gilera. On the afternoon of that same day the same bike, with only the gear ratios adjusted once more, won the World Championship race with ease, again in the hands of Hailwood we need hardly add. Apart from any other consideration, this was an undeniably effective demonstration of sound construction and mechanical robustness! Anyone interested in drawing conclusions from the way MV

had contested the '64 season could have maintained that the marque's strategy was to hold on as long as possible to its last line of defence – the 500 class – making use of what few arms it had left before surreptitiously leaving the field. A little like the famous Haydn symphony at the end of which the musicians stop playing one at a time, put down their instruments and leave in silence...

But anyone espousing such a point of view would have underestimated Count Domenico's pride and fighting spirit. For him, giving a little ground was one thing, full retreat another, especially as far as the big capacity classes were concerned: the big bikes had always represented the acme of motorcycle racing

and MV's half-litre machinery had ruled the roost for too many years to give up without making a fight of it. And to those who would say that the Italian marque had it too easy for too long against mediocre opposition, we say that such criticism forgets to consider the levels to which competition would have sunk in those years without the presence of MV: a pathetic collection of clapped out museum pieces, kept going with love and affection and not much else by their penniless owners.

And so, despite those for whom MV was doomed to resignation and decline, 1965 witnessed the birth of the most celebrated combination in the history of motorcycling: Giacomo Agostini and

With the arrival of Hailwood and Agostini, MV reached the apogee of its fame. Top left, the English star overtakes Marsovski (Matchless) at Mallory Park in 1963 (note the differences between Hailwood's fairing and the one on Surtees's bike); left, "Mike the Bike" at the end of his successful record attempt at Daytona in '64 (the enthusiastic semaphorist is Mike's father Stan); top centre, Agostini aboard the MV three, one of the most perfect combinations of man and machine ever seen; right Honda-mounted Hailwood and Agostini, teammates no longer.

the MV three. A rider who was then still very young but one whose promise had brought him to the attention of Count Domenico – a man with a quasi infallible nose for riding talent – and a bike that was in many ways unorthodox were to raise motorcycle racing to a level of popularity that had never been reached before.

The advent of the Tre Cilindri meant that the days of the old "Quattro" were numbered: in 1965 it was still used in 500 class competition, where its supremacy remained unchallenged (although by that time the 350 version was little more than a

102

reserve for the newer bike), but when the three-cylinder formula was adopted for the half-litre machine as well (on the occasion of the 1966 Dutch Grand Prix) then the time had come for the glorious veteran to bow out definitively: the career of the MV Quattro Cilindri had lasted for fifteen years, which would have been a remarkable stint for a touring bike never mind a sophisticated racing machine. The arrival of the three was a source of considerable controversy among the experts because a three-cylinder layout is easy to justify when designing a two-stroke, but less so in the case of a four-stroke. Nonetheless such a design is lighter, neater and more compact, all considerable advantages since at high speeds a difference of a few centimetres in width is the equivalent of a few more horses. But this decision was not made by an army of technicians armed with slide rules and complex calculations: everything sprang from the Count himself, who simply decided one fine day that his engineers would build an engine that was quite outwith current technical orthodoxy. A three-cylinder engine to be precise.

As we have already said, the first engine built according to the new formula was a 350, the class most at risk from Honda's unremitting assault. This engine was an under-square unit with the cylinders in-line across the frame and tilted forward at 10 degrees, double overhead camshafts driven by a gear train on the right, and four valves inclined at 22 degrees. A set of spur gears took the power to a seven-speed gearbox; lubrication was by a wet sump system with a gear-type pump; and ignition was by coil, while the engine breathed through three Dell'Ortos that were 31 or 32 mm instruments depending on the circuit. The frame was a duplex cradle made of tubing with a featherbed-type layout at the steering head and a wide triangulation at the back, as well as detachable bottom rails and a square-section swinging arm. In the first version the rear shock absorber struts could be anchored in various positions in order to modify the angle of inclination. The suspension struts, almost always made by Ceriani, featured manual adjustment. The wheels were shod with 3.00-18" wheels in front and 3.50-18" behind; the braking system, of MV's own make at first and later by Ceriani, was made up of a 230 mm 4LS drum fitted to the front wheel with a 240 mm 2LS brake bringing up the rear. The bike appeared for practice at some races fitted with a mechanically operated dual disc brake on the front wheel.

The new racer made a fleeting appearance during practice at Imola in the spring of '65 flaunting a handsome MV logo and with no trace of the legend "Privat", which would have been somewhat incongruous in any case given that this was a brand new design. It was sidelined for the first few races of the season until

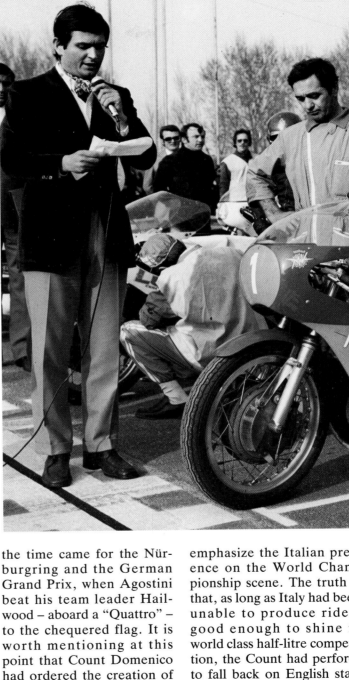

the time came for the Nürburgring and the German Grand Prix, when Agostini beat his team leader Hailwood – aboard a "Quattro" – to the chequered flag. It is worth mentioning at this point that Count Domenico had ordered the creation of the new machine with the precise intention of giving it to an Italian rider, so as to emphasize the Italian presence on the World Championship scene. The truth is that, as long as Italy had been unable to produce riders good enough to shine in world class half-litre competition, the Count had perforce to fall back on English stars but, while fully recognizing the contribution made to racing and development by the

A pregnant moment before the off. Agostini and mechanic Ruggero Mazza seem lost in thought as Sig. Costa makes his announcement.

103

likes of Graham, Surtees, and Hailwood, he had always hoped that one day his splendid creations would be ridden by Italians. When Agostini's star began to shine on the horizon the sporting Count was able to gratify these patriotic instincts at long last and, as we have already said, the MV-Agostini combination went on to build an enduring sporting legend.

Like all new machines, the three had to go through a fairly long tuning phase, which in this case lasted for most of the '65 season: brilliant results in East Germany and Finland, as well as at the Nurburgring and Monza alternated with more modest showings or retirements and at the end of the day the championship went to Redman-Honda; by way of compensation, however, Hailwood clinched the 500 title with the "Quattro".

Hailwood, by this time an established star, and the up and coming Agostini were to part company after only one season. At the end of 1965, tempted by the new Hondas and a mouth-watering contract, Hailwood agreed to join the Japanese team. He had already worked with Honda some years previously and, besides, he was already unhappy with the situation at MV.

Agostini was given the pick of the machinery available at Cascina Costa and for a while he rode both the three and the four: he won, for example, the opening race on the Italian championship calendar (a 500 event at Modena)

with the Tre Cilindri but he won several other important national championship events aboard the "Quattro".

In 1966 Agostini won his first world title victory in the toughest championship of all, the 500 class. Until the Belgian Grand Prix Agostini had picked up nothing better than a string of second places, both in the 350 and the 500 championships, in which he continued to ride the old four; but at a very wet Francorchamps circuit "Ago", as everybody called him by that time, won the day atop the faithful Quattro Cilindri. This was to be the last time that Agostini raced the four and from then on he preferred the three even for the 500 class.

Agostini's three had been created directly on the "field of battle" at Assen by scaling up a 350 to 377 cm^3 (the bike had also been fitted with a

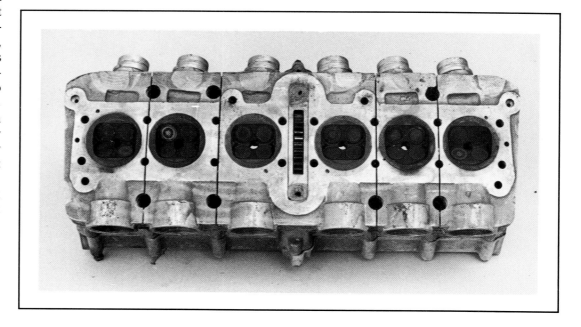

The duels between Agostini and Pasolini – shown here at Riccione in a 350 event in 1969 – inflamed the fans, who soon split into two opposing factions, in the finest Italian tradition. Right, the head of the 1969 version of the six-cylinder 350, which also had bronze combustion chambers. Note also the cuts made across the head to compensate for expansion.

104

350 4 cilindri - 1953-1965

1960 model - MV Museum, Gallarate

500

4 cilindri catena - 1952-1966

1965 model - MV Museum, Gallarate

600 4 cilindri - 1966-1970

1968 model - MV Museum, Gallarate

500 3 cilindri - 1966-1973

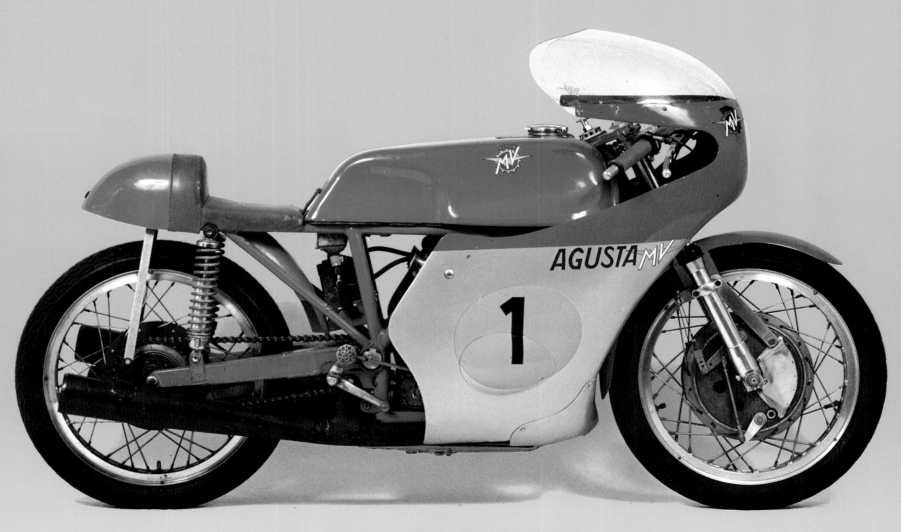

1970 model - MV Museum, Gallarate

bigger sump, lengthened at the front) and, as we have seen, it took second place behind Redman's Honda. After a disastrous fall in the East German Grand Prix MV had to cobble together a bike for the second round of the World Championship in Czechoslovakia. The mechanics mounted the three-cylinder engine in the bigger and heavier "Quattro" frame, and this unlikely hybrid was good enough to earn Agostini a second place. Then, at Monza, with an engine that had been beefed up to 474 cm³, Agostini finally managed to get the better of Hailwood on the Honda to take the title after a dramatic battle with the English ace, who had to retire when his overstressed engine gave up the ghost. By way of consolation Hailwood won the 350 championship, even though Agostini had won the TT and the Italian Grand Prix.

The '67 season looked set to develop into a duel between two men only: Hailwood on the Honda and Agostini on the MV. Both men went racing practically alone and only rarely enjoyed the luxury of a second rider paid to watch their backs. Agostini was scheduled to ride the 350 and 500 cm³ Tre Cilindri, both of which had been carefully overhauled and updated (the 500 had finally reached the ceiling for its capacity class); Hailwood would have a 500 four with more power on tap, as well as a splendid, spanking new six-cylinder 350.

At MV it was clearly understood that the new season

Left, Agostini in action on the 500 three and, below, with the 350. Although he rode with splayed knees, as decreed by the latest fashion, Agostini never played to the gallery but preferred to maintain that elegant style of his. "Ago" can fairly be described as the last great stylist on two wheels.

An interesting comparison between the crankshaft from a Quattro Cilindri of the Fifties (above) and the same component in its final form (centre), much more compact with power takeoff on the outside rather than between the cranks. Note the spartan design of the pistons. Below, the 16-valve head of the '71 version of the Quattro Cilindri.

was going to be no cakewalk and a suitable strategy was worked out. The Italian Championship was to be virtually ignored – Agostini won on his only outing at Zingonia – but the MVs were entered for all the traditional spring meetings held in the Romagna (Milano Marittima, Cesenatico, Rimini and Riccione) because these were races that attracted an international field and there was therefore a chance of finding out a little of what was going on in the enemy camp.

As things turned out the real surprise was provided by an unexpectedly sprightly Benelli 350 four with which Pasolini outpaced the MV at Cesenatico and Hailwood's Honda at Rimini. Then the 500 version of the same Benelli scored an unexpected victory at Modena, but this had been made easier by the retirement of Agostini's MV with mechanical troubles.

This event caused the Italian fans to divide into two camps, the fans of "Ago" and those of "Paso". This was a typical story of the handsome one; easy-going, lucky, and surrounded by girls, versus the shy, introverted, modest one seemingly condemned forever to play the underdog struggling away endlessly against adverse circumstances. It was the golden age of Italian motorcycling and no mistake!

The World Championship turned out to be a tumultuous affair, but it soon became clear that MV was going to have a rougher ride in the 350 class. The West German Grand Prix at Hockenheim was the first big test. In the 350 event the Honda six won by a clear minute, but Agostini won the 500 race after Hailwood had to withdraw in the closing stages. Agostini was beaten again in the Isle of Man and in Holland, but he got his revenge in Belgium and East Germany; it was Hailwood again in Czechoslovakia, then Agostini in Finland and Hailwood in Ulster. By the time Monza rolled round "Mike the Bike" had already wrapped up the 350 championship, but the 500 contest was still wide open. Hailwood unleashed all the considerable power of his four-cylinder engine to pull steadily away from Agostini, who was having some problems with the clutch. But a mere three laps from the finish the big Honda, which had been relentlessly thrashed throughout, began to misfire thus letting Agostini through to overtake his rival and win by a healthy margin. The last round of the championship, the Canadian Grand Prix, was of academic importance only: the title was already in Agostini's hands.

The following year, 1968, Honda quit racing although they did continue to supply Hailwood with bikes on what amounted to a private basis. Despite determined assaults by Benelli and the redoubtable Pasolini, it was a pretty easy year for MV, which carried off the world 350 and 500 titles with practised ease even though Agostini was practically their only representative in the field. The business of perfecting the bikes did not

cease, however, a fact borne out by the continuous stream of broken lap records on circuits everywhere. Unfortunately it has not been possible to find out much about the precise nature of the work carried out because at that time the strictest possible security measures were in force at MV; even in high summer the mechanics worked under heavy tarpaulins so that the bikes might be shielded from prying eyes, while MV staff skirmished with the paparazzi in time-honoured "Dolce Vita" style.

Nowadays, after so many years have gone by, even the mechanics can no longer remember much and the only things we can be sure about regard one or two modifications made to the fairings, which were obviously impossible to hide.

Sixty-nine, Seventy, Seventy-one. These are the legendary years in which the Agostini-MV combination won just about everything

there was to win with impressive, almost monotonous regularity on circuits all over the world. In all honesty we must add that, apart from some rare exceptions, the opposition was not particularly strong: we have already mentioned Pasolini and his Benelli, the works Yamahas, Suzukis and Kawasakis, and the various Italian and English specials. On the other hand, however, we should not forget that year after year and race after race the records were regularly broken, a fact that testifies to the degree of

Phil Read won at Imola in 1974 with the 500 four, but only after a tough fight to the finish with Agostini, who had left MV for Yamaha that season.

sporting and technical commitment which both rider and constructor were prepared to make. The same fact also suggests that a hypothetical opponent of a similar calibre would not have had an easy time of it and would probably have been beaten.

In any case, although MV racing was going through a tranquil moment, there was no question of resting on the large pile of laurels that the marque had collected and the firm never lost sight of the fact that a new opponent could appear from one moment to the next. With just such a possibility in mind work began in 1969 on a new 350 cm³ six-cylinder engine which was tested in comparative secrecy before being shelved two years later. The reason for this was not just that the engine had proved awkward to tune; but above all because the new rule book (due to come into force a short time after) called for a gradual reduction in the number of cylinders (and gears) for Grand Prix motorcycles: 50 cm³ bikes were limited to one pot, 125s and 250s could have two, while all the bigger capacity classes could have a maximum of four. It was therefore pointless to carry on with the preparation of a machine that, in all probability, would have been raced for a season at the most.

But work on a new four-cylinder unit was brought to a conclusion. The 350 version of this engine made its debut at the '71 Grand Prix of Nations, where it was ridden by Alberto Pagani, Nello's son,

who was put out of contention by a broken bearing (by way of consolation he won the 500 event aboard the Tre Cilindri). This was a memorable day in another sense because, apart from Pagani's failure to finish in the 350 event, bearing failures also obliged Agostini to retire in both the 350 and 500 races, something that had never happened before.

This was one of the first concrete signs that the old three was nearing the limits of its possibilities. Something new was urgently required.

At the end of '72 Agostini reached the hitherto unheard of total of twelve World Championship wins, but it had all been harder than expected. Suddenly the old three was feeling the pace and was struggling to keep up with the opposition, espe-

cially the rising Finnish star Saarinen and his spanking new water-cooled Yamaha 'stroker, while the new four had to go through the final phases of preparation right there in the field, with all the unknown quantities and risks involved in such an undertaking.

For the first races of the '72 season Agostini used – we are referring to the 350 class here – the faithful Tre Cilindri, but from the Austrian Grand Prix onwards – after Saarinen and the Yamaha had given the Italian combination a sound beating in Germany and France – the Italian champion switched over to the new "Quattro", which was not that much faster than the three but which could be banked over "until you can see the sky", as Agostini put it. A similar bike was then

given to Phil Read, because the threat posed by Yamaha was a very strong one and it had become necessary to field another rider to stop the Japanese squad from picking up too many useful points with high leaderboard placings.

The 350 three was not pensioned off immediately, however, and was kept in harness as a reserve; in the 500 class, on the other hand, its larger stablemate proved that it was still more than good enough for the duration of the season and so the problem of its replacement was put off until the next year – 1973. That, of course, was the year in which the strokers really made the grade, even in the large capacity classes.

In the years immediately preceding '73 the two-stroke engine – fortified with disc and

reed valves, transfer ports, expansion chambers and what not – had already shrugged off the air of inferiority that had traditionally distinguished it from four-stroke machinery to dominate small capacity class competition, while the four-stroke had continued to hold sway over the larger capacity classes. But in 1972, as we have already seen, the Yamaha strokers began to make themselves felt in 350 class competition too; this invasion was extended to the half-litre class the year after that, with Suzuki also making an entrance. At this point the most obvious thing to do as far as MV was concerned was to turn out a two-stroke power unit as fast as possible and thus hope to meet the enemy on an equal footing, but this was not an easy decision to make.

First of all MV had virtually no experience in the production of modern, large-capacity two-stroke engines, and so the time required for development would have been excessive; and then again the image of the marque was so tied up with four-stroke engines that a move away from their production might have been interpreted as a betrayal of the firm's tradition. A more recent example of this would be Honda's highly sophisticated but disappointing four with the "oval" pistons: an impossible attempt to go against the flow that sprang merely from loyalty to a principle. Be that as it may, in 1973 MV hastily prepared a 433 cm^3 four-cylinder engine (56 × 44 × 4), which developed about 80 hp at 14,000 rpm, and sent Phil Read along to the Paul Ricard circuit to see what it could do. For some time afterwards, however, Agostini preferred the Tre Cilindri, with which he felt far more at home. Agostini's three had been updated with the addition of a hydraulically operated front disc brake (by Lock-

On the previous page, the "monocross" frame prepared for the four in 1975, designed by Ing. Bocchi; above, the Quattro Cilindri with the 1975 frame and variable rake rear shock absorbers. Note the front forks with the external shock absorbers.

*Imola in the spring
of 1974.
Gianfranco Bonera,
called in to support
Phil Read, aboard
that glorious old
warhorse the 500
three.*

heed and Scarab) that was fitted to a classic wire spoked wheel at first and later to a wheel made of cast light alloy, which offers greater torsional rigidity.

In practice, the racing machinery was constantly varied throughout the season: the new "Quattro" was a fixture in the 350 class, but a new bike was prepared for the 500 class with an engine of nearly 500 cm^3 (as against the old 433 cm^3 unit), which promptly won its debut race at Hockenheim before being ousted by the Tre Cilindri. At the end of this season – a very dramatic affair full of tragic accidents, including the ghastly pile-up at Monza that cost the lives of Pasolini and Saarinen – Agostini and Read nevertheless managed to carry off the world titles in the 350 and 500 classes respectively, but by that time the writing was on the wall as far as MV were concerned and the end of an era was at hand.

In what seemed like confirmation of this fact, Agostini suddenly split with MV and signed for Yamaha in a move

that caused a sensation at the time. MV embarked upon the '74 season with Phil Read and new signing Bonera set to ride in the 500 class, the 350 championship having been abandoned.

By this time the marque's star machine was the Quattro Cilindri, and so we ought to take a closer look at it. The cylinders were tilted at 10 degrees, with square finning, while the engine dimensions were undersquare; gear-driven double overhead camshafts operated the valves (four per cylinder), which were inclined at 25 degrees. The engine was fed by four Dell'Ortos; normally the 350 was fitted with a 28 mm unit while the 500 breathed through a 32 mm carb, with the exception of certain circuits where slightly different instruments were used. The vital spark was supplied by a magneto mounted on the front of the crankcase and driven by a shaft and bevels; electronic ignition was later fitted to the 350. The wet sump lubrication system included a radiator mounted at the front behind the number holder on

The four-cylinder longitudinal boxer engine from 1976 that never competed owing to MV's definitive withdrawal from works racing.

the nose of the fairing, which was perforated to allow the passage of a cooling airstream.

Primary drive was by gears, while the clutch ran dry. The gearbox, originally intended to be an eight-speed unit, had only six speeds in deference to the new international regulations. The spaceframe chassis included a tubular duplex cradle and a square-section swinging arm; the forks and suspension struts were adjustable Ceriani components. The first versions of this bike had drum brakes laced into wire-spoked wheels; but, as we have already mentioned, these were replaced in 1973 by a disc brake carried on a wire- spoked wheel, before first the front and then the rear wheel was replaced by more modern cast alloy components. The front wheel was shod with a 3.00-18" tyre; 3.25-18", 3.50-18", and 3.75-18" tyres were used behind. Slicks also made their appearance in the course of 1974 while a fairing with little spoilers was tried out at Francorchamps.

In the case of the 350, the original output of 70 hp at 16,000 rpm was increased to 75 hp at 16,400 rpm (running on a compression ratio of 12.2:1) for the last version. The 500's power output was increased from 90 hp at 13,500 rpm (for the first 430 cm^3 model) to 102 hp at 14,600 rpm for the last model, which ran on a compression ratio of 11.5:1. A special bored-out 580 cm^3 version was also prepared for racing at Brand's Hatch.

The '74 season came to a close with a hard-won victory in the 500 class World Championship for the Phil Read-MV combination, which had had to fight all the way to get the better of the Yamaha team led by Read's ex teammate Agostini. The powers that be at MV then decided to concentrate all their efforts on improving the stability and handling of the Quattro Cilindri, and a lot of work was put in on the frame and the suspension. The propulsion unit had practically arrived at its peak of development and besides safety considerations had led modern circuits to encourage aspects of performance like acceleration and braking in preference to mere speed.

In the close season therefore a new frame was laid out featuring rear suspension units with an adjustable angle of inclination; then another frame was prepared for the German Grand Prix with "monocross"-type rear suspension and two small hydraulic shock absorbers flanking the wheels Despite the fact that the monocross frame got off to a promising start (Read had to give way to Agostini only in the closing stages of a race he had led virtually right from the start), its overall performance still left something to be desired and so it was decided to link the monocross suspension to a more traditional tubular duplex cradle. The lateral shock absorbers were retained, set at a steeper angle; while cast alloy wheels, disc brakes and slick tyres had become stan-

dard features by that time. But 1975 was not a happy year, and for the first time in many years MV racing did not manage to win any titles: Read and Toracca (called in on a temporary basis to replace Bonera, who had been injured at Modena) had to bow before the might of Agostini and his Yamaha. The only consolation for Cascina Costa took the form of Read's wins in Belgium and Czechoslovakia. It was the end of an era, and what had once been the world's most powerful racing team was now free only to mount a desperate defensive action in an attempt to leave the field with colours still flying.

And so we come to the last chapter, 1976, which opened with a sensation: Agostini – whose two-year contract with Yamaha had expired – decided to return to the fold. Apart from purely sentimental considerations, the return of the prodigal son was important for other, more practical, reasons: Agostini brought an important sponsor with him, Team Marlboro, and it was the tobacco giant's financial contribution that allowed MV to postpone its plans to abandon racing outright.

Officially the Quattro Cilindri earmarked for Agostini was to race for the Marlboro colours, while Cascina Costa was to provide technical assistance, mechanics and so on. Consequently the bike appeared clad in a red and white fairing – a very elegant one, if truth be told – upon which the glorious MV logo

was somewhat overshadowed by the cigarette company's trade mark, which occupied a prominent place on the flanks of the fairing.

The cycle parts had been altered yet again, with the addition of a new fork and new rear suspension, once more accompanied by teledraulic elements at each side of the wheel.

MV approached the new season in a mood of considerable optimism, so much so that they dusted off the old 350 – inactive for the previous two seasons – and things got off to a pretty good start. The first meeting on the calendar was at Modena and, although the 350 had to give up after a couple of laps, the 500 took the chequered flag to electrify the fans, who rediscover their enthusiasms as fast as they discard them.

Unfortunately, however, the display at Modena turned out to be little more than a flash in the pan: the 350 was dogged by a series of breakdowns, the only bright spots being a win at Assen and at the Mugello on the 26th of September, which was also the last race won by MV. In the senior category the 500 could do no better than a handful of very low placings, with the result that Agostini switched over to a Suzuki half way through the season in an attempt to recuperate a few points in the Individual Championship.

He had second thoughts when the time came for the German Grand Prix at the Nurburgring; and, in fact, it was here that he picked up a

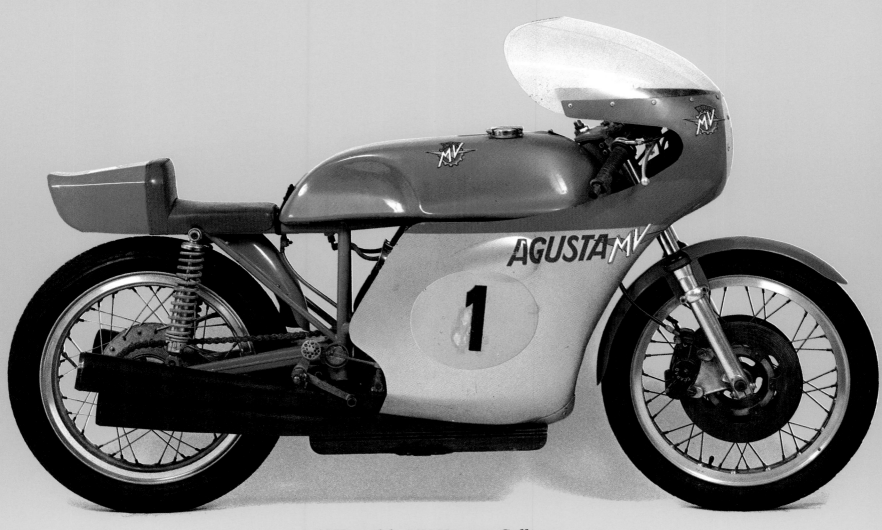

1973 model - MV Museum, Gallarate

500 4 cilindri - 1973-1976

1974 model - MV Museum, Gallarate

350 Sport "Ipotesi" - 1975-1980

1976 model - MV Museum, Gallarate

750 Sport America - 1975-1980

1976 model - MV Museum, Gallarate

win that was as unexpected as it was brilliant. That 29th of August is another date worth recording, because it was the last time that MV won a World Championship race.

By way of a postscript to the brief but intensely colourful history of MV we come to the last piece created by the technical staff, the boxer engine that should have replaced the "Quattro" in 1977. The brainchild of Ing. Bocchi – called in towards the end to run the experimental division and the man behind the frame with the monocross suspension, among other things – this engine had four horizontal cylinders with two facing forwards and two facing backwards. The design, known since the first decade of this century, offered a very low centre of gravity and minimal transverse dimensions. It was a water-cooled unit with two overhead camshafts per bank of cylinders and four-valve heads. Fuel supply was handled by four vertical carburettors specially designed by Dell'Orto, while the ignition was electronic. The six-speed gearbox was located beneath the cylinder block and driven by a gear pair. Final transmission was by a chain mounted on the right.

Research and development work was carried to a very advanced stage: a tubular spaceframe was all ready and the engine had already put in a good number of hours on the test bench, where output had arrived at something in the region of 100 hp.

Probably, and we say this in all objectivity, this engine would not have got the better of the best two-stroke machinery around at the time, for the reasons we have already made clear elsewhere; above all, four-stroke engines are decidedly penalized by current sporting regulations because only by spreading the cubic capacity over a large number of cylinders can such units reach the engine speeds that are indispensable to beat the best strokers.

Nevertheless it is a pity that we never got to see what this typically unconventional MV power unit would have been capable of in competition. A far greater pity still was the hauling down of a flag that had fluttered over the largest collection of laurels, victories and titles that the world had ever seen.

But the worst was yet to come, believe it or not. Ten years after MV's retirement from motorsport, we come to the very last page – as unexpected as it was unthinkable – in our story: the sale by auction of all the material left in the race shop: race-winning bikes, spares, machinery, everything. This material had in precedence been the subject of the most fantastic rumours, some even said that it had been buried so that no one else might ever have the use of it; but it still existed, some of it in the old premises near Gallarate and the rest in a warehouse in Borgomanero, near Novara.

The decision to sell off these items led to the dispersion of a heritage that belonged not just to the factory but to the entire nation. Furthermore, such a decision – whatever the reasons given by the state-run organization that took over the Agusta complex – represented a painful and insulting blow for all those people who had given freely of their ingenuity and labour over the years; not to mention those who laid down their lives for the marque and the country. Anyhow, the burocracy has always been synonymous with indifference, soullessness and short-sightedness; it is useless therefore to expect such people to possess so much as a crumb of sentiment, intelligence or love of country. Goodbye for ever, glorious MV!

6 NEVER SAY NEVER: THE RESURRECTION

...Just a moment, perhaps we, along with MV Agusta's liquidators, were a little hasty and categorical in writing off the great marque following the publication of the "clearance sale" notice (reproduced here) in the specialist press in the July of 1986.

Hurt and indignant, we railed against the money-men on the temple steps rather than demonstrating our faith in an, admittedly improbable, resurrection. As things have turned out, the facts have demonstrated that the ways of the Lord truly are infinite or, more prosaically, that we should never say never.

What has happened, in fact, is little short of a miracle and the Sleeping Beauty that is MV has, thanks to the idealism, rather than the fairy tale kiss, of Claudio and Gianfranco Castiglioni, entrepreneurs to be sure but first and foremost two great enthusiasts with a vocation for shoring up companies in difficulties. This they did firstly with Aermacchi Harley-Davidson at Varese, out of which Cagiva was born, and then with Ducati, taking the company to previously unimaginable heights in the fields of production and especially racing with the series of world Superbikes titles. The pair continued in the same vein by restructuring the Swedish Husqvarna firm and buying out the Moto Morini marque in view of a future relaunch.

These operations, however, all concerned "living" companies. In the case of MV Agusta, on the other hand, the resurrection was all the more remarkable because it involved a marque that has been dormant for no less than twenty years. There was more to restoring the glories of a name and producing a highly futuristic motorcycle than the realisation of a dream; a miracle had to be deliberately planned and put into effect.

Industrialists may work to commercial, profit-oriented ends, nurture ambitions of success and expansion and even perhaps enjoy a degree of personal popularity. The MV Agusta operation, however, given the consistency demonstrated, the magnitude of the investment, and above all the extreme and lucid desire to create a masterpiece embodying the entire MV Agusta story, reveals true passion. Passion recognised by the perceptive motorcycling public and reciprocated with faith and admiration. While many members of this public may lack the financial wherewithal to have any realistic hope of satisfying their ambition to own such a machine,

the warmth of their enthusiasm provides a priceless indicator of the universal approval for a product that stands out from the crowd.

However, we will discuss the latest MV creation later. For now we will linger a while longer in the limbo that preceded its appearance, retracing the course of events and filling in the gap that stretches from the liquidation of MV Agusta Corse in 1986 to the 15th of September, 1997, the historic date of the official presentation of the F4 (as the renaissance machine has been concisely baptised). The new motorcycle was then exhibited to the public at the Milan Motorcycle Show from the 16th to the 21st of September, where it received the full and enthusiastic reception mentioned above.

We will return now to the point at which we left the MV story, that is to say, with the closing remarks to the previous edition of this book following the disposal of the last of the racing stock in 1986, after the worthy Gruppo dei Lavoratori Anziani (the Senior Workers' Group) at MV Agusta had constituted the Museum of Technology and Labour in 1977, bringing together numerous relics from the racing department.

L'AGUSTA S.p.A. con sede a Milano - via Caldera 21,

vende le seguenti motociclette M.V. originali da competizione costruite dalla propria controllata M.V. Meccanica Verghera ed utilizzate nell'ambito del reparto corse della medesima Società

Nº 1	125 cc	1 CILINDRO	Campione del Mondo "Marche" anni 1952/1953/1955/1956/1958/1959/1960 e piloti con C. SANFORD e C. UBBIALI.
Nº 2	350 cc	4 CILINDRI	Campione del Mondo "Marche" anno 1952 e piloti con G. AGOSTINI.
Nº 1	500 cc	4 CILINDRI	Campione del Mondo "Marche" anni 1956/1958/1959/1960/1961/1962/1963 1964/1965/1967 e piloti con J. SURTEES, G. HOCKING, M. HAILWOOD e G. AGOSTINI.
Nº 3	500 cc	4 CILINDRI	Campione del Mondo Piloti anno 1974 con P. READ.
Nº 2	500 cc	3 CILINDRI	Campione del Mondo "Marche" anni 1967/1968/1969/1970/1971/1972/1973 e piloti con G. AGOSTINI e P. READ.
Nº 1	350 cc	3 CILINDRI	Campione del Mondo "Marche" anni 1968/1969/1970/1971 e piloti con G. AGOSTINI.
Nº 1	500 cc	4 CILINDRI	Prototipo
Nº 1	750 cc	4 CILINDRI	Tipo Daytona
Nº 1	500 cc		Prototipo boxer da montare.
Nº 6			Motori da montare (n. 1 mod. 250, n. 2 mod. 350, n. 3 mod. 500)
Nº 2		Telai	(n. 1 mod. 350, n. 1 mod. 500 boxer)

Per l'acquisto di singole motociclette oppure di tutto lo stock, le offerte devono essere inviate per lettera raccomandata a: AGUSTA S.p.A. (DGA), Via Caldera 21, 20153 Milano

GRUPPO AGUSTA

Recently deprived of its original home, the museum should reopen in a suitable location. It is our hope that in the meantime the odd... nut and bold does not go astray as, unfortunately, can all too easily happen in any move, and especially when precious objects are involved.

The announcement of the sale of the MV racing, motorcycles and the spare engines aroused enormous attention. Many newspapers criticised a decision that failed to respect the Italian technological and historical heritage and called on the government to intervene on behalf of the nation. Appeals were made to the Minister of Industry and the Minister of State Investments of the era but they did not appear to be particularly interested in the situation. Among the publications that took the matter to heart was the monthly magazine *Motociclismo* and in the November, 1986, edition it published an authoritative discourse on the MV case. In the middle of the article, however, an insert highlighted in yellow killed off all hopes. It read "As we go to press it is being rumoured that the MVs have been sold to Iannucci's Team Obsolete which will have the technical assistance of Roberto Gallina". That, in

fact, was exactly what happened. It was the Italo-American Roberto Iannucci, together with a partner, who scooped most of the material that was auctioned off for a sum said to be in the region of one and a half billion lire. As in any adventure worth its salt, the two ended up arguing as soon as they came to divide the booty and the collection was as a consequence conserved in store at La Spezia in the care of Roberto Gallina following a custodial order pronounced by the appropriate Italian authorities. The case was not resolved and the material released until 1993, and at that point it was swiftly sold off again, at least the greater part of it, on the occasion of the international exhibition "Moto Storiche in Grand Prix", an opportunity for collectors to gather organized by the 'Velocifero' at the Misano racing circuit in the July of that year. MV racing bikes had for some years, however, been seen at the various historic events held in Italy and abroad. These were machines from the motorcycle collec-

tion owned by Ubaldo Elli, an industrialist in the women's stocking sector from Busto Arsizio. He had been able, with much less clamour, to buy a great deal of spare parts from the racing department and over time, and thanks to the engagement of a number of very talented former members of the team, to patiently reconstruct example after example and to put together a mouth-watering collection of complete bikes in perfect working order. We are fortunate in that Ubaldo Elli, and subsequently his sons, having done everything legitimately and in the light of day, not only have had no hesitation in exhibiting their bikes wherever the tenor of the event merited the journey, but have also been truly prodigious in lending them to former racers, trusted friends and celebrities of the motorcycling world. In this way they have generated publicity for the marque of a form and immediacy which the company itself could only have dreamed of. Today, if Agostini is required at some impor-

tant international meeting he makes recourse to the Elli collection in order to put on a fitting demonstration. As he did, for example, when returning to the Isle of Man for a warmly applauded lap during the Historic Parade.

Apart from Elli's machines, further racing MV Agustas, some authentic other less so, have been making increasingly frequent appearances. How many they must have made in the various cylinder capacities and innumerable different versions in twenty years of production!

However, whilst the world of historic racing was being enlivened by the MV presence, a rather more significant and unexpected development took place. In the spring of 1992 Cagiva acquired the MV Agusta marque, rekindling the interest of all enthusiasts. The news was announced in a press release of which an extract is reproduced here.

The celebrated MV Agusta motorcycle marque is now part of the Cagiva stable: the Castiglioni brothers have acquired it from the former proprietors, the Agusta family, who decided to sell given the commercial value and the still intact appeal of the marque, above all among motorcycle racing enthusiasts. There were nu-

C. CASTIGLIONI

merous interested parties, some of whom had no connections with the two-wheeled world.

The brothers Gianfranco and Claudio Castiglioni won the race and the glorious MV badge will join those of the other marques they own: Cagiva, Ducati, Morini and Husqvarna.

"We have revived a tradition", explains Claudio Castiglioni, "and we will try to ensure that it is taken forwards. Those who love racing have never forgotten the victories of the company from Verghera, the fame of this marque is incommensurable, both in Italy and abroad".

text of his introductory speech given on the evening of the 15th of September, 1997, on the occasion of the presentation of the MV F4.

«One evening while discussing with my colleague and friend Massimo Tamburini on the topic that characterises nearly all of our encounters (motorcycles, naturally), the idea came about that was to give life to the F4 project.

Together we imagined an engine for a large-displacement motorcycle, a 4-cylinder engine that would give top performance.

The project was a complicated and difficult one, and, pressed by our respective commitments, we put the project aside for the time being, though promising to take up the subject again soon.

The idea of the engine kept coming back, until the confidence in the technical quality achieved by our projects and the experience gained in the area of development permitted us to consider this idea an actual possibility.

Among the individuals who were at my side during this arduous undertaking, I must mention Piero Ferrari, whose help was invaluable and of such fundamental importance to the realisation of the F4.

Naturally, the first step to-

Five years on from that courageous operation, it has to be said that Claudio Castiglioni's declaration has been respected in full. Arriving at the product presented in September, 1997 has by no means been easy and has required a complex process in terms of decisions, revisions, experimentation and testing to which Ferrari Engineering has made a valuable contribution. The design of the new bike is the work of the artist Massimo Tamburini.

Who better than Claudio Castiglioni to succinctly recount the story?

There follows, therefore, the

1997 first specimen - property of Count Riccardo Agusta

wards seeing the F4 project materialise coincided with Cagiva's acquisition of the glorious MV Agusta trademark, which possess the most fascinating history in world motorcycling.

Its victories on the racetracks of the world generated an indefinite number of enthusiasts throughout the globe, which no one has ever succeeded in equalling.

75 Rider and Make world championships, 270 Grand Prix victories and a total of 3027 victories in the various different biking disciplines have made the MV Agusta make a particular legendary myth.

We were then to make what was unquestionably the most difficult decision for the achievement of the project: to abandon world racing competitions in the 500 class - the most difficult in terms of technological effort and the most important in terms of stature, as well as an area that saw Cagiva as a major player and one of the leading performers.

This was a strategic decision, stemming from a precise intention to devote our specific knowledge and best men to a project that would stimulate the enthusiasm of everyone involved, and where excited just hearing the famed MV Agusta mentioned and eager

Thunders of applause welcome the new F4. Giacomo Agostini, between Claudio Castiglioni and Count Riccado Agusta, is visibly admired.

Witnessing of a champion

MV Agusta is part of my life, it represents for me a real symbol of many joys, hopes and great triumphs.

I have to share my greatest victories with this mythical make: as a matter of fact, 13 of my 15 world champion titles were won with an MV Agusta motorcycle.

During the years, MV Agusta has become popular all over the world among the sportsmen and sporting enthusiasts and has been able to incite admiration and great passion in conjunction with it's name. A real enthusiasm and an immeasurable competitive passion sustained the activity of the Agusta family, through a personal involvement.

The same interest and the same passion explains Cagiva's choice of giving new life to the mythical MV, the trade mark which has influenced most of the world motorcycling history.

The MV Agusta F4, besides a name famous and known world wide can boast an advanced technological research and high quality mechanical innovations.

I will be really moved and proud seeing again on the racetracks and roads the Italian motorcycle with its characteristic logo: the one of the inimitable MV Agusta.

Giacomo Agostini

Now it is official: great success at the presentation on September 16, 1997, at the Milan Motorcycle Show where the F4 has been unanimously crowned "queen".

to return it to its former fame. The Experimental Department in Varese was assigned the design and development of the engine, while the Cagiva Research Centre, directed by Massimo Tamburini, was given responsibility to create all the other components of the bike, in addition to its styling. The result of this joint effort is a product which will surely provoke comment for its exclusive features and sophisticated mechanics.

The "radial" valve timing system, a choice inspired directly from the F1, and the special removable gearbox, are clear examples of the commitment to create a racing inspired engine that is completely innovative.

The technical qualities, sportsmanship and competitiveness fused into an innovative design were the sole principles to guide us in our goal to give all enthusiasts and admirers of the MV Agusta trademark a product worthy of their expectations.

Through difficult, yet passionate work, we achieved the highest goal we had ever set for ourselves. The trademark cherished in the memories of all motorcycle enthusiasts has been revived, and with the F4, Cagiva has breathed new life into the legendary MV Agusta.»

In the light of what has come to bear, and trusting in the future, we are delighted to be able to conclude the latest edition of this book on a far happier note than in 1986. The MV Agusta story is far from over.

The making

The Cagiva Research Centre has had the privilege of working on a project of great importance and whose worth transcends the mere significance of a sport vehicle to which an engineer would normally make reference. The F4 has been a project involving a much deeper content, and I feel it my duty here to thank the President Claudio Castiglioni, who gave me the opportunity to dedicate all the resources of the Centre under my direction for the production of a vehicle destined to mark the rebirth of a make, which I have been a passionate fan of. The F4 for the rebirth of the MV Agusta: this idea immediately had a special significance for me, because the first bike to put me to the test as an engineer was an MV at the time of epic race-track duels of the silver and red bikes of Cascina Costa. Today, to have contributed to the creation of a complete motorcycle— incorporating an idea shared with the President to initiate a project for a new engine — is wholly satisfying not only in strictly professional terms, but also because of a passion for the world in which the MV Agusta is a cornerstone.

The concepts that my colleagues at the CRC and I have put into the F4 project are the result of years of activity in this field, but they are, above all, the work of persons that have been skillful in carrying out their work with total commitment and admirable dedication. The team spirit that can be felt in CRC and the irrepressible will to perform one's work to his fullest potential that permeates each and every department cannot help but have a result such as the F4 project.

I like to think that the special location of the Centre has in some way contributed to the success of this project. The opportunity — certainly not a common one — of working in an environment that has been specially set aside and organised has undoubtedly aided in the success of our research.

I am certain that the F4, for all its technical content, for the technological choices adopted, for the general quality achieved and for its "personal" design can be considered a vehicle par excellence.

I also think that the statement "beauty is objective", if applied to the F4, can provide a fertile ground for discussion.

Certainly, this motorcycle fully responds to the principles of "form follows function" that we had set for ourselves at the start of the study. I wish to thank all my colleagues at the CRC who worked at my side during this undertaking and Claudio Castiglioni who gave us the opportunity to make it a reality.

I also imagine with great satisfaction of the lucky enthusiasts who will be able to personally discover all the special features this high-performance motorcycle of such esteemed value has to offer.

Massimo Tamburini
Cagiva Research Centre

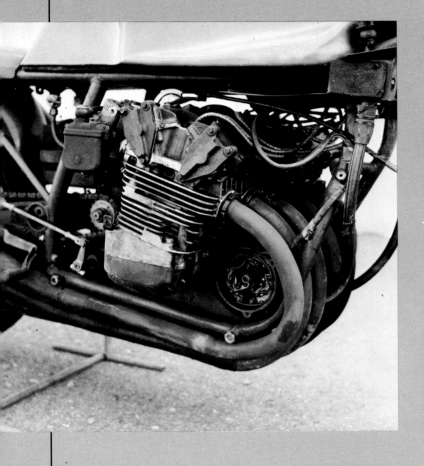

PART TWO

PRODUCTION CATALOGUE

The Production Bikes
The Prototypes
The Racing Bikes

NOTE: In the catalogue section of this book, the total duration of the production run of each model is indicated by a pair of dates in the title of each chapter. The dates given in the technical specifications files, on the other hand, refer to the production of the specific versions described in the said files. Given the frequent variation of the technical characteristics that occurred as models were developed, we have preferred to give detailed specifications of either the original model or the most significant version of it, while the reader is referred to the main text and captions for information regarding successive series or special versions. Certain titles may arbitrarily group different models together when these share a common architecture and major components.

TOURING BIKES

98 **1946-1949**

The first MV motorcycle, laboriously conceived during the difficult years of the Second World War, and born in the feverish period of post-war reconstruction, was an unpretentious utility machine, designed to cost little, consume less, and to be long lasting even in the hands of the most inexpert riders. In other words it was not aimed at the typical, exuberant and devil-may-care sporting rider of the pioneering pre-war days, but at all those doughty souls intending to use the machine as daily transport. The fundamental idea was to free these people from the effort of pedalling and the infuriating inefficiency and vagaries of public transport. The engine was therefore very simple; large enough to produce sufficient power without aspiring to be a speedster, and capable of doing its job without any need for particular riding skills. The MV 98 had all the indispensable prerequisites for serious and prolonged use: reliability, normal section tyres, and efficient suspension on both wheels at a time when rigid frames still had more than a few supporters. The engine following the classical two-stroke layout, with cross-flow scavenging and a deflector-crown piston; it was produced and sold with both two-speed and three-speed gearboxes (the latter soon became the only available option). The Turismo model was almost immediately joined by the Lusso, which was equipped with telescopic front forks that gave it a decidedly more modern and attractive appearance.

Power/rpm
3.5 hp at 3500 rpm
Dry weight
70 kg
Maximum speed
65 km/h

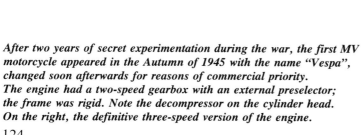

After two years of secret experimentation during the war, the first MV motorcycle appeared in the Autumn of 1945 with the name "Vespa", changed soon afterwards for reasons of commercial priority.
The engine had a two-speed gearbox with an external preselector; the frame was rigid. Note the decompressor on the cylinder head.
On the right, the definitive three-speed version of the engine.

124

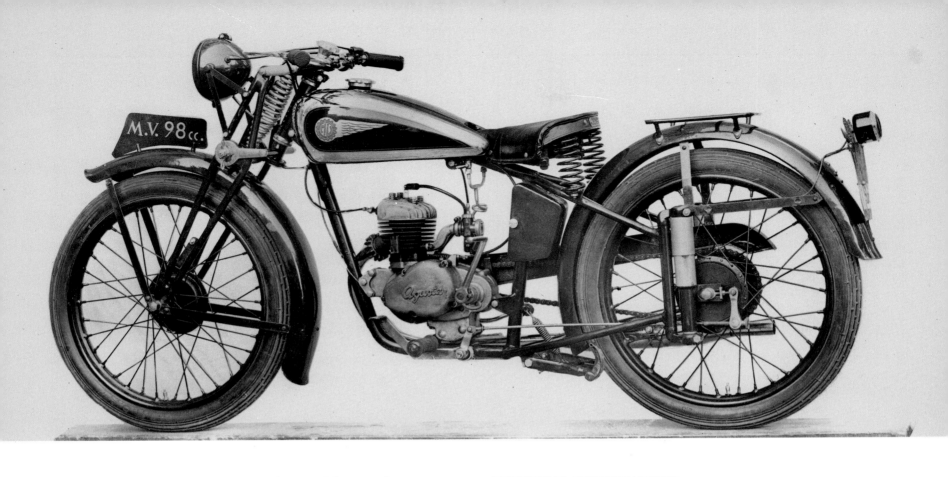

Above, the Turismo version with the sprung frame and three-speed gearbox; in 1947 it cost 135,000 lire. Below, the Lusso model with telescopic front forks was introduced at the end of 1946. These early models were painted dark brown.

TECHNICAL SPECIFICATIONS

Model/year	98 Turismo/Lusso - 98 cm^3 - 1946/1949
Engine	2-stroke single, 49 × 52 mm, 98 cm^3
Compression ratio	6 : 1
Cylinder head/barrel	Light alloy - cast iron
Valve configuration	–
Timing system	–
Ignition	Flywheel magneto
Carburettor	Dell'Orto TA 16 A
Lubrication	10 : 1 petroil
Clutch	Wet multiplate
Gearbox	Unit construction, two/three speeds
Transmission	Geared primary; final drive, chain
Frame/wheelbase	Closed tubular cradle - 1250 mm
Front suspension	Girder forks/telescopic forks
Rear suspension	Plunger-box
Wheels	Steel, wire spoked, 2.25 × 19"
Tyres	2.50 × 19 front and rear
Brakes	Lateral drum, front and rear 130 mm
Consumption	2.5 litres/100 km
Fuel tank capacity	9 litres
Oil tank capacity	–

125 Twin 1947

J ust a couple of years after its birth, MV was already an established marque and could allow itself the luxury of designing vehicles that – thanks to their by no means utilitarian character – could fairly be described as non-conformist in an era that was still economically depressed.
It was a sign of the Verghera firm's basic soundness that they were able to produce exclusive machines or even purely demonstrative prototypes, without the need for the financial cushion provided by mass production to absorb tooling costs. The presentation of the Zefiro model at the 1947 Milan Motorcycle Show was a case in point. It was a light and elegant 125, graced by a good two-stroke, twin-cylinder engine; which was an unusual configuration for an Italian machine even at a time when there was a wide variety of designs on the market. The finishing was painstakingly well done and the adoption of a four-speed gearbox was another notable feature that placed the Zefiro one step above most of the competition.

The whirring noise produced by the small, compact, and fairly lively engine soon resulted in the bike being nicknamed the Ra- netta or little frog. For the record it should be noted that the prototype was fitted with magneto ignition, which was later replaced by a flywheel magneto with a double contact breaker. In spite of the undoubted interest it aroused, the Zefiro never made it into production and was soon dropped from the catalogue.

Power/rpm	
5 hp at 5200 rpm	
Dry weight	
80 kg	
Maximum speed	
85 km/h	

TECHNICAL SPECIFICATIONS

Model/year	Zefiro - 125 cm³ - 1947
Engine	2-stroke twin 42 × 45 × 2 mm - 124.6 cm³
Compression ratio	6 : 1
Cylinder head/barrel	Light alloy - cast iron
Valve configuration	–
Timing system	–
Ignition	Flywheel magneto
Carburettor	Dell'Orto 22
Lubrication	16 : 1 petroil
Clutch	Wet multiplate
Gearbox	Unit construction, four speeds
Transmission	Geared primary; final drive, chain
Frame/wheelbase	Closed tubular duplex cradle - 1270 mm
Front suspension	Telescopic fork
Rear suspension	Plunger-box
Wheels	Steel, wire spoked, 2.50 × 19"
Tyres	2.75-19" front and rear
Brakes	Lateral drums
Consumption	3.5 litres per 100 km
Fuel tank capacity	12 litres
Oil tank capacity	–

The 125 twin had three ports, a deflector piston and transfer port inspection covers set into the cylinder barrel as on the 98. The engine breathed through a horizontal carb; a sporting and fashionable layout at the time.

The small Zefiro (nicknamed the "little frog" for its engine note) had very elegant and up-to-date styling, and was painted in metallic grey. Although the general layout was similar to the 98, the crankcase was slightly different, partly due to the adoption of a four-speed gearbox with an internal selector.

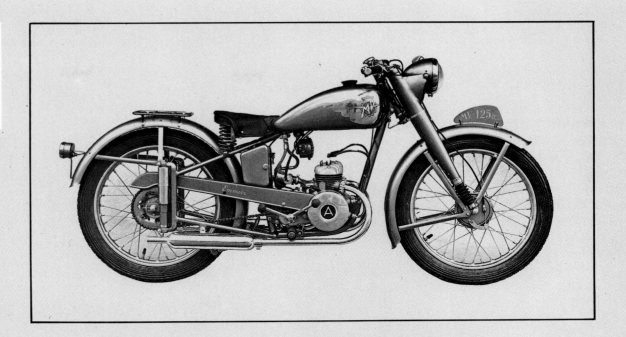

250

1947-1951

The 250, introduced in 1947, was developed at the same time as the Zefiro and, like the small 125 twin dealt with in the previous pages, it too was a brave challenge.

In those days the medium/large capacity bike market was a relatively small one dominated by a fairly considerable array of famous, well established names: apart from the big Moto Guzzi and Gilera models, there were the various Sertums, Bianchis and MMs. Armed with the courage (or was it the recklesness?) of youth, MV boldly launched itself into this difficult sector. In contrast to the radical design philosophy embodied by the Zefiro, the 250 stuck to tried and tested engineering, particularly in the case of the engine.

This was a straightforward vertical, pushrod single, with both head and barrel in cast iron.

The vital spark was provided by a magneto and the unit had a wet sump lubrication system.

More sophisticated touches were provided in the form of timing gears enclosed in an oil bath, and a unit gearbox; features that were still considered radical, if not exactly revolutionary.

With its duplex cradle and integral telescopic suspension the MV was among the avant-garde producers, at least in terms of frame design.

The prototype 250 first appeared in October 1946 when Egidio Conficoni rode it in a trials event at La Spezia, and then went into very limited production. It was painted metallic silver and cost 350,000 lire.

Power/rpm
10 hp at 5100 rpm
Dry weight
135 kg
Maximum speed
110 km/h

The classic 250 of 1947, inspired by the most famous of the English machines but with updated styling. In 1950 it retailed at 350,000 lire.

Note the differences between this model and the one on the facing page. The friction dampers have disappeared, the front brake is now on the left, and the fuel tank is chromed.

The long stroke engine with the cylinder head enclosed by the fuel tank, the valve gear, and the unit gearbox.

TECHNICAL SPECIFICATIONS

Model/year	250 - 250 cm^3 - 1947/1951
Engine	4-stroke single 63 × 80 mm - 249.2 cm^3
Compression ratio	6 : 1
Cylinder head/barrel	Cast iron
Valve configuration	Inclined overhead
Timing system	Pushrod
Ignition	Magneto
Carburettor	Dell'Orto MB 22 B
Lubrication	Wet sump
Clutch	Wet multiplate
Gearbox	Unit construction, four speeds
Transmission	Geared primary; final drive, chain
Frame/wheelbase	Closed tubular cradle with duplex bottom rails - 1390 mm
Front suspension	Telescopic fork
Rear suspension	Plunger-box with friction dampers
Wheels	Steel wire spoked, 2.50 × 19"
Tyres	3.00 - 19" front and rear
Brakes	Lateral drums, front 180 mm, rear 150 mm
Consumption	3 litres per 100 km
Fuel tank capacity	18 litres
Oil tank capacity	2 kg

125 3-Speed 1948-1949

In the spring of 1948 a new light motorcycle, equipped with a 125 cm³ single-cylinder engine was put into production. Produced in response to public demand, the newcomer was the logical development of the original 98, from which it had inherited both looks and general mechanical layout. Compared with the relatively sophisticated 250 twin introduced the previous year, the new product gave the impression of being a retrograde step in terms of engineering, but in reality

the 125 was simply a realistic response to market forces. A bike was needed that was a little faster and more powerful than the 98, but there was not yet sufficient demand to justify the production of excessively expensive machines. From an engineering point of view, however, the 125 engine introduced an important innovation: the

adoption of cross-flow scavenging with a flat piston, an undoubted improvement over the previous deflector-crown. The characteristic port inspection covers on the outside of the cylinder barrel continued to be fitted, but were triangular rather than rectangular. This model did not enjoy a long production run and was replaced the follo-

wing year by a new version, with a completely revised engine and frame; it is still an important bike, however, if only for the fact that the first true competition MV was developed from it.
The competition version (discussed in a later chapter) was to win the company's first important racing honours.

Power/rpm	
4.5 hp at 4500 rpm	
Dry weight	
75 kg	
Maximum speed	
82 km/h	

TECHNICAL SPECIFICATIONS

Model/year	125 Turismo - 125 cm³ - 1948/1949
Engine	2-stroke single 53 × 56 mm - 123.5 cm³
Compression ratio	6.2 : 1
Cylinder head/barrel	Light alloy, cast iron
Valve configuration	–
Timing system	–
Ignition	Flywheel magneto
Carburettor	Dell'Orto MA 17
Lubrication	20 : 1 petroil
Clutch	Wet multiplate
Gearbox	Unit construction, three speeds
Transmission	Geared primary; final drive, chain
Frame/wheelbase	Closed tubular cradle - 1390 mm
Front suspension	Girder fork
Rear suspension	Plunger-box
Wheels	Steel wire spoked, 2.25 × 19" or 2.50 × 19"
Tyres	2.75 - 19" or 3.00 - 19" front and rear
Brakes	Lateral drums
Consumption	2.5 litres per 100 km
Fuel tank capacity	12 litres
Oil tank capacity	–

The 1948 125 cm³ single was built along the lines of the earlier 98, but the engine employed crossflow scavenging and a flat piston. Note the reappearance of the tried and trusted girder forks.

125 TEL 1949-1954

In 1949 MV made what the Italians call "un salto di qualità" (a leap forward in terms of quality), with the introduction of the 125 TEL. Basically this model was the 125 cm³ lightweight, which practically formed the backbone of MV production, with a new engine: this was still a two-stroke, crossflow unit, but with a four-speed gearbox and a more compact, sleeker engine room, which had lost the dated-looking angular casing that had characterized earlier models. In addition the frame had also been comprehensively revised and now boasted a tubular front end combined with steel pressings at the rear; the rear suspension was also more efficient thanks to the adoption of a swinging arm and telescopic units. MV were to remain faithful to this layout for their production bikes for many years, virtually right up to the last models. The new 125 TEL was offered in two versions, Turismo and Sport, which differed in certain equipment details and, of course, in performance. Available in bright red or black finish, this was the first of the MV models to be identified by a series of letters, a policy that often caused confusion as the significance of the letters was often not immediately obvious and they were sometimes varied without appreciable modifications having being made to the model. The Turismo version cost 228,000 lire and the Sport could be had in exchange for 256,000 lire. The TEL remained in production, virtually unchanged, until 1954.

Power/rpm
5 hp at 4800 rpm
6 hp at 5500 rpm

Dry weight
85 kg

Maximum speed
80 km/h
85 km/h

In 1949 the 125 was completely revised with a new engine and frame. This is the 5 hp Turismo version (with a rear parcel rack), capable of 80 km/h.

The Sport version is identifiable by its 22 mm horizontal carburettor and different trim. It produced 6 hp and reached 85 km/h.

The 1949 engine, here in the Turismo version, with the four speed gearbox. The covers over the transfer ports are still fitted, but here they are triangular and disguised by the finning.

TECHNICAL SPECIFICATIONS

Model/year	125 TEL - 125 cm^3 - 1949/54
Engine	2-stroke single 53 × 56 mm - 123.5 cm^3
Compression ratio	6 : 1/7 : 1
Cylinder head/barrel	Light alloy - cast iron
Valve configuration	–
Timing system	–
Ignition	Flywheel magneto
Carburettor	Dell'Orto MA 17 / Dell'Orto MA 22
Lubrication	16 : 1 petroil
Clutch	Wet multiplate
Gearbox	Unit construction, four speeds
Transmission	Geared primary; final drive, chain
Frame/wheelbase	Open tubular duplex cradle and pressings - 1270 mm
Front suspension	Girder fork
Rear suspension	Rear s/arm with telescopic units and friction dampers
Wheels	Steel, wire spoked, 2.25 × 19"
Tyres	2.50 - 19" front and rear
Brakes	Lateral drums, front 150 mm, rear 130 mm
Consumption	2.7 litres per 100 km
Fuel tank capacity	12 litres
Oil tank capacity	–

125 B/C/CSL Scooter 1949-1951

In 1949 MV also decided to enter the scooter market. The scooter, an attempt to provide a more comfortable light motorcycle, was almost as old as the motorcycle itself, but it did not achieve worldwide popularity until after the Second World War, thanks to the "Italian school" that combined practicality with style. MV made an authoritative contribution to this trend with a series of models that was gradually expanded and updated and, even though these machines were not always particularly original, they were nevertheless able to command a healthy share of the market. The first MV scooter appeared at the Milan Trade Fair in the spring of 1949. It sported a brand new engine with a four-speed gearbox, housed in a monocoque pressed-steel body. The wheels were carried on stub axles and the bike used swinging arm rear suspension. This model was identified with the letter "B"; an "A" version also existed, but only in prototype form, and it never entered production. In 1950 a "C" version was introduced, later called the CSL ("C Super Lusso"); this machine had a tubular frame clad with unstressed body panels. The most obvious modification in terms of appearance was the presence of a tunnel (which channelled the air needed to cool the engine) running down the middle of the foot-rest platform.

Power/rpm
5 hp at 4800 rpm
Dry weight
85 kg
Maximum speed
80 km/h

The engine with forced air cooling.

The first MV scooter, the 125 cm³ model B from 1949, with open monocoque bodywork.

The C version from 1950, and the CSL from 1951 had tubular frames with a central tunnel.

TECHNICAL SPECIFICATIONS

Model/year	125 B/C/CSL - 125 cm³ - 1949/51
Engine	2-stroke single 53 × 56 mm - 123.5 cm³
Compression ratio	6 : 1
Cylinder head/barrel	Light alloy - cast iron
Valve configuration	–
Timing system	–
Ignition	Flywheel magneto
Carburettor	Dell'Orto MA 17
Lubrication	16 : 1 petroil
Clutch	Wet multiplate
Gearbox	Unit construction, four speeds
Transmission	Geared primary; final drive, chain
Frame/wheelbase	Pressed steel/single beam bearing body - 1130 mm
Front suspension	Stub axle trailing link
Rear suspension	Swinging arm with horizontal spring
Wheels	Steel discs, 3.25 × 10"
Tyres	3.50 - 10" front and rear
Brakes	Drums, 100 mm front and rear
Consumption	3 litres per 100 km
Fuel tank capacity	7 litres
Oil tank capacity	–

125 Motore Lungo

The 125 Motore Lungo ("long engine") as it was officially known, or "Carter Lungo" ("long crankcase") as it was more popularly known, was one of the small bikes most coveted by sporting riders, particularly those who were looking for a competitive but fairly inexpensive mount upon which to begin their racing careers. In 1950, when the "Carter Lungo" was introduced, there were already several single- or double-knocker four-strokes available, but their selling price and costly maintenance requirements put them out of most people's reach. A good two-stroke therefore, as long as it was really lively, represented the best alternative for a novice racer out to win his spurs. The name derives from the unusual forward extension of the crankcase required to house the Marelli magneto (a special twin-spark version) which had been adopted in place of the flywheel magneto that, at the time, was unable to rev beyond 7000 rpm.

The lightweight, all tubular frame was a closed duplex cradle with bracing at the rear to increase rigidity.

The brakes were large-diameter central drums. Although it was sold with normal road equipment including lights and a silencer, this bike was almost exclusively used for racing, both by works riders (in less important or long distance races), and by many privateers. Many of the future champions of the Fifties enjoyed their first taste of victory riding the fast and punchy "Carter Lungo".

Power/rpm	
9 hp at 8000 rpm	
Maximum speed	
120 km/h	
Fuel consumption	
4 litres per 100 km	

TECHNICAL SPECIFICATIONS

Model/year	125 Motore Lungo - 125 cm³ - 1950/53
Engine	2-stroke single 53 × 56 mm - 123.5 cm³
Compression ratio	9 : 1
Cylinder head/barrel	Light alloy - cast iron
Valve configuration	–
Timing system	–
Ignition	Magneto
Carburettor	Dell'Orto SS 25 A
Lubrication	16 : 1 petroil
Clutch	Wet multiplate
Gearbox	Unit construction, four speeds
Transmission	Geared primary; final drive, chain
Frame/wheelbase	Tubular full duplex cradle - 1300 mm
Front suspension	Telescopic fork
Rear suspension	S/arm with mechanical telescopic units
Wheels	Steel wire spoked, 2.50 × 19"
Tyres	2.75 - 19" front and rear
Brakes	Central drums, front 190 mm, rear 160 mm
Dry weight	95 kg
Fuel tank capacity	14 litres
Oil tank capacity	–

The characteristic engine of the "Carter Lungo", extended forwards to house the magneto. The example illustrated, now kept in the company museum, has been modified to use flywheel ignition.

1950-1953

The "Carter Lungo" had a lightweight tubular frame with reinforcing struts outboard of the swinging arm.

135

125 CGT Scooter 1950-1952

Power/rpm
5 hp at 4800 rpm
Dry weight
86 kg
Maximum speed
80 km/h

By 1950 MV had firmly committed themselves to scooter production and in 1950 the original "B" model – which had in the meantime become the CSL – was soon joined by a new machine that, while retaining the essential features of the preceding model, had a simplified specification intended to reduce production costs and, therefore, the retail price. This new scooter, introduced at the 1950 Geneva Show and known at first as the Popolare and then as the Normale and finally as the CGT (C Gran Turismo) used the mechanical organs of the CSL, and practically all of the front section of the latter's bodywork. The rear section, however, was omitted and the engine was therefore exposed for all to admire. The structure was completed by the rear-mounted fuel tank and a useful pannier, a feature which gave the decidedly spartan CGT at least one advantage over the more luxurious CSL.

The financial saving, however, was considerable: the new product was offered at 175,000 Lire, a very competitive price compared with its rivals.

In 1951 the powers that be at Cascina Costa decreed the introduction of a version with a larger, 150 cm³ engine, but it cannot be said that this model enjoyed much in the way of commercial success as the public preferred the CSL with its all-enclosed body. The CGT remained in production for practically two years, before making way for a completely different and even cheaper scooter: the Ovunque.

The CGT was the second MV scooter and was partially enclosed with a rear luggage box and a pedal gear change. It was usually finished in metallic green, but other colours were available.

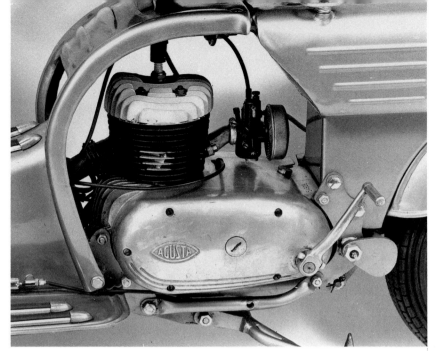

The 125 cm³ engine of the CGT had a four-speed gearbox and direct air cooling without a fan.

TECHNICAL SPECIFICATIONS

Model/year	CGT 51 - 125 cm³ - 1950/51
Engine	2-stroke single 53 × 56 mm - 123.5 cm³
Compression ratio	6 : 1
Cylinder head/barrel	Light alloy - cast iron
Valve configuration	–
Timing system	–
Ignition	Flywheel magneto
Carburettor	Dell'Orto MA 17
Lubrication	16 : 1 petroil
Clutch	Wet multiplate
Gearbox	Unit construction, four speeds
Transmission	Geared primary; final drive, chain
Frame/wheelbase	Step through single-beam and pressings -1132 mm
Front suspension	Trailing link
Rear suspension	S/arm with mechanical shock absorber
Wheels	Steel discs, 3.00 × 10"
Tyres	3.50 - 10" front and rear
Brakes	Drums, 100 mm front and rear
Consumption	3 litres per 100 km
Fuel tank capacity	7 litres
Oil tank capacity	–

500 Turismo 1950

The appearance of the four-cylinder MV 500 racer in the spring of 1950 created a sensation, but in retrospect this was clearly due to the fact that in racing, sensation was – and is – the norm. The road version on the other hand, presented at the Milan Motorcycle Show the following November, was truly breathtaking: it was the first time that such a projectile had been offered to the general public, a machine capable of offering mere mortals the chance to savour the high speed sensations that were usually the exclusive province of their favourite track stars. The machine had all the right ingredients to impress enthusiasts and experts alike: a four-cylinders, twin camshafts, shaft drive, and a duplex cradle frame. Furthermore, extremely accurate finishing and the extensive use of special materials ensured that the weight was kept well down, to a point below that of a comparable single-cylinder machine with the same engine capacity. It was a machine to be reckoned with, not just in Italy but throughout Europe, which in motorcycling terms in those days meant everywhere that counted. The bike had a list price of 950,000 lire, expensive for the time but not astronomical, and in keeping with the quality of the product. Despite the fact that there was considerable demand for the 500, MV never actually put it on sale, and after some time it was no longer even exhibited at the various bike shows where it had once been the major attraction.

Power/rpm
40 hp at 8500 rpm

Dry weight
155 kg

Maximum speed
170 km/h

The engine of the 500 four. The distributor can be seen under the carburettors. The clutch is mounted behind the gearbox.

TECHNICAL SPECIFICATIONS

Model/year	500 Turismo - 500 cm^3 - 1950
Engine	4-stroke four-cylinder 54 × 54 × 4 mm - 494.4 cm^3
Compression ratio	9 : 1
Cylinder head/barrel	Light alloy
Valve configuration	Inclined overhead
Timing system	Double overhead camshafts
Ignition	Battery and Coil
Carburettor	Dell'Orto SS1 27 DS, SS1 27 DD
Lubrication	Wet sump
Clutch	Dry single-plate unit, between gearbox and drive shaft
Gearbox	Unit construction, four speeds
Transmission	Primary via bevel gears, final drive by cardan shaft
Frame/wheelbase	Closed tubular duplex cradle - 1520 mm
Front suspension	Telescopic fork
Rear suspension	Twin swinging arms with torsion bar and friction dampers
Wheels	Light alloy, wire spoked; front 2.75 × 19", rear 3.25 × 19"
Tyres	Front 3.00-19", rear 3.50-19"
Brakes	Central drums, front 230 mm, rear 220 mm
Consumption	5 litres per 100 km
Fuel tank capacity	18 litres
Oil tank capacity	2.5 kg

The 500 four was painted in metallic silver. The instrument panel was integral with the fuel tank and contained a rev counter and odometer. The transverse gear pedal was operated with both feet.

Ovunque Scooter 1951-1954

Power/rpm

5 hp at 4800 rpm

Dry weight

74 kg

Maximum speed

80 km/h

In 1951 the battle for the conquest of the scooter market reached a peak of intensity, with the various companies involved wielding price cuts as if they were so many blunt instruments. Having presented the CGT the previous year, MV was eager to begin production of a new machine that, while adopting new technical featu-

res, could be sold at a still lower price. To this end the Ovunque ("Everywhere") was created, with a structure which was basically a step through frame made of large diameter tubing.

The engine used the same head and block as the previous four-speed models, but a gearbox offering only three speeds was fitted

along with a twistgrip change. The suspension layout was also of radically simplified design: the particular arrangement at the rear, where the engine was in-unit with the swinging arm, had made it possible to fit a surprisingly "modern" single-shock suspension system.

The Ovunque was put on sale at the very competiti-

ve price of 141,000 lire. There were two series, identified by the codes 0 51 and 0 52, the latter being characterized by twin exhaust pipes.

Above, the first version of the Ovunque with a single exhaust and below, the second version with twin pipes and silencers.

TECHNICAL SPECIFICATIONS

Model/year	Ovunque - 125 cm³ - 1951/54
Engine	2-stroke single 53 × 56 mm - 123.5 cm³
Compression ratio	6 : 1
Cylinder head/barrel	Light alloy, cast iron
Valve configuration	–
Timing system	–
Ignition	Flywheel magneto
Carburettor	Dell'Orto MA 17
Lubrication	16 : 1 petroil
Clutch	Wet multiplate
Gearbox	Unit construction, three speeds
Transmission	Geared primary; final drive, chain
Frame/wheelbase	Step through single-beam - 1240 mm
Front suspension	Trailing link
Rear suspension	S/arm in-unit with engine, mechanical damper
Wheels	Steel discs, 3.25 × 8"
Tyres	3.50 - 8" front and rear
Brakes	130 mm drums front and rear
Consumption	3 litres per 100 km
Fuel tank capacity	7 litres
Oil tank capacity	–

150 1952-1953

When, in 1951, the exemption from registration for light motorcycles of up to 125 cm³ was abolished, there was no longer any good reason not to exceed this capacity. In fact all the manufacturers quickly introduced bigger models of 150-160 or even 175 cm³, the traditional maximum capacity for pre-war lightweights. These modifications were initially made with the commendable intention of providing sturdier and more durable engines, though subsequently the increases in displacement were used to increase power and speed. MV too was quick to follow this path, and in 1952 their range was increased with the introduction of a new 150 that was produced in the traditional Turismo and Sport versions. The newcomer was fairly similar to the existing 125, with the additional benefits accruing from three years of production experience, and, above all, from the company's successful participation in trials competition. The new bike boasted substantial improvements to the suspension, now with hydraulic dampers, and to the braking system, which used light alloy central drums, as well as the usual internal modifications to the engine. List prices ranged from 200,000 to 240,000 lire. In 1953 a more economical version, equipped with girder forks, was produced and immediately pressed into service as a works trials iron. A number of tuned versions were also produced for long distance races such as the Milan-Taranto event.

Power/rpm
5.5 hp at 4800 rpm
6.2 hp at 5200 rpm

Dry weight
90 kg

Maximum speed
90 km/h 98 km/h

The Turismo version of the 150 with a rear parcel rack. The redesigned telescopic fork was by now mounted as standard on all MV products.

The Supersport version of the 150 with hydraulic rear dampers was presented in January 1952.

TECHNICAL SPECIFICATIONS

Model/year	150 Turismo/Sport - 150 cm^3 - 1952/53
Engine	2-stroke single 59 × 56 mm - 153 cm^3
Compression ratio	6 : 1 / 6.5 : 1
Cylinder head/barrel	Light alloy, cast iron
Valve configuration	–
Timing system	–
Ignition	Flywheel magneto
Carburettor	Dell'Orto MB 20 B
Lubrication	20 : 1 petroil
Clutch	Wet multiplate
Gearbox	Unit construction, four speeds
Transmission	Geared primary; final drive, chain
Frame/wheelbase	Open tubular duplex cradle plus pressings - 1270 mm
Front suspension	Telescopic fork
Rear suspension	Swinging arm with telescopic units
Wheels	Steel, wire spoked, 2.50 × 19"
Tyres	2.75 - 19" front and rear
Brakes	Central drum
Consumption	3 litres per 100 km / 3.5 litres per 100 km
Fuel tank capacity	14 litres
Oil tank capacity	–

The 150 Supersport engine equipped with a horizontal carburettor. Note the finning of the cylinder head, which was extended towards the rear. It had a four-speed gearbox.

In 1953 the blade fork was brought out of retirement and employed on this Turismo Economico model which was also used as a works entry in trials events.

A 150 Supersport prepared for long distance racing. Typical features are the rearsets for flat-out riding, and the megaphone exhaust, in stark contrast with present day technical orthodoxy.

175 CS 1953-1959

The single-cam 175, introduced in 1952 and put into production in 1953, was of fundamental importance to the technical, commercial and sporting evolution of the marque. From an engineering point of view the 175 CS was important because it was the first 4-stroke MV to go into volume production (the earlier 250, and 500 cm³ 4-stroke machines were little more than prototypes); as far as sport was concerned, the various versions and derivations of the 175 CS specially prepared for production bike racing – then enjoying one of its periodic spells of extreme popularity – made a considerable contribution to the marque's collection of racing honours; its commercial importance lay in the fact that, from that time on, MV's clientele was almost exclusively sporting. This situation arose because the designers of

The Turismo model presented at the Milan show in November 1952. There was also a version with larger section tyres. Below, the engine; in the first version, cylinder head and barrel had finning of practically identical diameter.

Power/rpm
8 hp at 5600 rpm
11 hp at 6700 rpm

Maximum speed
100 km/h
115 km/h

Consumption
2.5 litres per 100 km
3 litres per 100 km

TECHNICAL SPECIFICATIONS

Model/year	175 Turismo/Sport - 175 cm³ - 1953/59
Engine	4-stroke single 59.5 × 62 mm - 172.3 cm³
Compression ratio	6 : 1 / 7 : 1
Cylinder head/barrel	Light alloy
Valve configuration	Inclined overhead
Timing system	Single overhead camshaft
Ignition	Flywheel magneto
Carburettor	Dell'Orto MA 18B/Dell'Orto MB 22B
Lubrication	Wet sump
Clutch	Wet multiplate
Gearbox	Unit construction, four speeds
Transmission	Geared primary; final drive, chain
Frame/wheelbase	Open tubular duplex cradle plus pressings - 1300 mm
Front suspension	Teledraulic fork
Rear suspension	Swinging arm with hydraulic dampers
Wheels	Steel, wire spoked, 2.50 × 19"
Tyres	2.75-19" front and rear
Brakes	Central drums, front 180 mm, rear 150 mm
Dry weight	110 kg
Fuel tank capacity	14 litres
Oil tank capacity	1.8 kg

Below, the first Sport version, from November 1952. Bottom, the Turismo Lusso (CSTL). Also from November 1952, it had a dualseat and other differences in trim. On the right, the Sport (CS) from November 1955: the finning on the cylinder head is now more extensive.

the new lightweight had opted for performance rather than reliability and longevity, to the disadvantage of the ordinary user. The same could be said for virtually all the new bikes on the market at the time, but in the case of MV the phenomenon was more marked and, above all, longer-lasting. From then on a reputation for fragile brilliance accompanied the Lombard marque virtually to the end of its career. The MV 175 was on offer until 1959, with prices ranging from 235,000 to 300,000 lire for the normal versions.

The 1956 Turismo Lusso (CTSL) model adopted the engine with the extended finning. The form of the fuel tank is another modification that catches the eye.

The Sport (175 CS) from November 1958. The bodywork had been restyled and a new exhaust fitted. The drive for the rev counter was fitted to the cylinder head.

The Turismo Esportazione Lusso (175 CSTEL) was introduced in 1959. It is recognizable by the form of its (red and white) fuel tank, the silencer, and the filter fitted to the carburettor.

The 175 CSS or Supersport, better known as the "Disco Volante" or "Flying Saucer" – thanks to the shape of its fuel tank – in the version equipped with an Earles fork. It cost 275,000 lire.

The Squalo or "Shark" specifically prepared for racing. The 175 cm^3 single-cam engine was housed in a race-derived frame.

The Squalo was equipped with a silencer, headlight and starter for Formula sport production racing. Note the magneto ignition in place of the flywheel.

Pullman  1953-1956

At first it did not seem likely that the unassuming little Pullman would capture the imagination of the masses, an assumption reflected by MV's choice of the relatively unimportant Brussels Show for its launch in January 1953. It soon became clear, however, that odd-looking customer was a stroke of genius: apparently the public had been waiting for just such a vehicle; not fast or nippy, but simple, robust and – above all – comfortable. The fact of the matter is that, at that time, the ordinary daily user was still in the majority, and the desire for a means of transport that combined the comfort of a scooter with the characteristics of the traditional light motorcycle – large diameter wheels in particular – was fairly widespread. Furthermore the innovatory use of balloon tyres gave the Pullman a touch of originality that evidently appealed to the public eye. The Pullman's notable success also generated a wide range of imitations, as a number of other manufacturers produced "fat-wheeled" bikes. Mechanically, it was directly derived from the Ovunque scooter: a 125 cm^3 engine with a three-speed gearbox in-unit with the rear swinging arm; in this case, however, two spring-shock units were fitted on either side of the wheel, rather than the single unit fitted to the Ovunque. Front suspension was handled by a conventional telescopic fork. The Pullman was offered at a price that varied between 155,000 and 163,000 lire, depending on the specification.

Power/rpm	
5 hp at 4500 rpm	
Dry weight	
85 kg	
Maximum speed	
75 km/h	

The engine of the Pullman, here in a special version – now on show in the company museum – with direct fuel injection and a separate oil feed, with pump.

TECHNICAL SPECIFICATIONS

Model/year	Pullman - 125 cm^3 - 1953/1956
Engine	2-stroke single 53 × 56 mm - 123.5 cm^3
Compression ratio	6 : 1
Cylinder head/barrel	Light alloy - cast iron
Valve configuration	–
Timing system	–
Ignition	Flywheel magneto
Carburettor	Dell'Orto MA 17
Lubrication	16 : 1 petroil
Clutch	Wet multiplate
Gearbox	Unit construction, three speeds
Transmission	Geared primary; final drive, chain
Frame/wheelbase	Single beam - 1285 mm
Front suspension	Telescopic fork
Rear suspension	Rear s/arm in-unit with engine, hydraulic dampers
Wheels	Steel, wire spoked, 3.25 × 15"
Tyres	3.50-15" front and rear
Brakes	Central drums, front and rear 130 mm
Consumption	2.5 litres per 100 km
Fuel tank capacity	13 litres
Oil tank capacity	–

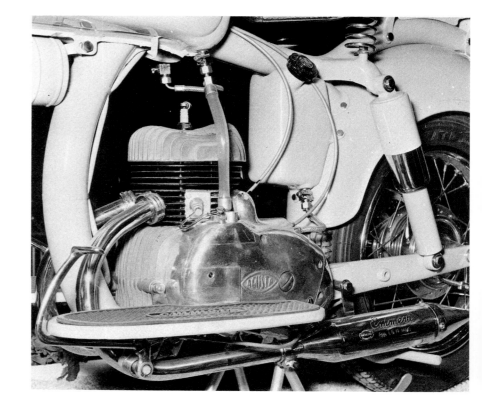

The first version of the Pullman, with the four-speed gearbox and twistgrip change (below), and the second version (on the right) with a rocker-arm pedal change. The bike was finished in light blue.

Two-stroke engines, which had played a part in the enormous diffusion of the utilitarian motorcycle in the post-war period, had begun to be less acceptable to the motorcycling fraternity by the mid-Fifties.

This was a reflection of the fact that, in the world of motorsport, the strokers had been outclassed by the four-stroke machines (this was before certain technical discoveries made after 1970 turned the tables altogether, as far as competition was concerned at

125 Turismo Rapido 1954-

least). Furthermore most people felt that four-strokes were "proper" engines, which lent both bike and rider a prestige beyond the gift of a humble two-stroke machine. Thus MV – in common with most other manufacturers – began to adopt the four-stroke engine for their utility bikes. The first result of this new trend

was the 125 Turismo Rapido, a calm, easy-going machine fitted with a sturdy pushrod engine and a four-speed gearbox.

The frame design was very much in the mainstream MV tradition: that is, an open duplex cradle, formed by tubes at the front in combination with pressed-steel elements at the rear. The Turismo Rapido

remained in regular production until 1958, and was constructed in a number of versions that differed only in certain details such as the form of the handlebars, the styling of the fuel tank or the paintwork. Prices varied from 180,000 to 200,000 lire, depending on the model and the year of production.

Power/rpm
6.5 hp at 6000 rpm
Dry weight
102 kgs
Maximum speed
90 km/h

The engine of the TR was one of the few MV units to have square rather than the company's traditional undersquare dimensions.

TECHNICAL SPECIFICATIONS

Model/year	Turismo Rapido - 125 cm³ - 1954/58
Engine	4-stroke single 54 × 54 mm - 123.6 cm³
Compression ratio	8.5 : 1
Cylinder head/barrel	Light alloy - cast iron
Valve configuration	Inclined overhead
Timing system	Pushrod
Ignition	Flywheel magneto
Carburettor	Dell'Orto MA 18B
Lubrication	Wet sump
Clutch	Wet multiplate
Gearbox	Unit construction, four speeds
Transmission	Geared primary; final drive, chain
Frame/wheelbase	Open tubular duplex cradle plus pressings - 1285 mm
Front suspension	Telescopic fork
Rear suspension	Swinging arm with hydraulic dampers
Wheels	Steel, wire spoked, 2.50 × 18"
Tyres	2.75-18" front and rear
Brakes	Central drums, front and rear 123.5 mm
Consumption	2 litres per 100 km
Fuel tank capacity	12 litres
Oil tank capacity	1.5 kg

1958

The first examples
of the TR had a
fully tubular frame
even at the rear.
This feature was
soon abandoned,
and so these
"pieces" are fairly
rare.

In 1955 the
Turismo Rapido
was produced with
box-section rear
frame components
following the
pattern established
for the other
models. The bike
was usually painted
black with a red
fuel tank.

Numerous versions of the TR were produced over the years. this is the Rapido Sport (RS) from 1956, which produced 8 hp and reached 105 km/h. It cost 198,000 lire.

The Turismo Rapido Extra (TRE) from 1958: standard 6.5 hp engine and a higher level of finish. It was painted red, with white bands on the fuel tank.

The Turismo Rapido Extra Lusso (TREL), again from 1958: black frame, red and white tank, larger front brake, and a higher level of finish.

The Turismo Rapido America (TRA): identifiable by its more humped tank, and different fork design. It was painted in red and white.

The Turismo Rapido Lusso (TRL) from 1957-58, with what was a fashionable fuel tank shape at the time, and larger mudguards. It cost 178,000 lire.

Moped 1955-1959

In 1955, following the T.R. four-stroke light motorcycle, MV launched another important novelty: their first "ciclomotore", or moped.

In the immediate post-war period the demand for mobility at absolute minimum cost had been met with the sale of "clip-on" micromotors that could be fitted to ordinary pedal cycles. In practice, however, these motorized bicycles soon revealed that they suffered from many limitations, considerable fragility, and an absence of even minimal comfort. As a result, true mopeds were not slow to appear. These were simple, lightweight vehicles designed to cope with the stresses imposed by the engine. By 1955 numerous moped manufacturers were already battling for a share of what was proving to be a very crowded and aggressive market, but very few of the motorcycle manufactoring companies were among them, almost as if they considered the production of such a small vehicle to be beneath their dignity: the MV company therefore was a notable exception. Their new vehicle had a very linear structure, based on a pressed-steel beam frame; the two-stroke engine was blessed with a three-speed gearbox, an extremely useful feature on the mountainous Italian roads.

The 48 moped was fitted with efficient suspension on both wheels, a feature that was not common to all contemporary mopeds, and it was therefore a very attractive proposition technically as well as financially: it was sold at just 79,000 lire.

Power/rpm	
2 hp at 5400 rpm	
Dry weight	
42 kg	
Maximum speed	
50 km/h	

TECHNICAL SPECIFICATIONS

Model/year	Moped - 48 cm^3 - 1955/59
Engine	2-stroke single 38 × 42 mm - 47.6 cm^3
Compression ratio	6 : 1
Cylinder head/barrel	Light alloy - cast iron
Valve configuration	–
Timing system	–
Ignition	Flywheel magneto
Carburettor	Dell'Orto T1 12 DA
Lubrication	20 : 1 petroil
Clutch	Wet multiplate
Gearbox	Unit construction, three speeds
Transmission	Geared primary; final drive, chain
Frame/wheelbase	Pressed-steel beam - 1160 mm
Front suspension	Leading links
Rear suspension	Plunger-box
Wheels	Steel, wire spoked, 2.00 × 20"
Tyres	2.25-20" front and rear
Brakes	Lateral drums, front and rear 96 mm
Consumption	1.5 litres per 100 km
Fuel tank capacity	3 litres
Oil tank capacity	–

The first MV moped with a pressed-steel sprung frame and a three-speed gearbox. It was painted deep blue.

Superpullman 1955-1957

Another novelty introduced in 1955 was the Superpullman, the last MV lightweight to be equipped with a two-stroke engine. The name of the bike gave the impression that it was a development of the successful Pullman model of two years before. In effect the new machine did spring from the same engineering philosophy that had inspired its predecessor – a blend of economy and simplicity – but in practical terms the two machines had little in common with each other. The Superpullman was more of a mainstream motorcycle, not only by virtue of the normal section tyres (2.75-18), but also the riding stance, footrest and handlebar layout, etc. The engine was a new design equipped with a four-speed gearbox. Despite these improvements the list price was kept low, actually less than that of the Pullman, at just 145,000 lire. This was achieved largely by redesigning the cycle parts: the machine was now built around a pressed-steel beam frame formed by two electrowelded half-shells from which the engine was cantilevered. The front fork was also a simplified leading link type, but springing was nevertheless more than comfortable. The Superpullman remained in the MV catalogue until 1957 even though its career was less successful than that of its predecessor, whose design proved more attractive as far as the public was concerned. The Superpullman was painted in deep blue, with a red band on the fuel tank.

Power/rpm
6 hp at 5200 rpm

Maximum speed
75 km/h

Fuel consumption
2.5 litres per 100 km

The Superpullman was a fairly traditional economical bike, which, for a while, was sold alongside the successful Pullman and eventually replaced it.

155

TECHNICAL SPECIFICATIONS

Model/year	Superpullman - 125 cm^3 - 1955/57
Engine	2-stroke single 53 × 56 mm - 123.5 cm^3
Compression ratio	6 : 1
Cylinder head/barrel	Light alloy - cast iron
Valve configuration	–
Timing system	–
Ignition	Flywheel magneto
Carburettor	Dell'Orto MA 17
Lubrication	20 : 1 petroil
Clutch	Wet multiplate
Gearbox	Unit construction, four speeds
Transmission	Geared primary; final drive, chain
Frame/wheelbase	Pressed-steel beam - 1245 mm
Front suspension	Leading link
Rear suspension	S/arm with hydraulic dampers
Wheels	Steel, wire spoked, 2.50 × 18"
Tyres	2.75-18" front and rear
Brakes	Lateral drums, 125 mm front and rear
Dry weight	82 kg
Fuel tank capacity	14 litres
Oil tank capacity	–

The cheapness of the Superpullman essentially derived from the wide use of pressed steel. Below, the compact and elegant engine. The cylinder was inclined forwards by 10 degrees.

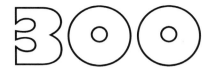 300 Twin 1955

As we have already seen, virtually all of MV's product range was designed in-house by the small group of technicians working directly under Count Domenico Agusta. One of the few external experts used by MV was a Roman engineer named Giannini, who cooperated with Verghera for a time during the mid-Fifties. The most important result of this association was a medium capacity double overhead camshaft, twin-cylinder engine, with battery ignition, a four-speed gearbox, and – a really avant-garde refinement this – electric starting. This engine, initially conceived as a 300 and bored out to 350 cm^3 at a later date, was housed in a hybrid full duplex frame made up of tubular and pressed steel elements rounded off by an Earles-type front fork, a layout that was very much in vogue at that time both for touring and competition machines.

Such a specification placed the 300 Twin firmly in the ranks of the decidedly sporting bikes, and in fact MV management hoped that it would relaunch the image of the high-performance medium-capacity class, at a time when it seemed in danger of being eclipsed by the swarms of small and ultra-rapid 175s which were so fashionable at the time.

Commercial success seemed assured but – as had happened before at MV – after the launch at the 1955 Milan Motorcycle Show the 300 Twin was not put into regular production and it disappeared from the scene shortly afterwards.

Power/rpm
20 hp at 8000 rpm

Dry weight
-

Maximum speed
-

The attractive 300 Twin, designed in 1955 by Giannini, unfortunately remained at the prototype stage.

TECHNICAL SPECIFICATIONS

Model/year	300 Twin - 1955
Engine	4-stroke twin 57 × 57.8 mm - 294.8 cm³
Compression ratio	8 : 1
Cylinder head/barrel	Light alloy - cast iron
Valve configuration	Inclined overhead
Timing system	Double overhead camshafts
Ignition	Coil
Carburettor	Two Dell'Orto units
Lubrication	Wet sump
Clutch	Wet multiplate
Gearbox	Unit construction, four speeds
Transmission	Geared primary; final drive, chain
Frame/wheelbase	Closed tubular duplex cradle plus pressings
Front suspension	Earles fork
Rear suspension	S/arm with hydraulic dampers
Wheels	Light alloy, wire spoked; front 2.75 × 19", rear 3.25 × 19"
Tyres	3.00-19" front and 3.50-19" rear
Brakes	Central drums
Consumption	–
Fuel tank capacity	18 litres
Oil tank capacity	2.5 kg

The 300 Twin and – below – its engine, enhanced by electric starting and twin overhead camshafts driven by a gear train between the two cylinders. The vertically mounted distributor can be seen behind the carburettors.

Raid 250-300 1956-1962

The 250 Raid made an entirely unexpected appearance at the 1956 Milan Trade Fair, where it aroused considerable interest and admiration. This was a modern motorcycle, designed according to the prevailing stylistic trends, with a reassuringly robust appearance. These were years dominated by the success of small but sporty 125s and 175s that could show a clean pair of heels to a traditional 500. A 250, therefore, as long as it was up-to-date, was considered to be a large capacity bike, not only restricted to a limited circle of motorcyclists – fans of long distance touring in particular – but also a machine which was capable of providing exceptional performance, at least as far as comfort and safety were concerned. In practice the Raid was not a particularly fast bike but in all other respects it lived up to its name, which in Italian is used to describe a long, fast, and somewhat adventurous trip by motorcycle or car. This name was chosen after polling the various MV concessionaires who had evidently been quick to identify what would be the most suitable use for the new product. The Raid was produced until 1962; the initial price was a decidedly moderate 290,000 lire. In 1959 the enlarged 300 cm³ version was presented but to all intents and purposes it enjoyed no real commercial success. The Raid also spawned a military motorcycle, of which only a very limited number of units was produced. These machines were fitted with the 300 engine.

Power/rpm
14 hp at 5600 rpm

Maximum speed
115 km/h

Fuel consumption
3 litres per 100 km

The Raid was a modern, medium-capacity bike. This is the 250 cm³ version from 1956-58.

Above, the Raid 250 again. The bike was finished in red and black and was sold at 286,000 lire. There was also an Extra version, with a higher level of finish that was sold at 290,000 lire.

Below, the Raid 300 from November 1959. It produced 16 hp at 5000 rpm, and could reach 120 km/h. Note the styling differences compared to the first model: exhaust, tank, and mudguards.

A Raid 300 "Special".

The Raid's compact four-speed propulsion unit was characterized by the heavy finning around the cylinder head and barrel.

TECHNICAL SPECIFICATIONS

Model/year	Raid - 250 cm^3 - 1956/62
Engine	4-stroke single 69 × 66 mm - 246.6 cm^3
Compression ratio	7.2 : 1
Cylinder head/barrel	Light alloy - cast iron
Valve configuration	Inclined overhead
Timing system	Pushrod
Ignition	Coil
Carburettor	Dell'Orto MB 22 B
Lubrication	Wet sump
Clutch	Wet multiplate
Gearbox	Unit construction, four speeds
Transmission	Geared primary; final drive, chain
Frame/wheelbase	Open tubular duplex cradle plus pressings - 1340 mm
Front suspension	Teledraulic fork
Rear suspension	Swinging arm with hydraulic dampers
Wheels	Steel wire spoked, 2.75 × 19
Tyres	3.00-19" front and 3.25-19" rear
Brakes	Central drums, 220 mm front and rear
Dry weight	145 kg
Fuel tank capacity	17 litres
Oil tank capacity	1.5 kg

Ottantatre 1958-1960

In 1958 the Ottantatre (Eighty-three) was introduced. This was a lightweight utility machine fitted with a four-stroke engine, despite its utilitarian nature, which owed its name to the highly unusual 83 cm³ cylinder capacity. In general, motorcycle manufacturers have always tended to respect the canonical engine capacity limits as set down in the sporting regulations, more out of habit than technical necessity; MV on the other hand had opted for logic in preference to tradition when it came to engineering its new lightweight. In fact, after various experiments, it was proved that this displacement was capable of developing enough power to transport not one but two people, while offering the minimum specific fuel consumption in relation to its technical characteristics. Of course performance was limited to levels that would provoke no little mirth these days, when a whole litre of capacity seems insufficient for solo touring. At that time, however, the public was different, with different needs, and above all slimmer wallets. The 83 cm³ capacity was therefore considered perfectly acceptable. The bike had an extremely simple tubular beam frame, but the suspension elements were teledraulic; a three-speed gearbox was fitted. Turismo and Sport versions were produced with slight differences in power output and top speed, as well as trim. The Ottantatre was available until 1960; list prices were 127,000 and 135,000 lire for the Turismo and Sport versions.

Power/rpm

3.7 hp at 6000 rpm
4.2 hp at 6400 rpm

Dry weight

83 kg

Maximum speed

75 km/h
80 km/h

TECHNICAL SPECIFICATIONS

Model/year	Ottantatre Turismo/Sport - 83 cm³ - 1958/1960
Engine	4-stroke single 46.5 × 49 mm - 83.2 cm³
Compression ratio	7 : 1 / 7.5 : 1
Cylinder head/barrel	Light alloy - cast iron
Valve configuration	Inclined overhead
Timing system	Pushrod
Ignition	Flywheel magneto
Carburettor	Dell'Orto MA 15B
Lubrication	Wet sump
Clutch	Wet multiplate
Gearbox	Unit construction, three speeds
Transmission	Geared primary; final drive, chain
Frame/wheelbase	Tubular single-beam - 1245 mm
Front suspension	Teledraulic fork
Rear suspension	Swinging arm with hydraulic dampers
Wheels	Steel, wire spoked, 2.25 × 19"
Tyres	2.50-19" front and rear
Brakes	Central drums 118 mm front and rear
Consumption	1.6 litres per 100 km/1.8 litres per 100 km
Fuel tank capacity	12 litres
Oil tank capacity	1.5 kg

The engine of the Ottantatre was cantilever mounted with the cylinder inclined at 10 degrees. This is the 4.2 hp Sport version.

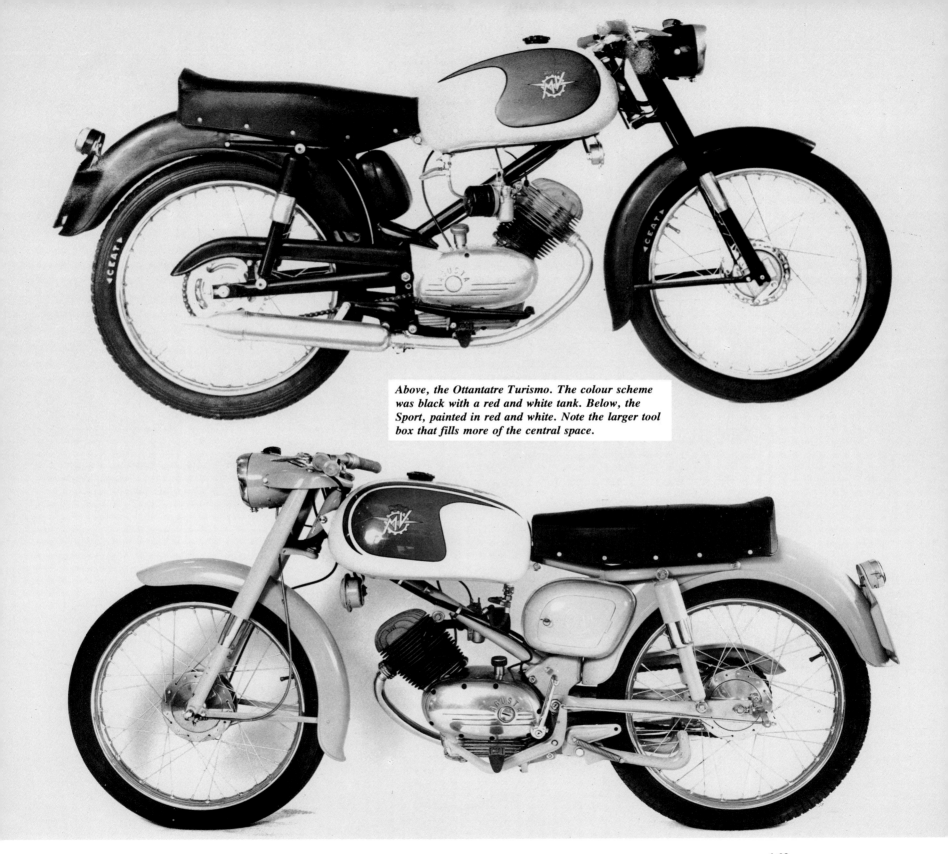

Above, the Ottantatre Turismo. The colour scheme was black with a red and white tank. Below, the Sport, painted in red and white. Note the larger tool box that fills more of the central space.

163

The 175 with the push-rod engine was a fairly modest, unexciting machine that was put on sale in 1957. It was introduced rather quietly, without any extensive publicity campaign, while the official launch did not come along until some time later. By 1960 it had disappeared from the catalogue. It was very similar in appearance to its better known – and more interesting – single overhead camshaft stablemate; in fact it was difficult to tell them apart at first glance. MV produced the pushrod 175 because it was felt that many fans of the lightweight category would cheerfully do without so-

175 A B 1958-1959

Power/rpm

7.5 hp at 5500 rpm

Dry weight

123 kg

Maximum speed

98 km/h

The 175 cm³ pushrod-engined Turismo Economico model. Note the simplified telescopic fork. Below, this engine can be easily distinguished from the overhead cam version by the more rounded finning on the top of the cylinder head. The barrel is also of a different design.

TECHNICAL SPECIFICATIONS

Model/year	175 AB - 175 cm³ - 1958/59
Engine	4-stroke single 59.5 × 62 mm - 172.3 cm³
Compression ratio	7 : 1
Cylinder head/barrel	Light alloy - cast iron
Valve configuration	Inclined overhead
Timing system	Pushrod
Ignition	Flywheel magneto
Carburettor	Dell'Orto MA 18 B
Lubrication	Wet sump
Clutch	Wet multiplate
Gearbox	Unit construction, four speeds
Transmission	Geared primary; final drive, chain
Frame/wheelbase	Open tubular duplex cradle plus pressings - 1300 mm
Front suspension	Teledraulic fork
Rear suspension	Swinging arm with hydraulic dampers
Wheels	Steel, wire spoked, 2.50 × 19"
Tyres	2.75-19" front and rear
Brakes	Central drums 185 mm front and 165 mm rear
Consumption	12.5 litres per 100 km
Fuel tank capacity	14 litres
Oil tank capacity	1.4 kg

me of the lively performance offered by the single-knocker bike in exchange for exemption from some of the undeniable technical inconveniences associated with single overhead camshaft designs. While such problems were of secondary importance to a strictly sporting clientele, they amounted to a considerable nuisance as far as ordinary riders were concerned. The pushrod 175 was produced in a number of versions in its fairly short life. These were all practically identical to one another apart from the finish and a series of somewhat cryptic code names whose mysteries have delighted, and occasionally confounded, enthusiasts and historians alike. These versions certainly included the Turismo, the America, the America Lusso, and the Turismo Extra Lusso and perhaps others. Prices ranged from 200,000 to 225,000 lire according to the model.

Three versions of the pushrod 175, all with slightly different accessories and trim: from top to bottom, the Turismo, the America with a rear mudguard similar to that of the Raid, and lastly, the America Lusso.

125 TREL - Centomila 1959-1963

During 1959 the four-stroke engine of the 125 light motorcycle was extensively revised, although from the outside these modifications were not very apparent.

The lubrication system was drastically improved by the adoption of a larger capacity sump and the introduction of a centrifugal oil filtering device which was driven off the crankshaft. The efficacy of this device was such that, shortly after the bike was launched in the spring, the company decided to exploit the publicity value of this interesting new device by extending the manufacturer's guarantee to an exceptional 100,000 km.

Thus the bike, originally known by the usual complicated acronym, in this case T.R.E.L. (which stood for "Turismo Rapido Extra Lusso"), was rebaptized the "Centomila" (One-Hundred-Thousand) to underline its exceptional reliability and longevity.

Unfortunately, we were unable to discover just how many examples of the Centomila actually reached this figure in perfect condition, but we can say that most of the bikes in this series gave excellent results. The number of crankcase stud bolts was also increased, in order to improve rigidity and compactness.

The Centomila remained in the catalogue until 1963, with a few variations in finish, colour schemes, and accessories, which in fact gave rise to the R.A. and E.L. models.

Prices for the different versions ranged from 157,000 to 187,000 lire.

Power/rpm	
7.5 hp at 6200 rpm	
Dry weight	
105 kg	
Maximum speed	
95 km/h	

TECHNICAL SPECIFICATIONS

Model/year	125 TREL/Centomila/RA-EL - 125 cm^3 - 1959/1963
Engine	4-stroke single 54 × 54 mm - 123.6 cm^3
Compression ratio	8.5 : 1
Cylinder head/barrel	Light alloy - cast iron
Valve configuration	Inclined overhead
Timing system	Pushrod
Ignition	Flywheel magneto
Carburettor	Dell'Orto MA 18B
Lubrication	Wet sump
Clutch	Wet multiplate
Gearbox	Unit construction, four speeds
Transmission	Geared primary; final drive, chain
Frame/wheelbase	Open tubular duplex cradle plus pressings - 1285 mm
Front suspension	Teledraulic fork
Rear suspension	Swinging arm with hydraulic dampers
Wheels	Steel, wire spoked, 2.50 × 18"
Tyres	2.75-18" front and rear
Brakes	Central drums
Consumption	2.5 litres per 100 km
Fuel tank capacity	13 litres
Oil tank capacity	1.5 kg

The 125 TREL, later known as the Centomila. The engine, equipped with a centrifugal oil filter, may be distinguished from its TR predecessor by the larger sump that projected below the crankcase.

166

150 4T 1959-1970

Not content with revising the 125, MV brought out a new 150 cm³ lightweight. The engine fitted to the newcomer was a bored-out descendant of the 125 engine, from which it had inherited some sophisticated technical innovations like the centrifugal oil filter.

As we mentioned before, the 150 cm³ capacity came into being around 1951, when new legislation made it obligatory for motorcycles of up to 125 cm³ to carry licence plates, and then fell into disuse in favour of the classic 175. The revised Italian Highway Code, introduced in 1959, brought the 150 back into fashion, as it forbade access to the motorway system to vehicles with cylinder capacities of less than 150 cm³. The MV 150 (which had an effective capacity of 150.1 cm³, and was therefore allowed to travel on the motorways) was very similar in appearance to the 125 cm³ Centomila: it shared the same general layout with a duplex cradle frame fashioned from tubes and steel pressings, a fuel tank that straddled the cylinder head, and a dualseat. Practically the only obvious difference was the exhaust system, which featured twin silencers mounted one above the other in order to improve efficiency without interfering with the flow of the exhaust gases. The 150 had a rather long life, and various versions were produced: the Gran Turismo (GT), the Rapido Sport (RS), and the Rapido Sport America (RSA). Prices were between 200,000 and 220,000 lire at first, but rose a little some time afterward.

Power/rpm

9 hp at 6000 rpm
10 hp at 6400 rpm

Maximum speed

110 km/h 115 km/h

Fuel consumption

2.5 litres per 100 km
3.0 litres per 100 km

TECHNICAL SPECIFICATIONS

Model/year	150 GT/150 RS - 150 cm³ - 1959/1965
Engine	4-stroke single 59.5 × 54 mm - 150.1 cm³
Compression ratio	8 : 1 / 8.5 : 1
Cylinder head/barrel	Light alloy - cast iron
Valve configuration	Inclined overhead
Timing system	Pushrod
Ignition	Flywheel magneto
Carburettor	Dell'Orto MA 18B/Dell'Orto MB 20 B
Lubrication	Wet sump
Clutch	Wet multiplate
Gearbox	Unit construction, four speeds
Transmission	Geared primary; final drive, chain
Frame/wheelbase	Open tubular duplex cradle plus pressings - 1300 mm
Front suspension	Teledraulic fork
Rear suspension	Swinging arm with hydraulic dampers
Wheels	Steel, wire spoked, 2.50 × 18"
Tyres	2.75-18" front and rear
Brakes	Central drums
Dry weight	110 kg
Fuel tank capacity	13 litres
Oil tank capacity	1.6 kg

The first version of the '59 version of the 150 is illustrated on the preceding page. Above, the Gran Turismo (GT) from 1961, with high handlebars and – unusually – a single silencer. The colour scheme was red and white. Below, the Rapido Sport (RS), with exposed rear spring/shock units. This version was usually painted red and silver.

Top, the 150 Rapido Sport America (RSA) with high handlebars and crash bars. Above, the engine. Right, the Rapido Sport again, with a different fuel tank, a fundamental element of MV styling.

Chicco Scooter 1960-1964

1959 was a particularly fertile year for MV, apart from the new products mentioned in the preceding pages, the company presented two all-new scooters at the Milan Motorcycle Show in November. The newcomers were baptized the Bik and the Chicco. Of the two, the Bik was undoubtedly the most interesting from a technical point of view. It was equipped with a 166 cm³ four-stroke twin-cylinder engine with semi-hydraulic tappets but, perhaps because it was too far ahead of its time, this model never made it into production. The Chicco, on the other hand, did make it into the MV catalogue, where it remained until 1964. It was a far more traditional machine than the Bik, but this is not to say that it did not possess some interesting mechanical features of its own – like having the driven wheel cantilevered directly onto the gearbox output shaft. The 155 cm³ two-stroke single engine had no connection with previous MV products and was designed specifically for this model: it had a horizontal cylinder with forced air cooling and chain-driven primary transmission. The body was a pressed-steel monocoque structure with a fixed front mudguard. The definitive version was a slightly modified version of the prototype seen at the Motorcycle Show, which had no engine covers. Whilst the styling was not particularly original, it was however harmonious and well proportioned. The Chicco was put on sale at 157,500 lire: at a time when 500 lire still meant something!

Power/rpm	
5.8 hp at 5200 rpm	
Dry weight	
121 kg	
Maximum speed	
75 km/h	

TECHNICAL SPECIFICATIONS

Model/year	Chicco - 155 cm³ - 1960/1964
Engine	2-stroke single 57 × 61 mm - 155.6 cm³
Compression ratio	7 : 1
Cylinder head/barrel	Light alloy
Valve configuration	–
Timing system	–
Ignition	Flywheel magneto
Carburettor	Dell'Orto MA 17
Lubrication	20 : 1 petroil
Clutch	Wet multiplate
Gearbox	Unit construction, four speeds
Transmission	Primary via duplex chain; final drive, direct
Frame/wheelbase	Pressed-steel monocoque - 1310 mm
Front suspension	Trailing link
Rear suspension	s/arm in-unit with engine, hydraulic damper
Wheels	Steel discs, 3.25 × 10"
Tyres	3.50-10" front and rear
Brakes	Drums, 150 mm front and rear
Consumption	2.3 litres per 100 km
Fuel tank capacity	8.5 litres
Oil tank capacity	–

The Chicco, a scooter with a pressed steel enclosure and a most unorthodox engine by MV standards. It had a horizontal cylinder and primary drive via a chain. A luggage compartment was created on the left-hand side of the bodywork. The scooter was painted ivory white.

Tevere 235 1959-1960

In 1959 MV built two vehicles carrying the name Tevere, a light motorcycle and a motorised tricycle. Whilst they shared the same cylinder capacity their structural architecture was of course completely different. The pushrod engine was basically that of the 175 AB model of which it retained the combustion chamber but not the cylinder bore dimension. The greater cylinder capacity was obtained by increasing the bore and leaving the stroke unchanged. In practice, the Tevere (motorcycle) had a number of features in common with the 175 AB, but was more powerful and consequently offered greater performance. The external styling was very similar, with the most obvious differences concentrated on the box concealing the battery and the air filter and an upper engine breather pipe. The Tevere did not enjoy a long commercial life. When it went on sale it failed to attract much interest, perhaps because it was overshadowed by its more attractive sister machine, the Raid, and consequently it was dropped after just a couple of years.

Power/rpm	
13 hp at 5600 rpm	
Dry weight	
140 kg	
Maximum speed	
105 km/h	

TECHNICAL SPECIFICATIONS

Model/year	Tevere - 235 cm³ - 1959/60
Engine	4-stroke single, 69 × 62 mm - 231.7 cm³
Compression ratio	7.2 : 1
Cylinder head/barrel	Light alloy - cast iron
Valve configuration	Inclined overhead
Timing system	Pushrod
Ignition	Flywheel magneto
Carburettor	Dell'Orto MB 22
Lubrication	Wet sump
Clutch	Wet multiplate
Gearbox	Unit construction, four speeds
Transmission	Geared primary; final drive, chain
Frame/wheelbase	Open tubular duplex cradle - 1350 mm
Front suspension	Teledraulic fork
Rear suspension	Swinging arm with hydraulic dampers
Wheels	Steel, wire spoked; front 2.50 × 19", rear 2.75 × 19"
Tyres	Front 2.75-19", rear 3.00-19"
Brakes	Central drums, 220 mm front and rear
Consumption	3 litres per 100 km
Fuel tank capacity	17 litres
Oil tank capacity	1.5 kg

The Tevere was an economical, medium sized motorcycle, placed somewhere between the 175 and the Raid. It is identifiable by its box-type air filter.

Checca 83-99-125

The Checca was MV's only new product for 1960, a fairly quiet year after the spate of new and updated models produced in 1959. It was presented in two cylinder capacities, 83 and 99 cm³, but even though it too was a four-stroke it bore no relation to the previous Ottantatre. The engine was derived from the new version of the 125 with the enlarged sump (as fitted to the Centomila series), and it was equipped with a four-speed gearbox. The frame was a classic MV open du-

Power/rpm
4 hp at 6000 rpm
5.1 hp at 6000 rpm

Dry weight
95 kg

Maximum speed
80 km/h 90 km/h

TECHNICAL SPECIFICATIONS

Model/year	Checca GT 38/GTE 99/S 99 - 83 cm³/99 cm³ 1960/69
Engine	4-stroke single, 46.5 × 49 mm - 83.2 cm³ - 50.7 × 49 mm - 98.8 cm³
Compression ratio	7.5 : 1
Cylinder head/barrel	Light alloy - cast iron
Valve configuration	Inclined overhead
Timing system	Pushrod
Ignition	Flywheel magneto
Carburettor	Dell'Orto ME 16 BS
Lubrication	Wet sump
Clutch	Wet multiplate
Gearbox	Unit construction, four speeds
Transmission	Geared primary; final drive, chain
Frame/wheelbase	Open tubular cradle plus pressings - 1350 mm
Front suspension	Teledraulic fork
Rear suspension	Swinging arm with hydraulic units
Wheels	Steel wire spoked, 2.25 × 17"
Tyres	2.50-17" front and rear
Brakes	Central drums, 123.5 mm front and 118 mm rear
Consumption	2 litres per 100 km / 2.5 litres/100 km
Fuel tank capacity	14 litres
Oil tank capacity	1 kg

Various versions of the Checca, a light motorcycle inspired by the Centomila series. Above, the 83 cm³ GT; on the facing page, from top to bottom, the GT Extra with the 99 cm³ engine; the more powerful 5.1 hp 99 cm³ Sport GT; and lastly, the 124, which never really got beyond the prototype stage.

172

1960-1969

plex cradle with tubular elements at the front and steel pressings at the rear. Three different models were originally available: the GT with the 83 cm³ engine, sold at 139,500 lire; the GT Extra, whose engine had been bored out to 99 cm³ but which was distinguishable only by the finish – given that performance was virtually identical – and the price, which was 149,000 lire; and the Sport GT whose 99 cm³ engine had been slightly modified to increase power output, and consequently top speed. The Sport GT was sold at 162,000 lire. In 1963 a version of the Checca was prepared with a 124 cm³ engine, which placed it alongside the Centomila, but this model remained at the prototype stage.

Liberty 1962-1969

Power/rpm

1.5 hp at 4500 rpm

Dry weight

58.5 kg

Maximum speed

40 km/h

After an absence of a number of years – the 48 Moped had been deleted in 1959 – MV returned to the small capacity sector in 1962 with the Liberty, a machine destined to remain in production until 1969. In effect the Liberty was a true motorcycle in miniature: as the revised Highway Code of 1959 had abolished the obligation to fit pedals, there was no longer any particular reason to remain faithful to the classic pedal cycle layout. Furthermore, the moped, originally an ultra-utilitarian means of transport, was fast becoming a favourite with youngsters who were not yet old enough to take out a driving licence. MV were shrewd enough to offer this new clientele a vehicle that, in spite of the performance restrictions imposed by the new legislation, gave them the impression of possessing a real motorbike that was in no way inferior to the one Dad used to get to work. The engine was a four-stroke, so similar in appearance to MV's larger units that it was possible for the uninitiated to confuse the two, while the frame was the usual tubular and pressed-steel duplex cradle that characterized the rest of the company's range. The Liberty was originally fitted with a three-speed gearbox with a twistgrip gear change that was replaced in 1967 by a pedal-operated four-speed unit. The usual three versions were available: Sport, Super Sport and Turismo. In 1964 a 70 cm³ version was produced but this came into the motorcycle category and had to be registered.

TECHNICAL SPECIFICATIONS

Model/year	Liberty - 50 cm³ - 1962/67
Engine	4-stroke single, 39 × 40 mm - 47.7 cm³
Compression ratio	7.5 : 1
Cylinder head/barrel	Light alloy
Valve configuration	Inclined overhead
Timing system	Pushrod
Ignition	Flywheel magneto
Carburettor	Dell'Orto SH 14/9/2
Lubrication	Wet sump
Clutch	Wet multiplate
Gearbox	Unit construction, three speeds
Transmission	Geared primary; final drive, chain
Frame/wheelbase	Open cradle - 1100 mm
Front suspension	Telescopic fork
Rear suspension	Swinging arm with telescopic units
Wheels	Steel, wire spoked, 1.75 × 18" or 1.75 × 16"
Tyres	2.00-18", or 2.00-16"
Brakes	Central drum, 104 mm
Consumption	1.5 litres per 100 km
Fuel tank capacity	9 litres
Oil tank capacity	0.6 kg

The Liberty's pushrod engine. With the exception of this particular version, the Liberty had a twistgrip gearchange. Note the heel-operated rear brake pedal.

174

Three versions of the Liberty: above left, the Turismo from November 1961, fitted with 16" wheels; above right, the Turismo T; on the left, the Sport Junior also from November 1961, with 16" wheels and a much more solid look. All of these models had twistgrip gear changes.

The Liberty was later equipped with 18" wheels that gave it a sleeker, sportier look. This is the Sport S version.

A 70 cm³ version of the Liberty was presented at the 1964 Milan Trade Fair, but it did not enjoy much commercial success.

The Super Sport from November 1965 was heavily restyled. Note the front fork with exposed springs and the brakes with the false ventilation louvres.

176

The America version, characterized by a distinctive fuel tank, wide handlebars and flashy chromed accessories like the crash bars, was also introduced in November 1965.

The Sport S was also produced with a pedal gear change on the left. In this case the rear brake pedal was placed on the right (see the detail photo of the engine) and was operated with the heel.

Germano 1964-1968

The Germano (Mallard) moped, introduced in 1963 and produced for almost five years, represents something of an anomaly in the history of MV in that the company relied heavily on outside suppliers for a number of its components, including the engine. These components were produced by the many firms that were then springing up with astonishing rapidity in the Emilia region of Italy. Some of these firms became so successful that the area began to acquire a reputation as the heartland of Italian motorcycling at the expense of the traditional industrial areas of Lombardy and Piedmont. There were many reasons behind MV's decision to adopt this particular form of production, but the most important of these was the desire to market a new product as quickly and as cheaply as possible. This meant that recourse had to be made to outside suppliers capable of mass producing standardized components at extremely competitive prices. The Germano – which with a hint of condescension, was nicknamed the "Bolognese" by the MV factory – was first constructed with a pressed-steel beam frame in Turismo and Sport versions, and later with a tubular frame in Gran Turismo, Sport and America versions. The latter undoubtedly appealed to youngsters far more than the versions with the heavier beam frame. Prices for the Germano were extremely competitive, ranging from 115,000 to 120,000 lire according to the version in question.

Power/rpm
1.5 hp at 4500 rpm

Dry weight
50 kg

Maximum speed
40 km/h

In order to contain costs and to speed up development of the Germano, MV – for the only time in its history – relied on an engine produced by one of the largest specialist factories of the Emilia region.

TECHNICAL SPECIFICATIONS

Model/year	Germano - 50 cm³ - 1964-65
Engine	2-stroke single 39 × 40 mm - 47.7 cm³
Compression ratio	7 : 1
Cylinder head/barrel	Light alloy - cast iron
Valve configuration	–
Timing system	–
Ignition	Flywheel magneto
Carburettor	Bing
Lubrication	20 : 1 petroil
Clutch	Wet multiplate
Gearbox	Unit construction, three speeds
Transmission	Geared primary; final drive, chain
Frame/wheelbase	Pressed-steel beam - 1100 mm
Front suspension	Telescopic fork
Rear suspension	Swinging arm with telescopic elements
Wheels	Steel wire spoked, 1.75 × 18"
Tyres	2.00-18" front and rear
Brakes	Central drum, 104 mm
Consumption	1.9 litres per 100 km
Fuel tank capacity	4 litres
Oil tank capacity	–

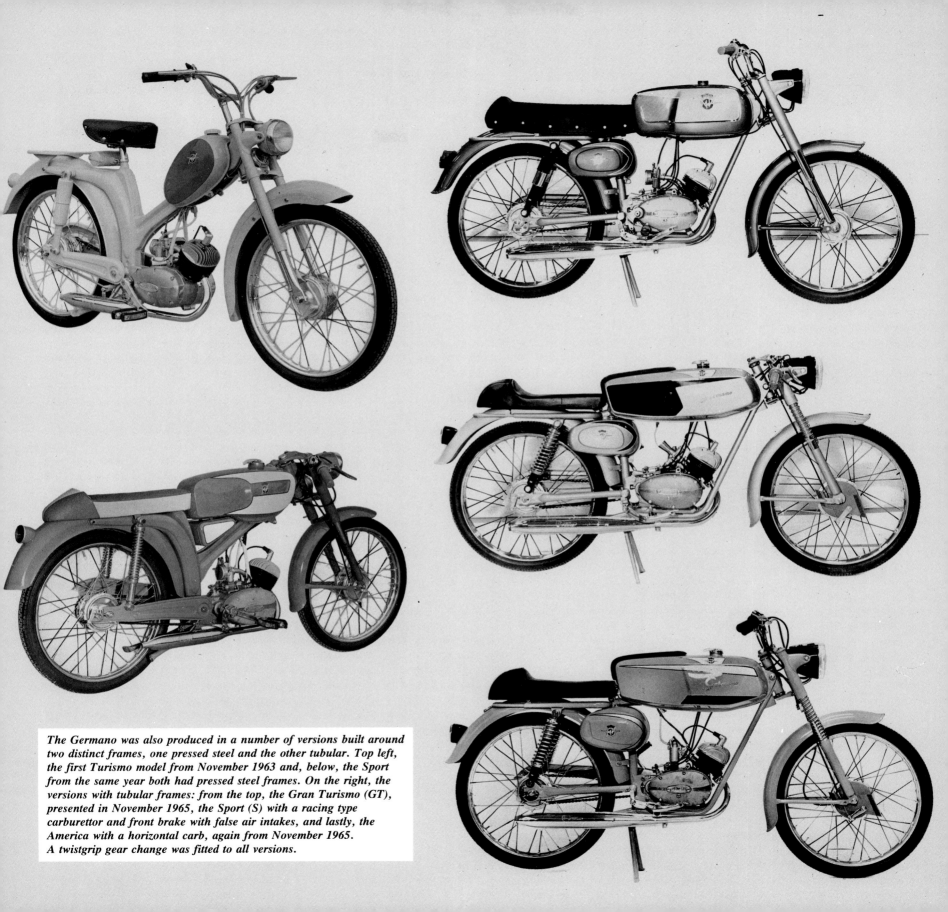

The Germano was also produced in a number of versions built around two distinct frames, one pressed steel and the other tubular. Top left, the first Turismo model from November 1963 and, below, the Sport from the same year both had pressed steel frames. On the right, the versions with tubular frames: from the top, the Gran Turismo (GT), presented in November 1965, the Sport (S) with a racing type carburettor and front brake with false air intakes, and lastly, the America with a horizontal carb, again from November 1965.
A twistgrip gear change was fitted to all versions.

Arno 166 GT 1964-1965

The Arno was born in November 1963, a rather bleak moment for the motorcycle industry, not only in Italy but throughout the world. The potential market for both sporting and utility motorcycles was steadily shrinking as improving economic conditions brought motor cars within the reach of an increasingly large segment of the population. The motorcycle tended to be regarded as an unwelcome reminder of harder times. On the other hand, economic progress had not yet reached the point where the motorcycle could be marketed as a recreational vehicle to be owned alongside a motor car. The presentation, therefore, of a four-stroke twin, even though it boasted a mere 166 cm³, was not only a declaration of faith in the future of the motorcycle, it was also a risky enterprise. At MV, where the manufacture of motorcycles was often a matter of the heart ruling the head, they pressed on regardless; and in this case the result was not just another show bike, but a model put into regular production and sold at 246,000 lire. This was not particularly cheap but not unreasonable considering the specification. It is true that the Arno was not one of MV's greatest successes, but it did serve to pave the way for subsequent twins of 250 cm³ or more, which became very popular when the fortunes of the motorcycle market eventually improved, and remained in the catalogue until the company wound up its motorcycle manufacturing division.

Power/rpm
7.5 hp at 6000 rpm

Maximum speed
105 km/h

Fuel consumption
3 litres per 100 km

TECHNICAL SPECIFICATIONS

Model/year	Arno - 166 cm³ - 1964/65
Engine	4-stroke twin 46.5 × 49 × 2 mm - 166.3 cm³
Compression ratio	7 : 1
Cylinder head/barrel	Light alloy
Valve configuration	Inclined overhead
Timing system	Pushrod
Ignition	Flywheel magneto
Carburettor	Dell'Orto MA 15 B
Lubrication	Wet sump
Clutch	Wet multiplate
Gearbox	Unit construction, four speeds
Transmission	Geared primary; final drive, chain
Frame/wheelbase	Open tubular cradle plus pressings - 1300 mm
Front suspension	Teledraulic fork
Rear suspension	Swinging arm with hydraulic dampers
Wheels	Steel, wire spoked, 2.50 × 18"
Tyres	2.75-18" front and rear
Brakes	Central drums, 170 mm front and 120 mm rear
Dry weight	145 kg
Fuel tank capacity	17 litres
Oil tank capacity	1.5 kg

The attractive Arno engine, with the cylinders inclined at 12 degrees and the spark plugs placed at the back of the cylinder head. The primary drive casing resembles that of the racing models.

The Arno was an up-market light motorcycle presented in a period when technically refined machines were not much in demand. Note the extrovert form of the fuel tank and the knee grips, once considered to be a useful accessory, but obsolete by that time. The twin carbs shared a central single float chamber. The bike was painted black with a metallic silver fuel tank.

125 GT-GTL 1964-1973

The 125 GT light motorcycle was originally intended to be the direct successor to the Centomila. In effect – apart from a few small differences in the paintwork – it was the same bike, but it was no longer sold with the incredible long distance guarantee. It was not long, however, before this motorcycle was restyled and improved mechanically to emerge as an entirely new product in its own right. The most important modification was the adoption of a five-speed gearbox, presented at the Milan Motorcycle Show in November 1965. At the same time a number of new versions were presented, the most noteworthy of which was perhaps the Scrambler, which had a different suspension layout and frame. The latter had a demountable lower cradle that also shielded the sump. Changes were also made to the mudguards, the exhaust system, the saddle, the handlebars etc. Finally, in 1969, the road models were also comprehensively facelifted involving the adoption of more modern styling including sleeker and lower fuel tanks. The side covers of the engine were also redesigned with more accentuated angles. The bikes were then equipped with a richer instrumentation pack including a rev counter. These modifications were also introduced on the 150 cm³ model described earlier. At first prices oscillated between 195,000 and 230,000 lire, but by 1973, when progressive devaluation had already begun to inflate the lira, these had leapt to 315-340,000 lire.

Power/rpm

9.5 hp at 8000 rpm

Dry weight

95 kg

Maximum speed

105 km/h

TECHNICAL SPECIFICATIONS

Model/year	Gran Turismo - 125 cm³ - 1964/65
Engine	4-stroke single 53 × 56 mm - 123.5 cm³
Compression ratio	10.5 : 1
Cylinder head/barrel	Light alloy - cast iron
Valve configuration	Inclined overhead
Timing system	Pushrod
Ignition	Flywheel magneto
Carburettor	Dell'Orto MB 22 B
Lubrication	Wet sump
Clutch	Wet multiplate
Gearbox	Unit construction, four-speeds
Transmission	Geared primary; final drive, chain
Frame/wheelbase	Tubular open duplex cradle plus pressings - 1280 mm
Front suspension	Teledraulic fork
Rear suspension	Swinging arm and hydraulic dampers
Wheels	Steel, wire spoked, 2.50 × 18"
Tyres	2.75-18" front and rear
Brakes	Central drums. 158 mm front, and 123.5 mm rear
Consumption	2.5 litres per 100 km
Fuel tank capacity	15 litres
Oil tank capacity	1.7 kg

In 1964 the Centomila was renamed even though nothing much had been changed, especially in the engine room. A year later, however, a five-speed gearbox was adopted.

The 125 Gran Turismo Lusso (GTL) from 1964. This version still had the four-speed gearbox.

The 125 Gran Turismo (GT), again from 1964. Note the different fuel tank.

The Gran Turismo Lusso (GTL) from November 1965, with the five-speed gearbox.

The 125 Scrambler was also introduced in November 1965. The cradle is closed under the engine.

184

The 125 Super Sport seen at the 1969 Milan Trade Fair. The GTLS and the 150 RS were virtually identical.

The 125 GT from 1971. As can be seen from the photograph, the design of the crankcase has been changed.

The 150 was also updated in line with the new styling trends: this is the 1971 GT, fitted with a five-speed gearbox.

125 Regolarità 1965-1970

Power/rpm
10 hp at 8000 rpm
Dry weight
98 kg
Maximum speed
100 km/h

MV were actively involved in trials competition from the very beginning, and in fact one of their first sporting victories was achieved in this speciality. By 1949 the firm was taking a more active part in such events, which provided some important wins in internationally famous competitions such as the "Sei Giorni" (ISDT). But then, as the marque became more involved in track competition, less and less attention was paid to trials until the point was reached where the activity was abandoned altogether. After 1960, however, MV reviewed their trials policy, largely in view of the fact that the sport was going through a period of particular popularity, both with the public and with the major Italian and European manufacturers. Things had changed over the previous decade, however, and production bikes were no longer adequate: specifically designed machines were required. The 125 Regolarità was produced to satisfy this need and, after a certain period of testing, it was also made available to privateers. The Regolarità was no adaptation of an already existing production bike, but a purpose-built machine. Proof of this, lies in the standard five-speed gearbox, a feature that did not appear on production tourers until some time later. The Regolarità remained available up until the end of 1970, with the list price gradually increasing from 310,000 to 380,000 lire.

The 125 Regolarità, specifically designed for competition, had benefitted from particular attention to detail: note the QD wheels, the stoneguard over the headlight, the folding footrests and the air filter.

The 125 Regolarità was equipped with long-travel Ceriani forks – the best available at the time. The fuel tank was spring mounted.

The engine of the 125 trials iron with the large air filter, and the cut-away crankcase cover which gave better access to the chain sprocket. Note also the sump guard that completes the cradle.

TECHNICAL SPECIFICATIONS

Model/year	125 Trials - 125 cm³ - 1965/70
Engine	4-stroke single 53 × 56 mm - 123.5 cm³
Compression ratio	10.5 : 1
Cylinder head/barrel	Light alloy
Valve configuration	Inclined overhead
Timing system	Pushrod
Ignition	Flywheel magneto
Carburettor	Dell'Orto MB 22 B
Lubrication	Wet sump
Clutch	Wet multiplate
Gearbox	Unit construction five-speeds
Transmission	Geared primary; final drive, chain
Frame/wheelbase	Tubular open duplex cradle plus pressings - 1330 mm
Front suspension	Teledraulic fork
Rear suspension	Swinging arm and hydraulic dampers
Wheels	Steel, wire spoked; front 2.50 × 19", rear 2.75 × 19"
Tyres	2.75-19" front and 3.25-19" rear
Brakes	Central drums. 180 mm front, and 150 mm rear
Consumption	3.3 litres per 100 km
Fuel tank capacity	13 litres
Oil tank capacity	1.7 kg

250 Twin 1966-1971

Power/rpm

19 hp at 7800 rpm

Dry weight

140 kg

Maximum speed

135 km/h

In 1965 the motorcycle market began to give the first encouraging signs of recovery. Many people, even those inhabiting the higher social echelons, had discovered the motorcycle as a badge of a certain socially acceptable nonconformism in a world where the motor car was no longer a rarity but a truly ubiquitous presence. Naturally such people could not be contented with a moped; something exclusive, large, powerful and sophisticated was required. Those were the last golden years of the British motorcycle industry as, at that time, the British were practically the only manufacturers of large bikes and therefore the only ones capable of satisfying the desires of the new class of élite motorcyclists. But the Italians, and also the Japaneses, were quick to see which way the wind was blowing and they entered the big bike sector with new and attractive products. The rest is history. MV, with the four-cylinder 600 described in the following pages, was one of the first companies to produce a model that reflected the spirit of the times; at the same time they also introduced an excellent 250 twin with very attractive performance and styling that was perfect for all those who were not interested in the bigger machines.

The 250, which actually entered production in 1967, was produced in a number of versions including the Scrambler, a bike adapted for light off-road work; by the end of the production run prices had risen from the original 320,000 to 474,000 lire.

The 1966 250 twin readdressed the theme introduced with the Arno a couple of years earlier, but in an economic climate rather more suited to larger bikes.

The Scrambler version of the 250 twin. Noteworthy details include the eyecatching exhaust pipes, the sump guard and the front fork.

The engine of the 250 twin had a different crankcase design from the Arno, while the plugs had been moved to the side of the cylinder.

TECHNICAL SPECIFICATIONS

Model/year	250 Twin - 250 cm^3 - 1967-71
Engine	4-stroke twin 53 × 56 × 2 mm - 247 cm^3
Compression ratio	10 : 1
Cylinder head/barrel	Light alloy
Valve configuration	Inclined overhead
Timing system	Pushrod
Ignition	Coil
Carburettor	Dell'Orto UB 22, Dell'Orto UB 22 S
Lubrication	Wet sump
Clutch	Wet multiplate
Gearbox	Unit construction five-speeds
Transmission	Geared primary; final drive, chain
Frame/wheelbase	Tubular open duplex cradle plus pressings - 1330 mm
Front suspension	Teledraulic fork
Rear suspension	Swinging arm and hydraulic dampers
Wheels	Steel, wire spoked, 2.25 × 18"
Tyres	2.75-18" front and 3.25-18" rear
Brakes	Front 180 mm twin-cam drum; rear 158 mm drum
Consumption	5.9 litres per 100 km
Fuel tank capacity	13 litres
Oil tank capacity	2 kg

4 Cylinder series 1965-1980

The rebirth of the Italian motorcycle industry began with the Milan Motorcycle Show of November 1965 where numerous new products were presented by the various manufacturers. The vast majority of those were attractive propositions, but the most sensational of them all was undoubtedly the MV 600 four. At last enthusiasts were able to buy a bike that was unlike anything else on the market, and one that was closely related to the most famous racing machines of the day into the bargain: the same machines that the likes of Surtees, Hailwood and the rising star Agostini had been riding to victory after victory for years. Despite this, the company intended the 600 to be a tourer and took a number of steps – the unusual cylinder capacity, for example – to discourage its use on the circuits. But the very name was enough to attract sporting riders like moths to a flame. As a matter of fact, the 600 four always suffered from something of an identity crisis: it was too much of a touring bike for some, too much of a racer for others, too expensive for everybody, and it was never completely convincing. The displacement was gradually increased to 800 cm³ for the final version. This big four was also the last bike – together with the Ipotesi – to be sold by MV.

Now that it is no longer in production the 600 form is enjoying sweet revenge over its one-time rivals as it has become one of the most sought-after and expensive collector's bikes in the world.

Power/rpm
50 hp at 8200 rpm
Dry weight
221 kg
Maximum speed
170 km/h

TECHNICAL SPECIFICATIONS

Model/year	600 Four - 600 cm³ - 1966/70
Engine	4-stroke four 58 × 56 × 4 mm - 591.5 cm³
Compression ratio	9.3 : 1
Cylinder head/barrel	Light alloy
Valve configuration	Inclined overhead
Timing system	Double overhead camshafts
Ignition	Coil
Carburettor	Dell'Orto MB 24, MB 24 S
Lubrication	Wet sump
Clutch	Wet multiplate
Gearbox	Unit construction five-speeds
Transmission	Geared primary; final drive, shaft
Frame/wheelbase	Tubular closed duplex cradle - 1390 mm
Front suspension	Teledraulic fork
Rear suspension	Swinging arm and hydraulic dampers
Wheels	Light alloy, wire spoked, 3.25 × 18"
Tyres	3.50-18" front and 4.00-18" rear
Brakes	Front, 216 mm mechanically operated dual discs; rear 200 mm drum
Consumption	5 litres per 100 km
Fuel tank capacity	20 litres
Oil tank capacity	3 kg

Despite the modifications made to adapt it to road use, the engine of the 600 four clearly revealed that it had sprung from the competition units of the same period. The transverse gearbox was linked to the final drive shaft via bevel gears.

On the right, the first version of the 600 four presented at the Milan Motorcycle Show in November 1965. Below, the second version, with siamesed silencers. The large rectangular headlight, the humped fuel tank and the stepped saddle were expressly requested by Count Domenico Agusta. Note the mechanically operated twin-disc front brake. The machine was painted black, and sold for 1,060,000 lire in 1966.

In November 1969 the Sport (left) appeared with an uprated 750 cm³ engine with four single silencers. It was finished in red, blue and white, and cost 1,980,000 lire. Below, the GT from November 1971, with slightly less sporting trim. It was painted white and bronze and sold for 1,950,000 lire.

TECHNICAL SPECIFICATIONS

Model/year	750 Sport - 750 cm³ - 1970/75
Engine	4-stroke four 65 × 56 × 4 mm - 742.9 cm³
Compression ratio	9.5 : 1
Cylinder head/barrel	Light alloy
Valve configuration	Inclined overhead
Timing system	Double overhead camshafts
Ignition	Coil
Carburettor	Two Dell'Orto UB 24 B2, two Dell'Orto UB 24 BS2
Lubrication	Wet sump
Clutch	Wet multiplate
Gearbox	Unit construction five-speeds
Transmission	Geared primary; final drive, shaft
Frame/wheelbase	Tubular closed duplex cradle - 1390 mm
Front suspension	Teledraulic fork
Rear suspension	Swinging arm and hydraulic dampers
Wheels	Light alloy, wire spoked, 3.25 × 18"
Tyres	3.50-18" front and 4.00-18" rear
Brakes	Front 230 mm four-cam drum; rear 200 mm drum
Consumption	6.5 litres per 100 km
Fuel tank capacity	24 litres
Oil tank capacity	3 kg

The dynamotor, located beneath the final drive shaft bevel gearing, was equipped with differentiated twin belts and served as both starter and generator.

Power/rpm	69 hp at 7900 rpm
Dry weight	230 kg
Maximum speed	200 km/h

Below, the November 1973 version of the 750 Sport. As well as the fuel tank paintwork, the shape of the saddle was altered. A 4LS front drum brake was still fitted as was the four silencer exhaust system. The price remained at 1,980,000 lire.

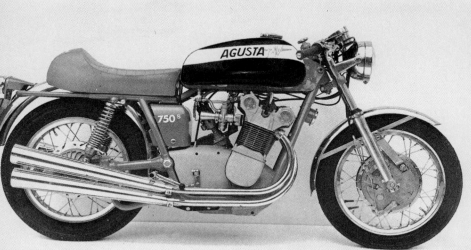

In the summer of 1974 the 750 Sport received a fairing and a Scarab hydraulic twin-disc front brake (above). On the right, the Super Sport of November 1971, credited – a little optimistically – with a top speed of 260 km/h. Price: 2,500,000 lire.

193

The ultimate version, the 750 S America with a 790 cm³ engine. On the right, as it was first presented (1975), and below, the 1976 model with black exhaust pipes. Cast alloy wheels and a rear disc brake were available as optional extras.

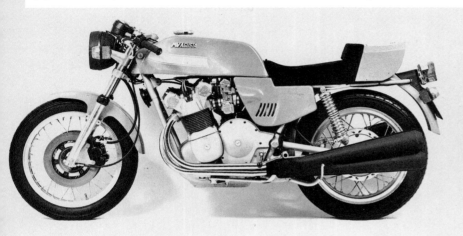

TECHNICAL SPECIFICATIONS

Model/year	750 Sport America - 800 cm³ - 1975/80
Engine	4-stroke four 67 × 56 × 4 mm - 789.3 cm³
Compression ratio	10 : 1
Cylinder head/barrel	Light alloy
Valve configuration	Inclined overhead
Timing system	Double overhead camshafts
Ignition	Coil
Carburettor	Four Dell'Orto VHB 26 D
Lubrication	Wet sump
Clutch	Wet multiplate
Gearbox	Unit construction five-speeds
Transmission	Geared primary; final drive shaft
Frame/wheelbase	Tubular closed duplex cradle - 1390 mm
Front suspension	Teledraulic fork
Rear suspension	Swinging arm and hydraulic dampers
Wheels	Light alloy, wire spoked, 3.25 × 18"
Tyres	3.50-18" front and 4.00-18" rear
Brakes	Front 280 mm twin discs; rear 200 mm central drum
Consumption	8 litres per 100 km
Fuel tank capacity	19 litres
Oil tank capacity	3 kg

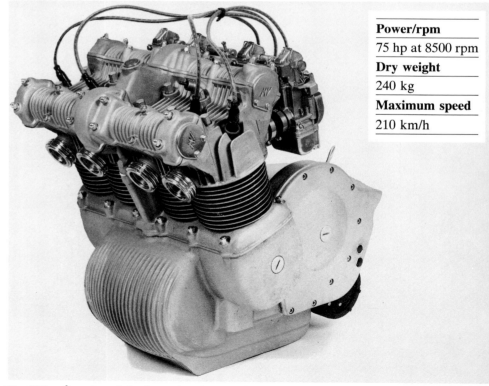

The 790 cm³ engine of the Sport America was fed by four carburettors with concentric float chambers.

Power/rpm
75 hp at 8500 rpm
Dry weight
240 kg
Maximum speed
210 km/h

350 Twin 1970-1974

The 350 twin was introduced in November 1969, at the Milan Motorcycle show. The designers of this attractive newcomer had taken the power unit from the old 250 and increased the bore from 53 to 63 mm in order to obtain an undersquare engine with extra power and pick-up by courtesy of the higher engine revolutions. The bike was the inevitable reply to the demands of the new clientele, who wanted sparkling acceleration and high top speeds from medium-sized bikes too. The 350 joined the lineup alongside the 250, but it eventually replaced the latter completely in the MV range, an incontrovertible sign that the public clearly preferred the bike that guaranteed the most spectacular results.

During its fairly short life – it was to be replaced in 1975 by a new (in terms of styling at any rate) and, as we shall see, very interesting model – the 350 was produced in a number of variants: apart from a Scrambler version with typical off-road trim that appeared in November 1971, we also ought to mention the introduction of electronic ignition in the spring of 1972, and a snappy boy-racer version fitted with a full fairing (made in conformity with the dimensions stipulated in the sporting regulations, but equipped with a headlight), which was also presented in 1972. The list prices of the 350 reflected the galloping inflation that typified those years and they soon rose from the initial 560,000 lire to the 678,000 lire of the last year of production.

Power/rpm
28 hp at 8400 rpm

Dry weight
149 kg

Maximum speed
155 km/h

The 350, presented in November 1969, was derived from the 250 Twin. The bike shown here is the Sport (S) version with coil ignition. The colour scheme was red and white and the price was 560,000 lire.

Top left, the GT presented at the Milan Trade Fair in 1971; it cost 550,000 lire and was painted black and red with chromed mudguards. Top right, the Scrambler model of the same year with upswept exhaust pipes.

Above left, a different version of the Scrambler from November 1971. Right, the restyled Sport fitted with electronic ignition presented at the 1972 Trade Fair. It was sold at 605,000 lire.

Left, the GT Elettronica (GTE) fitted with cowhorn handlebars and direction indicators. The Sport Elettronica was also available with a fairing that resembled the one used in competition.

TECHNICAL SPECIFICATIONS

Model/year	350 Sport - 350 cm³ - 1970/74
Engine	4-stroke twin 63 × 56 × 2 mm - 348.9 cm³
Compression ratio	9 : 1
Cylinder head/barrel	Light alloy
Valve configuration	Inclined overhead
Timing system	Pushrod
Ignition	Coil
Carburettor	Dell'Orto UB 24 BS 2, Dell'Orto UB 24 B2
Lubrication	Wet sump
Clutch	Wet multiplate
Gearbox	Unit construction five-speeds
Transmission	Geared primary; final drive, chain
Frame/wheelbase	Tubular open duplex cradle plus pressings - 1330 mm
Front suspension	Teledraulic fork
Rear suspension	Swinging arm and hydraulic dampers
Wheels	Light alloy, wire spoked, 1.85 × 18"
Tyres	Front 2.75-18", rear 3.25-18"
Brakes	Front 200 mm twin-cam drum; rear 200 mm drum
Consumption	5.2 litres per 100 km
Fuel tank capacity	13 litres
Oil tank capacity	2 kg

Above, a police version of the GT Elettronica fitted out with pannier bags, crash bars, windscreen, siren and direction indicators.

350 Ipotesi 1975-1980

Power/rpm

34 hp at 8500 rpm

Dry weight

150 kg

Maximum speed

170 km/h

In 1973 the situation at MV began to become confused: those who believed the firm ought to abandon motorcycle manufacture were steadily gaining ground; but pride, and the desire to continue the glorious tradition of the marque were still strong. For the time being this permitted those in favour of soldiering on to win the day with the result that MV got to work on the preparation of new versions of the four-cylinder bike and a new middleweight, whose styling was destined to arouse a great deal of interest. This was the birth of the Ipotesi (Hypothesis); a motorcycle first presented as a styling exercise – but one that the firm intended to develop further – at the Milan Motorcycle Show in November 1973. The design was by Giorgio Giugiaro, and was based on horizontal lines and very angular shapes. The open duplex cradle frame was a new design with the top frame rails running in a straight line from the steering head to the rear suspension, but shaped to follow the lines of the fuel tank. The engine was based on the previous 350 twin with electronic ignition, but it looked completely different on the outside thanks to the new-style squarish outer casings. Cast-alloy wheels and disc brakes completed this extremely modern look. The Ipotesi, which entered production in 1975, was a popular bike but the decision to abandon production prevented it from obtaining the degree of success with the public that it undoubtedly deserved.

TECHNICAL SPECIFICATIONS

Model/year	350 Sport - 350 cm³ - 1975/80
Engine	4-stroke twin 63 × 56 × 2 mm - 349 cm³
Compression ratio	9.5 : 1
Cylinder head/barrel	Light alloy
Valve configuration	Inclined overhead
Timing system	Pushrod
Ignition	Dansi electronic flywheel magneto
Carburettor	Dell'Orto VHB 24 B, VHB 24 BS
Lubrication	Wet sump
Clutch	Wet multiplate
Gearbox	Unit construction five-speeds
Transmission	Geared primary; final drive, chain
Frame/wheelbase	Tubular open cradle - 1400 mm
Front suspension	Teledraulic fork
Rear suspension	Swinging arm and hydraulic dampers
Wheels	Cast light alloy, front 2.50 × 18", rear 3.00 × 18"
Tyres	Front 2.75-18", rear 3.25-18"
Brakes	Front 230 mm twin discs; rear 230 mm disc
Consumption	4.3 litres per 100 km
Fuel tank capacity	19 litres
Oil tank capacity	2 kg

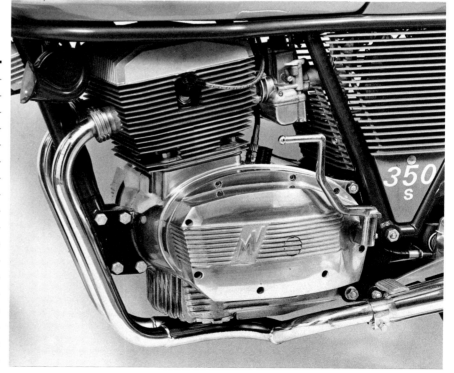

The engine of the '75 350 Sport, better known as the Ipotesi. It had been completely redesigned externally, but the internal mechanical parts were unchanged.

With the introduction of the Ipotesi the 350 was brought dramatically up-to-date as far as design was concerned. The idea was to adapt function to modern concepts of form without plunging headlong into futuristic styling.

The design of the Ipotesi was the work of Giorgio Giugiaro. In this example note the black exhaust pipes – the latest racing technology. It cost 1,232,000 lire.

125 Sport 1975-1980

Following in the footsteps of the 350 Sport – better known to most people as the Ipotesi, as the original prototype had been called – came the 125 Sport. This was introduced in 1975 and can fairly be described as the marque's swansong.

To tell the truth the relationship with the Ipotesi was more apparent than real and derived mainly from the new angular design of the engine casings and a few bodywork details. The engine was a pushrod single with the traditional MV engine dimensions of 53 x 56 mm, which the Verghera-based company had used even for their earliest strokers. The frame, which also had straight top rails, was a full rather than an open duplex cradle; wire wheels were fitted in preference to the cast-alloy variety and the rear brake was a drum. Despite these differences this model too eventually became known as the Ipotesi. The basic model was later joined by a version fitted with a dolphin fairing, just as had happened previously in the case of the four-cylinder and the 350 twin. The 125 Sport went on sale at 784,000 lire; by the time the last examples were sold in 1980 the price had gone up to 840,000 lire, without the fairing. By this time production had ceased and all that remained were a few parts in the stores. Once these have been sold the final curtain will fall for the last time on a machine that for a few brief years had succeeded in becoming, at least in the sporting field, the most celebrated motorcycle in the world.

Power/rpm
12 hp at 8500 rpm
Dry weight
103 kg
Maximum speed
115 km/h

TECHNICAL SPECIFICATIONS

Model/year	125 Sport - 125 cm^3 - 1975/80
Engine	4-stroke single 53 × 56 - 123.5 cm^3
Compression ratio	9.8 : 1
Cylinder head/barrel	Light alloy
Valve configuration	Inclined overhead
Timing system	Pushrod
Ignition	Dansi electronic flywheel magneto
Carburettor	Dell'Orto VHB 22
Lubrication	Wet sump
Clutch	Wet multiplate
Gearbox	Unit construction five-speeds
Transmission	Geared primary; final drive, chain
Frame/wheelbase	Tubular closed duplex cradle - 1300 mm
Front suspension	Teledraulic fork
Rear suspension	Swinging arm and hydraulic dampers
Wheels	Light alloy, wire spoked, 1.6 × 18"
Tyres	Front and rear 2.75-18"
Brakes	Front 230 mm disc; rear 136 mm drum
Consumption	2.7 litres per 100 km
Fuel tank capacity	19 litres
Oil tank capacity	2 kg

The engine of the 125 was also restyled along the lines of the Ipotesi: squared crankcase cover and rectangular head and barrel.

F4-750 1997-...

THE ENGINE

The 4 cylinders of the MV Agusta F4 represent the standard for comparison in the Supersport category. The size of the head and its cover have made it possible to reduce the dimensions of the fuel tank to a level never seen before with a 4-cylinder.

The block with removable gearbox

A removable gearbox has been adopted based on the experience of the Cagiva Racing Department during the years of the 500 World Championship.

It will be therefore possible for both the road user and the racing pilot, of all levels, to optimise the distancing of the ratios of the motorcycle depending on the track or the average usage conditions.

GENERAL FEATURES

Dimensions, weight, capacities	wheelbase mm 1.412 overall length mm 2.026 overall width mm 685 saddle height mm 79 min. ground clearance mm 130 trail mm 103,7 dry weight Kg 180 fuel tank capacity l 22 transmission oil l 3,5
Performances	maximum speed Km / h 275 average fuel consumption Km / l 13 max. horse power - r.p.m. (at the crankshaft) KW 93 / 12.200 - CV 126 / 12.200 max. torque Nm 72 / 9.000 Kgm 7,3 / 9.000

TECHNICAL DATA

Engine	four cylinder, four stroke
Bore	mm 73,8
Stroke	mm 43,8
Total displacement	cm³ 749,4
Compression ratio	12 : 1
Starting	electric
Cooling system	liquid cooled, water - oil heat exchanger
Timing system	"d.o.h.c.", radial valve
Lubrication	wet sump
Engine management system	"Weber - Marelli" 1,6 M ignition injection integrated system; induction discharge electronic ignition; "Multipoint" electronic injection
Clutch	wet, multi - disc
Gearbox	six speed, constant mesh

The radial valve cylinder head

And for the first time on a high-performance road bike a timing system has been adopted with four radial valves per cylinder with direct control of the valves by means of tappets and tapered cams. The increased fluxing of the flow has resulted in a perfect harmony of torque and horsepower, which grant the motorbike a smooth supply of power without troughs.

The timing system with transmission

Nothing was spared in the search for performance: to attain a highly compact combustion chamber and the smallest angle between the valves in the category (22 degrees) without running up against a decrease in the resistance of the middle zone of the driving shaft, a specially designed transmission system was adopted to control the timing chain. In this way, the toothed wheels on the camshafts could be reduced to the current diameter, thereby allowing for the most compact head and cover unit in the category.

Fuel supply-intake system

The F4 uses a sophisticated fuel supply-intake system whose most valuable component is the electronic injection utilising a special processing unit that grants the vehicle optimum fuel supply performance, thus giving reduced fuel consumption and emissions.

Rolling chassis	steel tubular trellis with light alloy plate rear swing arm fulcrum
Front suspension	"upside down" telescopic hydraulic fork with rebound - compression damping and spring preload adjustment fork leg dia. mm 49 travel on leg axis mm 113, manufacturer "Showa"
Rear suspension	progressive, with light alloy single sided swing arm single shock absorber with rebound - compression damping and spring preload adjustment wheel travel mm 120, shock absorber manufacturer "Öhlins"
Front brake	double steel floating disc with light alloy flange, disc dia. mm 310 "Nissin" six pot caliper with 0.89 - 1.00 - 1.19 in. dia.
Rear brake	single steel disc; disc dia. mm 210 "Nissin" four pot caliper with 1.00 in. dia.
Front rim	material light alloy size 3,50"x 17"
Rear rim	material light alloy size 6,00"x 17"
Front tire	manufacturer and type "Pirelli" / "Michelin" size 120 / 65 - ZR 17
Rear tire	manufacturer and type "Pirelli" / "Michelin" size 190 / 50 - ZR 17
Electrical system	voltage 12 V lamp wattage double polyellipsoidal head light low beam 55 W high beam 60 W pilot light 5 W tail light with double bulb pilot light 5 + 5 W stop light 21 + 21 W turn signals 10 W battery 12 V - 9Ah alternator 650 W A / at 5.000 r.p.m. ignition - Injection system 45 W

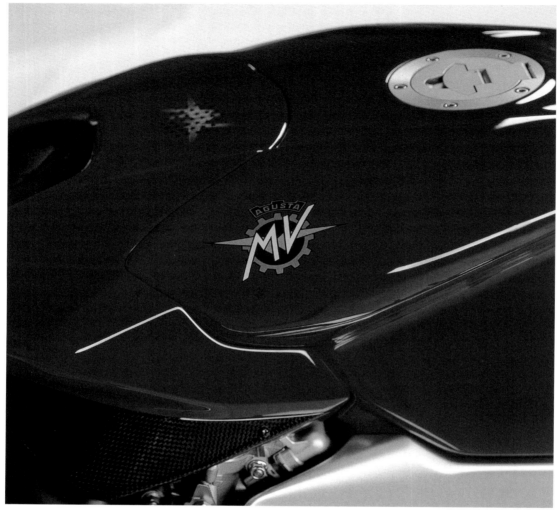

allowing the separation in the trellis/plate connecting points to enable the division of the bike into two distinct sections: the front end with the steel cage connected to it; and the rear part with the swing-arm pivot point plates and the tail end, leaving the engine free from any superstructures.

Swing-arm

The F4 single-sided swing-arm cast in a light alloy was the object of intensive scientific analyses which led to the creation of a superior component. The values of torsional and bending rigidity, the low weight, the highly resistant section of the curved arm, whose innovative "arc" with integrated truss grants the component uncommon individual style, giving an outstanding component.

Suspension

At the front, the F4 has an upside down fork with 49 mm diameter legs for a 113 mm wheel travel, generous adjustments for compression, rebound and spring preloading and above all a system for fixing the front wheel spindle with quick-release clamps all to endow this component with top-rate performance.

The steering head, cast in an open-sectioned light alloy, has a characteristic diamond-patterned prism de-

Cooling system

The large-sized concave radiator has been conceived to obtain a high number of "elements" and has been equipped with a system of "high efficiency turbolators"; that provide a high level of thermal exchange.

The radiator is assisted by an electric fan that is activated by means of a flow conveyor and by a "heat exchanger."

Exhaust system

The four pipes exiting the engine take a sinuous course that envelopes the engine, perfectly copying its forms, to lead to a totally original expansion/silencing system.

This system is composed of symmetrical "elements" in which the two expansion units, specially fitted with a diaphragm, open out by means of silencer "organ pipe."

CHASSIS

The F4's frame is made up of a "mixed" steel and aluminium structure. The main section is composed of a trestle in round chromemolybdenum steel tubes that wrap round the engine and connects at the rear to light alloy plates that provide a pivot point for the swing-arm.

What most characterises the "mixed" frame of the F4 is its special feature of

sign that gives greater stiffness while the lower yoke, also cast in light alloy but with a closed section is meant to support the greater stresses it is subject to.

The rear end features a "floating" suspension unit based on a single air/oil shock absorber driven by kinematic motion operating with a "progressive articulation" that ensures the rear wheel with a travel of 120 mm.

The shock absorber, which can be adjusted for compression, rebound and spring preload, is activated by a special rocker that can be placed on two different pivot points, which allow different "progression curves"; the rocker is moved by the swing-arm by means of a special counteracting structural element with a variable length.

This allows the bike's set-up to be varied.

Steering head angle adjustment device

On the F4 it is possible to adjust the steering head angle while keeping the wheelbase invaried.

This is achieved through an eccentric support of the steering bearings. With just a simple adjustment, different steering head angles are obtained to conform to the personal specifications.

Wheels

F4's front has the classic 3.50" x 17" sized rim with a five "star."

At the rear, however, a rim measuring 6.00" x 17" has been chosen.

Though its form echoes the pentagonal star shape of the front, its design is deliberately different from its twin at the front.

The attachment to the rear wheel spindle is the job of one large, central nut that is similar in terms of its functional concept and size to the one used for all the current F1 vehicles.

As for the tyres, which where specially designed for the F4, the CRC engineers together with the technicians from the supplying companies, concluded on a very particular size for the front tyre of 120/65 ZR 17 where as the rear is 190/50 ZR 17.

Braking system

The front brake consists of calipers each of which has 6 opposed different diameter cylinders derived from Cagiva's racing expertise.

The front brake set up is served by two 310mm diameter floating disks.

The rear boasts a 4 pistoned caliper and a single 210mm disk.

Steering damper

Clearly derived from the racing bikes, the steering damper is located transver-

sally in relation to the forward direction of the vehicle. This is to allow the greatest performance with perfectly symmetrical responses for left and right movement of the steering unit.

Lights

The twin stacked polyellipsoidals are very effective and give an unmistakable character rendering possible a very narrow fairing for obvious aerodynamic (small frontal area) and styling advantages. At the rear there is a twin-lamp

light with triangular lenses set into the tail's end section.

Instruments

The "mixed" composition of the instruments includes an "analogue" electronic rev counter, a multifunctional display and a set of warning lamps. The rev counter, with a maximum count of 17,000 r.p.m., has a large dial to ensure legibility even a high speeds.

The display oversees the tachometer, odometer, double trip, water temperature and clock.

The parameters can be set in kilometres/hour and Celsius degrees in addition to miles per hour and Fahrenheit degrees.

The warning lamps signal the lights, high beams, neutral, direction indicators, sidestand, current generator, rev-limiter and oil pressure.

Controls

Light alloy semi-handlebars anchored into fork sleeves by means of practical "bracelet" clamps.

The optimum slant, the perfect grip, the ergonomic, adjustable levers give the F4's cockpit absolute efficiency. As for the pedal controls, the bike is equipped with precious supports pressed in aluminium alloy which allow the set-up of the foot pegs through a practical eccentric system. The gear change and brake levers are also fitted with an adjustment system.

Styling

The work of Massimo Tamburini and his CRC staff is composed of parts of a mosaic connected together with racing-inspired quick fasteners. The study of the entire frame led to the production of a sharp, elegant exterior with overall dimensions comparable to those of motorcycles having a much smaller displacement. The pointed headlight fairing, which enfolds and extends to the front, the tank, the single-seater tail to top off the rear section graced with an exhaust system anticipate style and technology for years to come.

COMMERCIAL VEHICLES

Commercial vehicles 1947-68

In common with the majority of Italian motorcycle manufacturers, MV were also involved in the commercial vehicle sector, for which they produced a small number of those curious little delivery tricycles ("motocarri") still a common sight on Italian roads to this day. This was already a growth area before the second World War and it continued to flourish for many years afterwards. As far as MV was concerned the production of goods vehicles was always of marginal importance, but nevertheless a number of models were produced. The first appeared as early as 1947, when the company was still finding its feet: this was a vehicle with a front-mounted loading platform, and a 98 cm³ two-stroke engine, of which only a few examples were produced. The theme was taken up again in 1955 and this time the result was a vehicle with a rear loading platform, a design by then accepted as the most rational layout; the engine was derived from the single overhead camshaft unit used to power the contemporary light motorcycle of the same capacity. In 1959 two further vehicles were introduced in quick succession; these were more fully developed products complete with metal cabs and reverse gear; the first – the Centauro – was powered by a 150 cm³ four-stroke engine, the second – the Tevere – was fitted with a 235 cm³ engine and reduction gearing (the four-speed gearbox was still used). MV commercial vehicle production ended in 1968. Just for the record, we ought to mention the fact that the Verghera-based manufacturer also laid plans for a small delivery tricycle with a "regulation" 50 cm³ engine, but this tiddler was abandoned at the prototype stage and never made it into production.

Power/rpm	
3.5 hp at 4500 rpm	
Dry weight **Loading capacity**	
160 kg/250 kg	
Maximum speed	
40 km/h	

TECHNICAL SPECIFICATIONS

Model/year	Delivery Tricycle - 98 cm³ - 1947/48
Engine	2-stroke single 48 × 54 mm - 97.7 cm³
Compression ratio	6 : 1
Cylinder head/barrel	Light alloy - cast iron
Valve configuration	–
Timing system	–
Ignition	Flywheel magneto
Carburettor	Dell'Orto TA 16 A
Lubrication	16 : 1 petroil
Clutch	Wet multiplate
Gearbox	Unit construction, 3-speed + reverse, reduction gears
Transmission	Geared primary; final drive, chain
Frame/wheelbase	Tubular and pressed steel
Front suspension	Leaf spring
Rear suspension	Rigid frame
Wheels	Steel discs, 3.75-8"
Tyres	4.00-8" front and rear
Brakes	Hydraulic drum
Consumption	4 litres per 100 km
Fuel tank capacity	8 litres
Oil tank capacity	–

The first MV transport vehicle, introduced in 1947, had a tubular frame integrated with pressed-steel elements, steering via a car-type wheel, rear-wheel drive, hydraulic brakes, and a wooden loading box.

Power/rpm
8 hp at 5600 rpm
Dry weight
Loading capacity
250kg/350kg
Maximum speed
50 km/h

In 1955 a delivery tricycle with a single-cam 175 cm³ engine with forced-air cooling was produced. It cost 375,000 lire.

Power/rpm
7hp at 5500 rpm
Dry weight
Loading capacity
270kg/350kg
Maximum speed
60 km/h

The Centauro delivery tricycle from 1959. The traditional motorcycle-type structure was abandoned and we now have a decidedly rational vehicle from the point of view of driving comfort as well as utility.

TECHNICAL SPECIFICATIONS

Model/year	Delivery Tricycle - 175 cm³ - 1955/1958
Engine	4-stroke single 59.5 × 62 mm - 172.3 cm³
Compression ratio	6.6 : 1
Cylinder head/barrel	Light alloy
Valve configuration	Inclined overhead
Timing system	Overhead camshaft
Ignition	Flywheel magneto
Carburettor	Dell'Orto MA 18 B
Lubrication	Wet sump
Clutch	Wet multiplate
Gearbox	Unit construction, 4-speed + reverse
Transmission	Geared primary; final drive, shaft
Frame/wheelbase	Tubular - 1800 mm
Front suspension	Teledraulic fork
Rear suspension	Leaf spring
Wheels	Front, steel, wire spoked 2.25-17"; rear, discs 4.00-15"
Tyres	Front 3.50-17", rear 4.25-15"
Brakes	Drum
Consumption	4.5 litres per 100 km
Fuel tank capacity	14 litres
Oil tank capacity	1.8 kg

TECHNICAL SPECIFICATIONS

Model/year	Centauro - 150 cm³ - 1959/1966
Engine	4-stroke single 59.5 × 54 mm - 150.1 cm³
Compression ratio	7 : 1
Cylinder head/barrel	Light alloy - cast iron
Valve configuration	Inclined overhead
Timing system	Pushrod
Ignition	Flywheel magneto
Carburettor	Dell'Orto MA 18 B
Lubrication	Wet sump
Clutch	Wet multiplate
Gearbox	Unit construction, 4-speed + separate reverser
Transmission	Geared primary; final drive, shaft
Frame/wheelbase	Tubular and pressed-steel - 1720 mm
Front suspension	Trailing links
Rear suspension	Leaf spring
Wheels	Steel discs 3.75 × 8"
Tyres	4.00-8" front and rear
Brakes	Drum
Consumption	3 litres per 100 km
Fuel tank capacity	12 litres
Oil tank capacity	2 kg

TECHNICAL SPECIFICATIONS

Model/year	Tevere Trasporto - 235 cm³ - 1959/68
Engine	4-stroke single 69 × 62 mm - 231.7 cm³
Compression ratio	6.5 : 1
Cylinder head/barrel	Light alloy - cast iron
Valve configuration	Inclined overhead
Timing system	Pushrod
Ignition	Flywheel magneto
Carburettor	Dell'Orto MB 22
Lubrication	Wet sump
Clutch	Wet multiplate
Gearbox	Unit construction, 4-speed + reverse + reduction gearing
Transmission	Geared primary; final drive, shaft
Frame/wheelbase	Tubular and pressed steel - 1936 mm
Front suspension	Leading links and teledraulic elements
Rear suspension	Leaf spring
Wheels	Steel discs 4.50-10"
Tyres	5.00-10" TL front and rear
Brakes	Drum
Consumption	6 litres per 100 km
Fuel tank capacity	15 litres
Oil tank capacity	2 kg

The mechanical components of the Centauro, with the 150 cm³ engine, four-speed gearbox, shaft drive and separate reverser.

Power/rpm

9 hp at 5500 rpm

Dry weight
Loading capacity

396kg/700kg

Maximum speed

54 km/h

RACING BIKES

 **Two-Stroke 1946**

MV had only been in business for a few months when their modest, innocuous looking machines began to be used – victoriously it should be noted – in more than a few sporting events. This may well have been the point at which MV management (another way of saying Conte Domenico Agusta) contracted the racing "bug", we do not know; the fact is that these early wins were soon followed by the appearance of the first true MV racer, which was introduced to the pu-

blic at the Milan Motorcycle Show in November 1946. This proto-projectile from Cascina Costa was not that different from the contemporary touring bike: the engine was still a 98 cm³ unit construction affair with three ports and a three-speed gearbox; the frame was still a tubular single-loop and even the long chainguard for the fi-

nal drive chain was still fitted. Power output had been increased by about 1.5 hp compared to the production bike and top speed approached 100 km/h, a figure that would make even a cyclist chuckle today. But it was quick enough for those days and above all there were a number of "competition-type" features to please

the enthusiast: brand new telescopic forks, an enlarged fuel tank, footrests set well aft and a generously proportioned saddle and pillion pad. The bike took part in various races in 1947, often with victorious results; but, with public interest focused on the larger capacity machines, it was replaced for 1948 by a faster and "meaner" 125.

Power/rpm
5 hp at 5400 rpm
Dry weight
65 kg
Maximum speed
95 km/h

The sleek and seductive lines of the first MV racer, the 98 from 1948, and the engine of the same bike. It was painted red.

TECHNICAL SPECIFICATIONS

Model/year	98 Sport - 98 cm³ - 1946/47
Engine	2-stroke single 49 × 52 mm - 98 cm³
Compression ratio	7 : 1
Cylinder head/barrel	Light alloy - cast iron
Valve configuration	–
Timing system	–
Ignition	Flywheel magneto
Carburettor	Dell'Orto RAO 20
Lubrication	10 : 1 petroil
Clutch	Wet multiplate
Gearbox	Unit construction, three speeds
Transmission	Geared primary; final drive, chain
Frame/wheelbase	Tubular closed cradle - 1250 mm
Front suspension	Telescopic fork
Rear suspension	Plunger-box
Wheels	Light alloy, wire spoked, 2.25 × 19"
Tyres	2.50-19" front and rear
Brakes	Lateral drums 130 mm front and rear
Consumption	–
Fuel tank capacity	13 litres
Oil tank capacity	–

213

125 2-stroke 3-speed 1948

Power/rpm

9 hp at 6900 rpm

Dry weight

55 kg

Maximum speed

120 km/h

At the same time as the new MV 125 cm³ single appeared on the market, development began on a racing version of the same cubic capacity. Light motorcycle racing had very quickly become enormously popular, so much so that the Italian Motorcycling Federation decided to enliven the Championship by reintroducing the 125 category. This amounted to a death-knell for the local events run in the shadow of the parish church tower for the benefit of a few enthusiasts; now the races were highly organized affairs and it was necessary to prepare for them seriously. At first, to tell the truth, the various manufacturers felt that production bikes, after only a few modifications, would be sufficiently competitive and consequently the first MV racer was not very different to the standard models. During the course of the season, however, the pressing need to produce results led to a revision of this opinion and substantial modifications were rapidly made: the first externally visible change was the adoption of a cylinder head with considerably extended finning, which allowed MV to win the first really important race of its career, the Grand Prix of Nations held in Faenza in 1948. The three-speed 125 had a fairly short life – it was replaced in 1949 by a new model with a four-speed gearbox – but it still occupies an important place in the history of the company, not least because it allowed several future MV stars to win their spurs, including the great Carlo Ubbiali.

TECHNICAL SPECIFICATIONS

Model/year	125 Three-speed - 125 cm³ - 1948
Engine	2-stroke single 53 × 56 mm - 123.5 cm³
Compression ratio	8.5 : 1
Cylinder head/barrel	Light alloy - cast iron
Valve configuration	–
Timing system	–
Ignition	Flywheel magneto
Carburettor	Dell'Orto SS 25 A
Lubrication	8 : 1 petroil
Clutch	Wet multiplate
Gearbox	Unit construction, three speeds
Transmission	Geared primary; final drive, chain
Frame/wheelbase	Tubular closed cradle - 1260 mm
Front suspension	Girder fork
Rear suspension	Plunger-box
Wheels	Light alloy, wire spoked, 2.25 × 21"
Tyres	2.50-21" front and rear
Brakes	Lateral drums
Consumption	–
Fuel tank capacity	14 litres
Oil tank capacity	–

The compact engine of the 125 Three-speed, directly derived from the touring machines, in its last version with the enlarged cylinder head. Note the unusual legend "Agusta Milano".

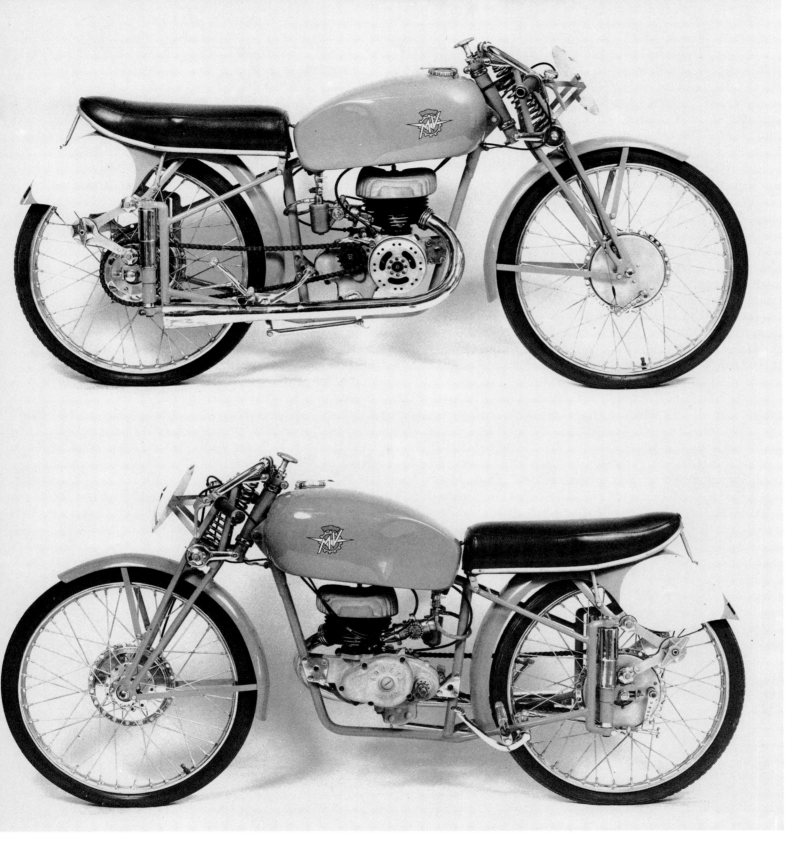

The MV 125 as it appeared at the 1948 Grand Prix of Nations at Faenza with an enlarged fuel tank and dualseat. The cylinder head/barrel assembly was larger than the crankcase.

The structure of the MV 125 was typified by lightness and simplicity – note the frame and wheels.

215

125 Two-Stroke Four-speed 1949-50

The programme of renewal carried out by MV in the production bike sector during 1949 naturally had an effect on what was happening in the racing department: the racing 125 made its appearance at the beginning of the season also had the power egg engine, the four-speed gearbox, and the frame with the swinging arm rear suspension. Somewhat strangely, this version was also fitted with old fashioned girder forks, still apparently more reliable than the telescopic forks mounted on the 98, which were technically very interesting but not yet fully developed. The 125 competition bike was offered for sale to the general public at a price somewhere in the region of 400,000 lire, but it was also used – after certain obvious modifications had been made to the tuning of course – by the works riders.

At that time there was no doubt that the new MV speedster was the fastest stroker around and, thanks to its all-round ability, it proved an ideal machine for privateers. However, in the more important races such as the Italian and World Championships (held for the first time in the 1949 season), it had no option but to give way to the greater power of the new four-stroke models which MV's rivals had produced specifically for the occasion, and which were sweeping all before them on circuits all over the country. Thus the 125 remained available to the public, but in 1950 the works team dropped it in favour of a new four-stroke model.

Power/rpm	
10.5 hp at 6700 rpm	
Dry weight	
65 kg	
Maximum speed	
130 km/h	

TECHNICAL SPECIFICATIONS

Model/year	125 Four-speed - 125 cm³ - 1949/50
Engine	2-stroke single 53 × 56 mm - 123.5 cm³
Compression ratio	10 : 1
Cylinder head/barrel	Light alloy - cast iron
Valve configuration	–
Timing system	–
Ignition	Flywheel magneto
Carburettor	Dell'Orto SS 25 A
Lubrication	8 : 1 petroil
Clutch	Wet multiplate
Gearbox	Four-speed in-unit
Transmission	Geared primary; final drive, chain
Frame/wheelbase	Tubular closed duplex cradle - 1270 mm
Front suspension	Girder fork
Rear suspension	Swinging arm with telescopic units and friction dampers
Wheels	Light alloy, wire spoked, 1.75 × 21"
Tyres	2.00-21" front and rear
Brakes	Lateral drums
Consumption	4.5 litres per 100 km
Fuel tank capacity	14 litres
Oil tank capacity	–

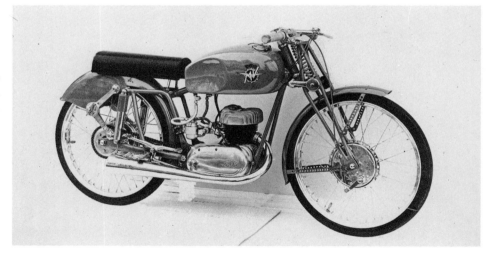

The 125 two-stroke from 1949, with redesigned engine, gearbox, frame and rear suspension. Note the horizontal carb with a separate float chamber.

125 Twin-cam 1950-1960

The 125 twin-cam of 1950 represented a real step forwards in terms of quality, as well as a breakaway from its two-stroke origins. From that time onwards the marque's racing machines were expressly designed to achieve the best possible results regardless of any merely commercial considerations. The 125 cm³ twin-cam engine was the base unit from which all the successive single and twin-cylinder competition engines used in the small/medium capacity classes were developed. For a long time a similar role was played by the contemporary four-cylinder engine as far as the larger categories were concerned. The twin-cam 125 remained in harness until 1960, and in this eleven year career it inevitably went through a series of modifications, after which it was very different from the original bike: it was modified structurally; the ignition system, gearbox, frame and suspension were all altered; it was fitted with progressively more "scientific" and extensive fairings; but throughout this process it never lost its original general layout. After a fairly lengthy period of testing and tuning, it became, in 1952, the first MV to win a world title; the first of a long series of triumphs spanning more than twenty years. Resurrected, in 1964, after a few years in retirement, it managed to win the 1964 Italian championship before being definitively consigned to the museum. The same bike also spawned a single-knocker variant, which we shall deal with a little later.

Power/rpm
13 hp at 10,000 rpm
Dry weight
78 kg
Maximum speed
140 km/h

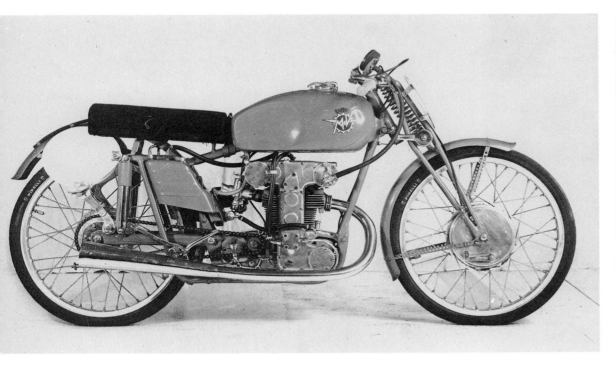

The 125 four-stroke, introduced in 1950, was expressly designed for racing and had nothing in common with the production bikes, which were still two-strokes. This bike had an interesting closed duplex cradle frame, with reinforcing struts outboard of the rear fork.

The first version of the 125 twin-cam engine with the straight camshaft cover and the oil pump housed on the timing gear casing. The magneto was mounted at the front.

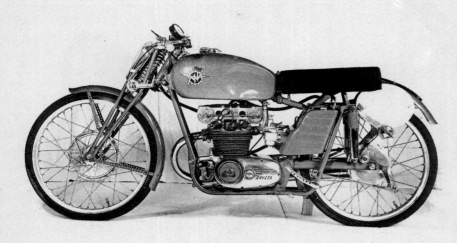

The 1950 engine had a small external flywheel. The oil tank was under the saddle.

The 1952 version had the oil pump assembly at the same height as the magneto.

The 1952 World Championship winning model, with a telescopic front fork and hydraulic dampers at the rear.

A Formula Two 125 twin-cam that took part in the 1955 "Motogiro". Note the spare valve springs.

The aluminium integral fairing prepared for the Grand Prix of Nations held at Monza in 1953.

The 1955 model had teledraulic forks with exposed springs and a front-mounted oil tank.

The transitional version from 1956, with the new demountable cradle frame (the couplings can be seen under the steering head), and the 1954 – type engine with magneto ignition and no flywheel.

An experimental engine prepared for fuel injection. The pump was housed in the square protruberance on the timing gear casing, visible above the drive chain sprocket.

TECHNICAL SPECIFICATIONS

Model/year	125 twin-cam - 125 cm^3 - 1950/51
Engine	4-stroke single 53 × 56 mm - 123.5 cm^3
Compression ratio	9.5 : 1
Cylinder head/barrel	Light alloy
Valve configuration	Inclined overhead
Timing system	Double overhead camshafts
Ignition	Magneto
Carburettor	Dell'Orto SS 25 A
Lubrication	Geared pressure pump
Clutch	Wet multiplate
Gearbox	Unit construction, four-speeds
Transmission	Geared primary; final drive, chain
Frame/wheelbase	Tubular closed duplex cradle - 1250 mm
Front suspension	Girder fork
Rear suspension	S/arm with telescopic units and friction dampers
Wheels	Steel, wire spoked, 1.75 × 21"
Tyres	2.00-21" front and rear
Brakes	Lateral drums 180 mm front and 150 mm rear
Consumption	–
Fuel tank capacity	15 litres
Oil tank capacity	2 kg

219

The last edition of the 125 twin-cam (from 1959) with coil ignition and arched camshaft cover. Note the new position of the oil pump.

Full view of the 1959 machine. The closed duplex cradle frame is in two parts bolted together. The oil tank is in front of the fuel tank.

Again the 1959 engine, this time seen from the primary drive side with the new cover and the distributor. Note the rubber mounted float chamber.

The 125 twin-cam with the last type of dolphin fairing, adopted after the abolition of dustbin fairings at the end of the 1957 season.

 **Shaft-drive Four 1950-53**

The 500 cm³ four-cylinder racing bike, unexpectedly presented at the 1950 Milan Trade Fair – a rare, if not unique example of a racing machine being presented to the public before it appeared on the circuits – marked MV's sensational entry into the large capacity classes. The company clearly intended to do things properly and to play a leading role right from the start. The bike, which was designed in the space of a few months by a small group of technicians headed by Pietro Remor, possessed a number of features not often found in a competition machine, such as shaft drive and torsion bar suspension. It made its debut at the Belgian Grand Prix, where it arrived just in time for practice after a long and eventful road trip in the company's transporter. Ridden by Arciso Artesiani, the newcomer managed a fourth place behind the battle-hardened Gilera and AJS entries, despite the fact that pre-race tuning and preparation amounted to no more than a twenty minute session on the test bed just before leaving Cascina Costa. The 500 four was always a very fast bike, but it suffered from some roadholding problems, and for the following year it was equipped with conventional telescopic suspension. Finally, in 1952, chain drive was adopted and a new version of the four-cylinder racer was created. The shaft-driven model, however, continued to be used occasionally. A shaft-driven version fitted with an Earles fork was used as a back-up for the new chain-driven model.

Power/rpm
50 hp at 9000 rpm
Dry weight
118 kg
Maximum speed
190 km/h

The 500 four with torsion bar suspension at front and rear. This extremely elegant version was prepared for the 1950 Milan Trade Fair. It was painted in metallic silver with light blue flashes.

TECHNICAL SPECIFICATIONS

Model/year	500 shaft-drive four - 500 cm^3 - 1950/51
Engine	4-stroke four-cylinder 54 × 54 × 4 - 494.4 cm^3
Compression ratio	9.5 : 1
Cylinder head/barrel	Light alloy
Valve configuration	Inclined overhead
Timing system	Double overhead camshafts
Ignition	Magneto
Carburettor	Dell'Orto SS 28 DS/SS 28 DD
Lubrication	Wet sump
Clutch	Single dry-plate, between gearbox and drive shaft
Gearbox	Unit construction, four-speeds
Transmission	Primary via bevel gears; final drive, cardan shaft
Frame/wheelbase	Tubular and pressed-steel closed duplex cradle - 1520 mm
Front suspension	Girder fork and torsion bars
Rear suspension	Twin swinging arms with torsion bars and friction dampers
Wheels	Steel, wire spoked, 2.75 × 20"
Tyres	Front 3.00-20", rear 3.25-20"
Brakes	Central drums, 230 mm front, and 220 mm rear
Consumption	–
Fuel tank capacity	18 litres
Oil tank capacity	2.5 kg

222

In 1951 a telescopic fork was adopted although the rear torsion bars were retained for a while longer.

The engine with shaft drive was fed by twin carbs. The clutch was located at the back of the gearbox.

Another shot of the early 1951 version. During the course of the season the rear torsion bars were eliminated and a four-carb set up was adopted.

The shaft-drive four was still used in 1953, with rear torsion bars and an Earles front fork. Note the faired disc in front of the steering head.

223

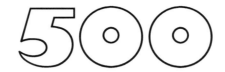 **Chain-drive Four**

The four-cylinder MV, introduced in 1950, was substantially modified for the 1952 season; the most important innovations included the adoption of chain drive and a five speed gearbox. MV's longest serving competition campaigner, the 500 four remained in harness for a good fifteen seasons, during which time it was subjected to continuous modification. A high achiever if ever there was one, this bike loaded many of the greatest riders of the time with fame and titles.

It would be virtually impossible to catalogue all of the modifications that were introduced over the years, largely because of the cloak of silence that the marque began to draw around its racing activities; for the same reason it has not been possible to supply the comprehensive photographic documentation that we would have liked.

Only the most important developments may be noted here therefore: the Earles fork used by Graham during 1952; the demountable cradle from 1954, which was later modified so that only the bottom rails could be detached for simpler engine removal; the adoption of the swinging arm with an eccentric pivot, and lastly a

vast array of fairings. From 1961 onwards the 4-cylinder chain-drive model was raced under the Privat name after MV had announced its official retirement from racing. It ended its career by passing the torch on to another of the MV's most famous and successful machines; namely the Tre Cilindri, the bike that Agostini made famous.

Power/rpm
56 hp at 10,500 rpm
Dry weight
140 kg
Maximum speed
230 km/h

TECHNICAL SPECIFICATIONS

Model/year	500 chain-drive four - 500 cm^3 - 1952/53
Engine	4-stroke four-cylinder 53 × 56.4 × 4 mm - 497.5 cm^3
Compression ratio	10 : 1
Cylinder head/barrel	Light alloy
Valve configuration	Inclined overhead
Timing system	Double overhead camshafts
Ignition	Lucas magneto
Carburettor	Four Dell'Orto SS 28
Lubrication	Wet sump
Clutch	Wet multiplate
Gearbox	Unit construction, five-speeds
Transmission	Geared primary; final drive, chain
Frame/wheelbase	Tubular closed duplex cradle - 1370 mm
Front suspension	Teledraulic fork/Earles fork
Rear suspension	Swinging arm with teledraulic dampers
Wheels	Light alloy, wire spoked, front 2.50 × 19"; rear 3.00 × 18"
Tyres	Front 3.00-19", rear 3.50-18"
Brakes	Central drums
Consumption	10 litres per 100 km
Fuel tank capacity	24 litres
Oil tank capacity	3 kg

The chain-driven 500 four can be distinguished from its shaft-drive predecessor mainly by the form of the crankcase, which differed due to the transverse location of the gearbox and clutch. Note the magneto behind the carburettors.

The first attempts at streamlining in 1952: the small cupola over the steering head was swept back to join the fuel tank.

In 1953 experiments were made with exposed spring rear suspension units.

1953 was also the year of the Earles fork. Note the generous dimensions of the frame.

The bike was equipped with a supplementary oil tank, located under the saddle, for the Isle of Man T.T.

Top left, a dustbin from 1957. The frame has been lowered and has detachable top rails for engine removal. On the right, the 1959/60 version with detachable lower rails. Above left, the new fairing and the Privat badge for the early '60s.

Above, the last version (1964/65). On the left, a detail of the square-section swinging arm tested in 1965; the eccentric pivot was first introduced in 1960.

125 Sohc 1953-1956

In 1953, with a view to allowing as many enthusiasts as possible to participate in motorcycle racing with reasonable hopes of success, the Motorcycling Federation revived Sport class racing for production-derived bikes on sale to the general public. Basically, the move was aimed at redressing the balance in favour of the privateers, who could no longer compete against the specially designed factory racers. Formula Sport enjoyed considerable success, but the regulations were gradually relaxed as time went by with the result that, in terms of looks, performance and unfortunately price, the bikes began to get more and more like the works racers they were supposed to be replacing. For 125 class racing, MV prepared and marketed a model that was virtually identical to the bike they had fielded in the Italian and World Championships. About the only difference was that the engine had a single camshaft as required by the original rules for this type of event. It was also equipped with an electrical lighting system (run off a flywheel magneto mounted on the left hand side) for events like the "Motogiro d'Italia" where the regulations demanded a full set of "street legal" accessories including lights, starter and registration plates. This model was a considerable success and remained in production until 1956. But this was by no means the end of the road for this sporty 125, which continued to be raced for some time afterwards in the hands of various privateers.

Power/rpm
16 hp at 10,300 rpm
Dry weight
75 kg
Maximum speed
150 km/h

227

TECHNICAL SPECIFICATIONS

Model/year	125 Single cam - 125 cm^3 - 1953/1956
Engine	4-stroke single 53 × 56 mm - 123.5 cm^3
Compression ratio	9.2 : 1
Cylinder head/barrel	Light alloy
Valve configuration	Inclined overhead
Timing system	Single overhead camshaft
Ignition	Magneto
Carburettor	Dell'Orto SS 27 A
Lubrication	Geared pressure pump
Clutch	Wet multiplate
Gearbox	Unit construction, four-speeds
Transmission	Geared primary; final drive, chain
Frame/wheelbase	Tubular closed duplex cradle - 1250 mm
Front suspension	Telescopic fork with a central hydraulic damper
Rear suspension	Swinging arm with hydraulic dampers
Wheels	Light alloy, wire spoked; front 1.75 × 19", rear 2.25 × 19"
Tyres	Front 2.00-19", rear 2.50-19"
Brakes	Central drums, front 180 mm, rear 150 mm
Consumption	–
Fuel tank capacity	14 litres
Oil tank capacity	2 kg

Above and overleaf, the 125 single-cam prepared for circuit racing.

The single-cam engine was directly derived from the works twin-cam unit. Note the oil pump.

The 125 single-cam in typical Formula Sport trim, with number plate, stand, starter, and electrical system powered by a small flywheel. This is the version prepared for the "Motogiro" of 1954.

Racing scooter equipped with the 125 cm³ single-cam engine. There was also a twin-cam version. An opening of just a few centimetres between the steering head and the fuel tank was enough to comply with the regulations.

350 Four 1953-1965

Power/rpm

42 hp at 11,000 rpm

Dry weight

145 kg

Maximum speed

210 km/h

The four-cylinder 350 was introduced without much fanfare in 1953. At first it was not seen as a serious class contender but more as a means of allowing the works riders to get better acquainted with courses – such as the Isle of Man – where the number of practice laps was never enough. But as things turned out the bike went on to make a very important contribution to the company's sporting image, particularly abroad where the 350 class attracted a strong following. The first 350 four, which actually made its debut at the T.T., was equipped with an engine that had been obtained by sleeving the bores of a 500. The makers did not get round to designing a new engine for this bike until later, and even then it had the familiar MV-type layout. Nevertheless, the 350 four obtained excellent results right from its debut season, when it romped home an easy winner in the German Grand Prix despite its not inconsiderable weight. Following Ray Amm's death it was sidelined for a while, only to reappear in a leading role in the hands of John Surtees, who was the first rider to take it to a World Championship title. From then on it starred in all the most important races, where it benefitted from the frame, fairing, and engine modifications made to the 500. Its domination only began to show signs of weakening in 1962 with the appearance of the Japanese bikes. Subsequently its appearances became rarer until it was replaced in 1965 by the lighter, more compact and manoeuverable three-cylinder model.

TECHNICAL SPECIFICATIONS

Model/year	350 Four - 350 cm^3 - 1953/55
Engine	4-stroke four 47.5 × 49.3 × 4 mm - 349.3 cm^3
Compression ratio	10.4 : 1
Cylinder head/barrel	Light alloy
Valve configuration	Inclined overhead
Timing system	Double overhead camshafts
Ignition	Lucas magneto
Carburettor	Dell'Orto SSI 28 A
Lubrication	Wet sump
Clutch	Wet multiplate
Gearbox	Unit construction, five speeds
Transmission	Geared primary; final drive, chain
Frame/wheelbase	Tubular closed duplex cradle - 1400 mm
Front suspension	Teledraulic fork
Rear suspension	Swinging arm with hydraulic dampers
Wheels	Light alloy, wire spoked; front 2.75 × 19", rear 3.25 × 19"
Tyres	Front 3.00-19", rear 3.25-19"
Brakes	Central drums, front twin-cam 240 mm, single-cam rear
Consumption	8.5 litres per 100 km
Fuel tank capacity	24 litres
Oil tank capacity	3 kg

The 350 cm^3 four-cylinder engine, structurally identical to the 500 from which it was derived in 1953.

The 350 prepared for the 1953 Grand Prix of Nations. Compare the structure of the Earles fork with that used on the 500 of the same period.

The 350 in the early Sixties, with partial fairing and detachable top rails. This example, conserved in the company museum, has had the Privat badging removed.

231

175 Twin-cam 1955-1958

Power/rpm

25 hp at 11,500 rpm

Dry weight

90 kg

Maximum speed

160 km/h

The "production derived" Formula Sport category was gradually transformed into Formula Two, open to Junior riders, in which the restrictions on technical developments were reduced to the point that even a bike like the MV 500 four could qualify. But the queen of this speciality, clearly intended for young riders, was the 175 class where the most famous marques of the moment were locked in mortal combat – Morini, Mondial, and – of course – MV. For these races, where works teams now competed openly, MV put aside the "Disco Volante"-type single overhead camshaft engine, and developed a new machine with a bigger double overhead camshaft engine (obtained by increasing the bore of the 125 unit from 53 to 63 mm) housed in a closed duplex cradle frame. The bike lived up to all expectations and notched up numerous wins, which culminated in outright victory in the Motogiro of 1957, the last year in which this prestigious race was held. As, in the meantime, the 175 class had been introduced to the Italian Senior Championship, MV also prepared a Grand Prix version of the new twin-cam with a dustbin fairing and without the various restrictions (carburettor diameter, etcetera) imposed by the Formula Two regulations. It lived up to its sparkling reputation and noble lineage in this specification as well, and in fact Masetti won the 1955 Championship with this bike. The Junior version was successfully raced until 1958.

TECHNICAL SPECIFICATIONS

Model/year	175 twin-cam - 175 cm^3 - 1955/1958
Engine	4-stroke single 63 × 56 mm - 174.5 cm^3
Compression ratio	9.5 : 1
Cylinder head/barrel	Light alloy
Valve configuration	Inclined overhead
Timing system	Double overhead camshafts
Ignition	Coil
Carburettor	Dell'Orto SS 25 A
Lubrication	Geared pressure pump
Clutch	Wet multiplate
Gearbox	Unit construction; five-speeds
Transmission	Geared primary; final drive, chain
Frame/wheelbase	Tubular closed duplex cradle - 1235 mm
Front suspension	Teledraulic fork
Rear suspension	Swinging arm with hydraulic dampers
Wheels	Light alloy, wire spoked, 2.25 × 19"
Tyres	2.50-19", or 2.75-19"
Brakes	Central drums, front 180 mm or 200 mm, rear 150 mm
Consumption	–
Fuel tank capacity	18 litres
Oil tank capacity	3 kg

One of the last versions of the 175 cm^3 twin-cam engine, which also had an arched camshaft cover and coil ignition.

The 175 twin-cam was specifically created for the Formula Two category derived from the earlier Formula Sport. This is the bike that won the Motogiro d'Italia in 1957 with Remo Venturi. The frame is similar to that of the 250 G.P.

It is interesting to note the preparations necessary for a long distance race: cushions on the tank, tool bag on the number plate, spare valve spring, a pear-shaped bulb horn. The oil tank is in front of the saddle.

203 250 Single

Power/rpm

29 hp at 9800 rpm

Dry weight

96 kg

Maximum speed

200 Km/h

MV's debut in the 250 class dates from the Shell Gold Cup event held at Imola in 1955, when a 203 cm³ machine derived from the 175 twin-cam was entered. Despite the undersized engine, its greater lightness and ease of handling compared with its full 250 cm³ rivals – most of which were not particularly modern in conception – allowed the MV to go straight to the top of its class. In its first year the new bike won the World Constructors' Championship after wins in the T.T., in Holland, and at Monza. In spite of these remarkable early results, it would not have been sensible to continue to give away all those cubic centimetres to the opposition, and therefore the engine was gradually bored out to the full capacity. At the beginning of 1956 it was increased to 220 cm³, and then a 249 cm³ engine was prepared for the World Championship races. This version (it was raced with either the dustbin or the full fairing) was also very successful, racking up a good number of wins, which culminated in the World Championships of 1956 and 1958. Stripped of its fairing and modified to comply with the other restrictions, it also competed in the Italian Junior Championship. Experiments with fuel injection were also carried out on this engine. Pressure from increasingly strong competition led the company to adopt new and more radical technology however, and in 1959 the men in charge at Cascina Costa decided it was time to move on to a twin-cylinder engine.

TECHNICAL SPECIFICATIONS

Model/year	250 single - 250 cm³ - 1956/1958
Engine	4-stroke single 72.6 × 60 mm - 248.2 cm³
Compression ratio	10 : 1
Cylinder head/barrel	Light alloy
Valve configuration	Inclined overhead
Timing system	Double overhead camshafts
Ignition	Coil
Carburettor	Dell'Orto SS 25 A
Lubrication	Geared pressure pump
Clutch	Wet multiplate
Gearbox	Unit construction, five-speeds
Transmission	Geared primary; final drive, chain
Frame/wheelbase	Tubular closed duplex cradle - 1230 mm
Front suspension	Teledraulic fork
Rear suspension	Swinging arm with hydraulic dampers
Wheels	Light alloy, wire spoked, 2.25 × 19"
Tyres	Front 2.50-19", rear 2.75-19"
Brakes	Central drums, front 220 mm rear 180 mm
Consumption	–
Fuel tank capacity	16 litres
Oil tank capacity	2 kg

The medium capacity single-cylinder engine started out as a 203 cm³ unit before it was bored out to 250 cm³. A classic small capacity MV engine design.

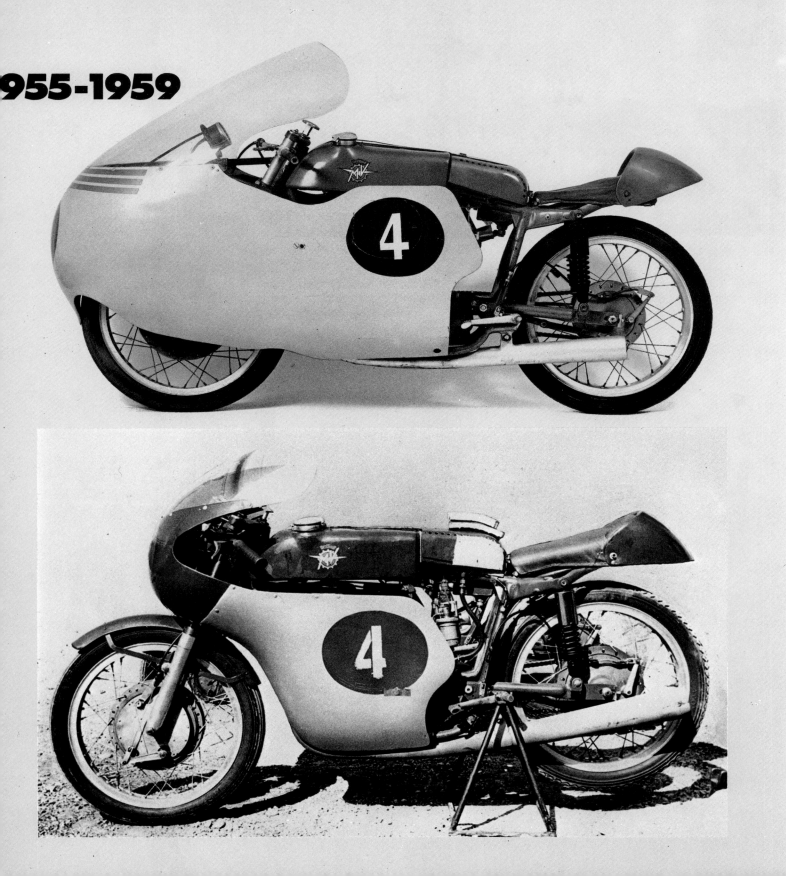

955-1959

The 250 single with the dustbin fairing used in 1957. For fast circuits such as Monza this bike was fitted with an integral fairing with a rear tail section, like the one seen on the 125 twin-cam.

The partial fairing adopted after 1957. The oil tank was located in front of the saddle. The rear section of the frame was a modified version of the 125 layout.

350 Twin 1957

The twin-cylinder twin-cam engine designed by Giannini in 1955 – described in the section dedicated to touring bike production – served as the base, two years later, for the creation of a new racing motorcycle with some rather unusual structural and technical features. The 350 cm³ engine retained the cylinders inclined at 45 degrees and the fan-like finning on the cylinder head, but it had been transformed by the adoption of magneto ignition and a dry sump lubrication system with a double gear pump; furthermore the gearbox now had five speeds. It was the frame, however, that constituted the most original part of this machine: it was a spaceframe structure made up of small diameter tubes that partially enclosed the engine, following a pattern derived from aeronautical practice. This kind of layout was enjoying widespread popularity at the time, for example in Formula One racing cars, as it assured both considerable rigidity and remarkable lightness. The front fork was an Earles-type unit which was also made up of small diameter tubing. The bike underwent lengthy testing, both privately and during practice sessions at various Grand Prix meetings, where it was generally entrusted to the talented but sometimes inconsistent Australian rider Ken Kavanagh. In the end, however, it was abandoned in preference to the tried and tested four. The latter may well have been a far less handy machine than the twin but it could offer a lot more horsepower.

Power/rpm	
47 hp at 12,000 rpm	
Dry weight	
132 kg	
Maximum speed	
-	

TECHNICAL SPECIFICATIONS

Model/year	350 Twin - 1957
Engine	4-stroke twin 62 × 57.8 × 2 mm - 348.8 cm³
Compression ratio	10.5 : 1
Cylinder head/barrel	Light alloy
Valve configuration	Inclined overhead
Timing system	Double overhead camshafts
Ignition	Magneto
Carburettor	Two Dell'Orto SS 29 A
Lubrication	Geared pressure pump
Clutch	Dry multiplate
Gearbox	Unit construction, five-speeds
Transmission	Geared primary; final drive, chain
Frame/wheelbase	Tubular spaceframe - 1380 mm
Front suspension	Modified Earles fork
Rear suspension	Swinging arm with hydraulic dampers
Wheels	Light alloy, wire spoked; front 2.75 × 19", rear 3.75 × 19"
Tyres	Front 3.00-19", rear 4.00-19"
Brakes	Central drums, front twin-cam 230 mm, rear single cam 180 mm
Consumption	–
Fuel tank capacity	24 litres
Oil tank capacity	3 kg

The 350 twin was inspired by the 300 cm³ touring unit produced at the time. The timing gear was in the centre. Note the typical fan-like finning around the cylinder head.

236

Both the frame and the Earles fork had a tubular spaceframe structure. Note also the considerable height of the rear of the bike, the adjustable rear swinging arm springs, and the large rear sprocket.

Unusually, the engine was fitted with two small external flywheels, one on either side. The oil tank was in the centre, under the saddle. The brake system, with a twin-cam 4LS unit at the front, was quite something for those days.

The first 250 cm³ twin was developed at Cascina Costa in 1955 by siamesing two 125 cm³ cylinders, but the results did not come up to expectations and the experiment was shelved for the time being. The idea of a twin-cylinder engine for the 250 class was revived in the winter of 1958/59, as the single-cylinder unit was beginning to feel the opposition breathing down its neck. This time, however, a completely new engine was produced, which had nothing in common with the company's previous products. While the engine was still undersquare, the cylinders were now tilted forwards at 10 degrees, a wet sump lubrication system was used and the bike was fitted with coil ignition: the valves, needless to say, were actuated by twin camshafts. The new engine immediately produced 5 hp more than the old unit and top speed promised to be around 220 km/h despite the reduced fairing imposed by the new regulations. The 250 twin won the World Championship in 1959 and 1960, and, had its development continued, it undoubtedly would have been capable of competing effectively for some time with the swarms of Japanese bikes that were beginning to appear. But Count Domenico's decision to withdraw from works racing in 1961, which was followed by the decision to concentrate on the larger capacity classes, took the bike off the race tracks, and subsequently it made only occasional appearances. Its last outing was at Alicante in 1966 when Agostini rode it to victory.

250 Twin 1959-1966

Power/rpm

36 hp at 12,000 rpm

Dry weight

109 kg

Maximum speed

220 km/h

TECHNICAL SPECIFICATIONS

Model/year	250 Twin - 250 cm³ - 1959/1966
Engine	4-stroke Twin 53 × 56 × 2 mm - 247 cm³
Compression ratio	10.8 : 1
Cylinder head/barrel	Light alloy
Valve configuration	Inclined overhead
Timing system	Double overhead camshafts
Ignition	Coil and twin spark plugs
Carburettor	Two Dell'Orto SS 31 A
Lubrication	Wet sump
Clutch	Wet multiplate
Gearbox	Unit construction, seven-speeds
Transmission	Geared primary; final drive, chain
Frame/wheelbase	Tubular closed duplex cradle - 1310 mm
Front suspension	Teledraulic fork
Rear suspension	Swinging arm with hydraulic dampers
Wheels	Light alloy, wire spoked, 2.50 × 18"
Tyres	2.75-18"
Brakes	Central drums, front twin-cam 210 mm, rear single-cam
Consumption	–
Fuel tank capacity	15 litres
Oil tank capacity	2 kg

Wet sump lubrication was a new feature for lightweight MV racing engines. The cylinders were inclined at 10 degrees. Note the large contact breaker for the twin-spark ignition.

While it had the so-called featherbed layout at the steering head, the cradle had an unusual shape that closely followed the line of the engine unit.

The 250 twin was equipped with pivots mounted ahead of the fork struts and a square-section swinging arm, features that are still current today. The front brake was a twin-cam 4LS unit.

The 250 twin with the usual fairing. At that time the fairings were hand-beaten from aluminium or elektron. The colour scheme was the typical MV red and silver.

500 Six 1957-1958

Power/rpm

75 hp at 15,000 rpm

Dry weight

145 kg

Maximum speed

240 km/h

A new six-cylinder MV 500 made its debut at the Monza autodrome during practice for the 1957 Grand Prix of Nations. Technical honours that year were divided between the Gilera four and the eight-cylinder Guzzi – the maximum expression of the multi-cylinder concept ever applied to a motorcycle – and it was logical for MV's research and development squad to follow the same route in the search for higher rev limits and therefore greater performance. The layout of the six-cylinder engine resembled that of the earlier MV four: the cylinders were set across the frame and inclined forwards at 10 degrees, primary drive was via a gear train driven off one end of the crankshaft, the gearbox was a six-speeder, and the spark was provided by a magneto. The use of chrome-bore cylinder barrels was a particularly interesting feature. The frame was modelled on those used at the time for the Quattro Cilindri, with a tubular double triangulation at the rear, and a demountable cradle to enable the propulsion unit to be removed with the minimum of effort. The 500 cm³ six appeared in practice at a number of other races and took part in the Monza Grand Prix in 1958 with Hartle in the saddle. The absence of a worthy adversary however (after the withdrawal of Guzzi, Gilera, and Mondial from the sporting arena), rendered further development of the bike superfluous, and it was abandoned before it had the chance to demonstrate its full potential.

The first six-cylinder MV was created in 1957: a remarkable machine, it was rendered virtually pointless by the absence of a worthy adversary and wound up on the shelf before it had the opportunity to express its full potential.

The six-cylinder had a spaceframe structure at the rear with a detachable lower cradle, a design that was also used for the four-cylinder model. The front brake had four cams.

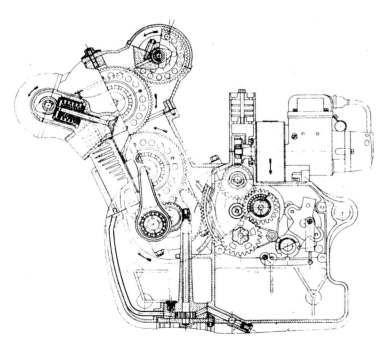

The structure of the six-cylinder engine was virtually identical to that of the four. Note the magneto drive taken off the transmission gearing.

TECHNICAL SPECIFICATIONS

Model/year	6 - 500 cm^3 - 1957/1958
Engine	4-stroke six 48 × 46 × 6 mm - 499.2 cm^3
Compression ratio	10.8 : 1
Cylinder head/barrel	Light alloy
Valve configuration	Inclined overhead
Timing system	Double overhead camshafts
Ignition	Magneto
Carburettor	Six Dell'Orto SSI 26 A
Lubrication	Wet sump
Clutch	Wet multiplate
Gearbox	Unit construction, six-speeds
Transmission	Geared primary; final drive, chain
Frame/wheelbase	Tubular closed duplex cradle - 1350 mm
Front suspension	Teledraulic fork
Rear suspension	Swinging arm with hydraulic dampers
Wheels	Light alloy, wire spoked; front 2.75 × 18", rear 3.25 × 18"
Tyres	Front 3.00-18", rear 3.50/5.20-18"
Brakes	Central drums, front quad-cam 260 mm, rear twin-cam 190 mm
Consumption	–
Fuel tank capacity	22 litres
Oil tank capacity	3 kg

125 Disc Valve 1965

Power/rpm

21 hp at 12,000 rpm

Dry weight

69 kg

Maximum speed

–

In the mid-Sixties the two-stroke engine began, with increasing success, to challenge the domination of the four-stroke: technical innovations and above all the remarkable technological progress made in the early part of that same decade had bridged the gap in performance between the two and even promised to turn the tables before long. In fact it was in 1965 that MV, very aware of the latest developments as usual, began working on a new small racing motorcycle with a 125 cm³ two-stroke engine featuring all the technical developments that a mere ten years later would come to be seen as essential for success in the dog-cat-dog world of top-flight competition: these included a chromed cylinder barrel with a ringless piston, a disc valve, lubrication via a separate tank and pump, and water cooling. Furthermore, as far as the cycle parts were concerned, the bike, which had a closed duplex cradle frame and teledraulic suspension, also boasted a front disc brake, albeit a mechanically controlled one. The new sportster appeared for the first time during practice at Cesenatico in the spring of 1965, and was occasionally seen at other events although it never actually appeared on the grid.

As you would expect, it needed the usual lengthy spell of testing and development, but after a number of experiments this promising project was abandoned, partly because Count Domenico Agusta had never displayed much enthusiasm for it.

TECHNICAL SPECIFICATIONS

Model/year	125 2-stroke - 125 cm³ - 1965
Engine	2-stroke single 54.2 × 54 mm - 124.5 cm³
Compression ratio	14 : 1
Cylinder head/barrel	Light alloy
Valve configuration	–
Timing system	–
Ignition	Coil
Carburettor	Dell'Orto SSI 29 D
Lubrication	Separate oil and piston-type pump
Clutch	Wet multiplate
Gearbox	Unit construction, seven speeds
Transmission	Geared primary; final drive, chain
Frame/wheelbase	Tubular closed duplex cradle - 1275 mm
Front suspension	Teledraulic fork
Rear suspension	Swinging arm with hydraulic dampers
Wheels	Light alloy, wire spoked, 2.25 × 18"
Tyres	Front 2.50-18", rear 2.75-18"
Brakes	Front mechanically-operated 230 mm disc, rear 150 mm central drum
Consumption	–
Fuel tank capacity	16 litres
Oil tank capacity	1.5 kg

The extremely advanced two-stroke engine introduced – with out any great conviction to tell the truth – in 1965. The disc valve is on the right, the oil pump is partly hidden under the base of the radiator.

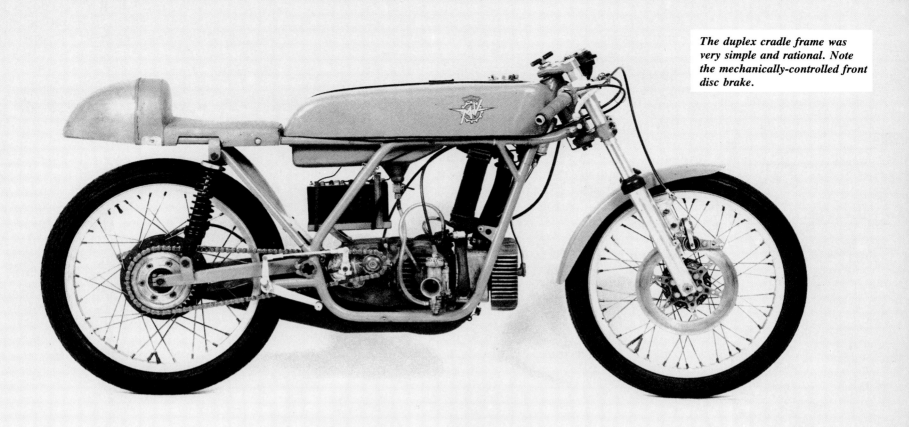

350 Three 1965-1973

The 350 three-cylinder was brought out in 1965, when the old four had begun to feel the pace, at least in this capacity class. It was an all-new machine, with an unusual engine format, particularly for a four-stroke, that was destined – along with its 500 cm³ stablemate – to become one of the most famous racing motorcycles of all time, forever linked with the name of Giacomo Agostini and his legendary exploits. It made its debut at Imola in 1965, and its last appearances were in 1973: this was the period of greatest success and popularity for MV and also the beginning of its decline. At first the three-cylinder engine produced a few less horses than the old four, but it was lighter, smaller and nimbler, which made it immediately competitive. In its first few seasons, however, a number of unfortunate circumstances prevented it from getting the better of its Japanese rivals – which had recently entered the international racing arena in strength – but as soon as the MV reached its peak of development it was good enough to win four consecutive world titles from 1968 to 1971. The intense development work was a continuous process always carried out in the strictest secrecy, which makes it next to impossible to retrace all the phases today. Furthermore false information was often spread in order to keep the competition guessing. The data that we have published, however, are the fruit of long and patient research and can be considered as official and reliable.

Power/rpm

62.5 hp at 13,500 rpm

Dry weight

116 kg

Maximum speed

240 km/h

TECHNICAL SPECIFICATIONS

Model/year	350 Three-cylinder - 350 cm³ - 1965/1966
Engine	4-stroke in-line three 48 × 46 × 3 mm - 343.9 cm³
Compression ratio	11 : 1
Cylinder head/barrel	Light alloy
Valve configuration	Inclined overhead
Timing system	Double overhead camshafts
Ignition	Coil
Carburettor	Three Dell'Orto SS 28 B
Lubrication	Wet sump
Clutch	Dry multiplate
Gearbox	Unit construction, seven speeds
Transmission	Geared primary; final drive, chain
Frame/wheelbase	Demountable tubular duplex cradle - 1310 mm
Front suspension	Teledraulic fork
Rear suspension	Swinging arm with hydraulic dampers
Wheels	Light alloy, wire spoked, 2.75 × 18"
Tyres	Front 3.00-18", rear 3.25-18"
Brakes	Central drums, front quad-cam 240 mm, rear twin-cam 230 mm
Consumption	–
Fuel tank capacity	16 litres
Oil tank capacity	3 kg

Without doubt one of the most famous racing engines of recent times, the 350 version of the three-cylinder MV was produced in 1965. See the first section of the book for photographs of the internal details.

The large photo below shows the first version of the 350 Tre Cilindri, fitted with drum brakes. On the right, a lightened example with twin hydraulic front discs, fitted in 1973. The same modification was also made to the 500. Here the fuel tank has a slightly different form.

 **Three 1966-1974**

In 1966 the three-cylinder format was also adopted for the new 500, in order to meet the threat posed by Honda. The first example was practically constructed on the battlefield, during the practice sessions for the Dutch Grand Prix.

The cylinders of a 350 cm³ engine were bored out to 55 mm, thus obtaining a total capacity of 377 cm³; this was further increased to 420 cm³, and then again to a point near the limit for the category at 497.9 cm³. The three- cylinder 500 – perhaps even more so than the 350 – was linked to the golden years of Giacomo Agostini, who rode the bike to his first world title in 1966, overcoming his ex-teammate Mike Hailwood; his domination was to last unbroken until 1973, an exploit unique in the history of motorcycle racing. Researchers interested in the history of the 350 tend to encounter the same problems as those interested in the 500; its development was also veiled in the most absolute secrecy, broken only by occasional – and usually deliberately inexact – "leaks", most of which concerned bore and stroke measurements, the numbers of valves and gear ratios in particular. Many secrets have now been revealed, but the passage of time has left no trace of much of the work carried out, and so now even the factory is unable to reconstruct an exact chronology of the various modifications.

These pages contain all the information we have been able to find that might be of interest to our readers.

Power/rpm	
78 hp at 12,000 rpm	
Dry weight	
118 kg	
Maximum speed	
260 km/h	

TECHNICAL SPECIFICATIONS

Model/year	500 Three-cylinder 500 cm³ - 1967/1972
Engine	4-stroke in-line three 62 × 55 × 3 mm - 497.9 cm³
Compression ratio	11 : 1
Cylinder head/barrel	Light alloy
Valve configuration	Inclined overhead
Timing system	Double overhead camshafts
Ignition	Coil
Carburettor	Three Dell'Orto MASSI 27 A
Lubrication	Wet sump
Clutch	Dry multiplate
Gearbox	Unit construction, seven speeds
Transmission	Geared primary; final drive, chain
Frame/wheelbase	Demountable tubular duplex cradle - 1310 mm
Front suspension	Teledraulic fork
Rear suspension	Swinging arm with hydraulic dampers
Wheels	Light alloy, wire spoked, 2.75 × 18"
Tyres	Front 3.00-18", rear 3.25-18"
Brakes	Central drums, front quad-cam 240 mm, rear twin-cam 230 mm
Consumption	–
Fuel tank capacity	18 litres
Oil tank capacity	3 kg

The 500 cm³ three-cylinder engine was virtually identical to the 350 unit. The reader is again referred to the first section of the book for detail photographs.

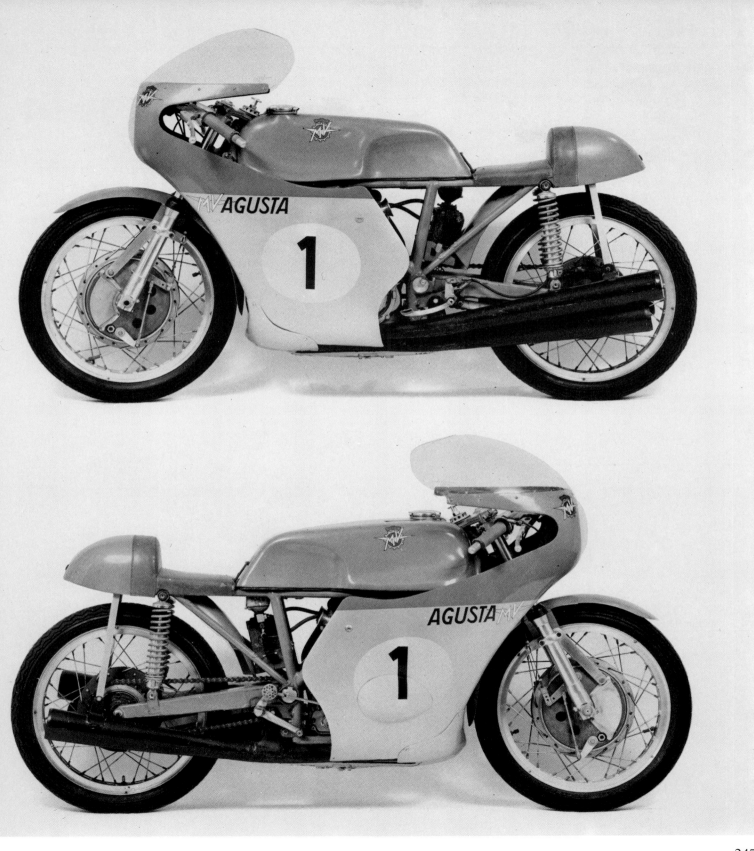

A half-litre version of the Tre Cilindri with drum brakes; the four-cam front brake was produced by MV or Ceriani: Ceriani also supplied the forks and most of the rear elements.

The cycle parts were also virtually identical to the 350; therefore the photographs of the 350 frame structure also apply to this model. Both bikes were painted red and silver.

247

350 Six 1969

The 350 six-cylinder is, without doubt, one of the most mysterious of the MV racing bikes. It was built in 1969 and tested during practice sessions at some of the Grand Prix meetings. Very few photographs of the six are known to exist, just a few fortuitous snapshots taken here and there. In all probability, those we have chosen to publish are probably the only ones that show the bike without the fairing. The engine assembly with its practically vertical cylinders (they were inclined forwards at just 10 degrees) was a forerunner of the later four-cylinder units that were to win the marque's last racing honours. It had double overhead camshafts driven by a gear train at the centre of the block, while the primary drive was taken – as it was with the 500 six – from one end of the crankshaft. This motorcycle underwent lengthy development testing which revealed, as you would expect, that it was no easy bike to tune. For example, it was found necessary to abandon the futuristic electronic ignition in favour of the tried and tested coil. The results would certainly have been worth the trouble (right from its very first outings the engine had been producing over 70 hp) had the machine been able to complete its apprenticeship, but then new international sporting regulations were introduced that limited the number of cylinders in the 350 and 500 classes to four, in an attempt to discourage over-sophisticated engineering. Needless to say, the experiments with the six came to an abrupt halt.

Power/rpm
72 hp at 16,000 rpm
Dry weight
125 kg
Maximum speed
250 km/h

The imposing yet sleek structure of the 350 six. The frame was a closed cradle with detachable bottom rails.

The battery of six carburettors, the large-bore oil breather pipe, and the dry clutch. The ignition distributor was on the right, in front of the cylinder block (see the photo on the facing page).

The timing gear was in the centre; note the narrow valve angle and the oil cooler in front of the fuel tank.

TECHNICAL SPECIFICATIONS

Model/year	350 six - 350 cm^3 - 1969
Engine	4-stroke six 43.3 × 39.5 × 6 mm - 348.8 cm^3
Compression ratio	11 : 1
Cylinder head/barrel	Light alloy
Valve configuration	Inclined overhead
Timing system	Double overhead camshafts
Ignition	Coil
Carburettor	Six Dell'Orto SS 19
Lubrication	Wet sump
Clutch	Dry multiplate
Gearbox	Unit construction, seven speeds
Transmission	Geared primary; final drive, chain
Frame/wheelbase	Demountable tubular duplex cradle - 1350 mm
Front suspension	Teledraulic fork
Rear suspension	Swinging arm with hydraulic dampers
Wheels	Light alloy, wire spoked, 2.75 × 18"
Tyres	Front 3.00-18", rear 3.25-18"
Brakes	Central drums, front quad-cam 240 mm, rear twin-cam 230 mm
Consumption	–
Fuel tank capacity	18 litres
Oil tank capacity	3 kg

350 Four 1971-1976

At the begining of the Seventies MV's domination of the larger capacity classes was still fairly solid, but clouds were beginning to appear on the eastern horizon. The Japanese were bringing the two-stroke engine to output levels that would have been unthinkable just a few years earlier. The manoeuverability of the three-cylinder MV was no longer sufficient, as the Japanese bikes were lighter still. The only available course of action was to augment power output by increasing the rev limit and the number of cylinders. The brand new four-cylinder machine had its first outing at the Grand Prix of Nations in 1971 but tuning it was a time consuming business, so much so that it was used alternately with the three-cylinder model for the whole of the following season. It won the world title just the same, and in 1973 it carried Agostini to the riders' title. By now, however, the supremacy of the strokers was complete; and furthermore the first signs of uncertainty were appearing at MV as a prelude to the company's pulling out of motorcycle production altogether, so that it was impossible to undertake long term projects. The 350 four-cylinder was improved as far as possible by fitting electronic ignition and carrying out a good deal of work on the frame and suspension. After Agostini's dramatic defection, the 350 four was sidelined for a couple of years, following which it reappeared to snatch two victories at Assen and Mugello before retiring for good.

Power/rpm	
70 hp at 16,000 rpm	
Dry weight	
115 kg	
Maximum speed	
250 km/h	

The four-cylinder engine from 1971 had a number of features in common with the six.

TECHNICAL SPECIFICATIONS

Model/year	350 four - 350 cm³ - 1971/1976
Engine	4-stroke four 53 × 38.2 × 4 mm - 349.8 cm³
Compression ratio	12.2 : 1
Cylinder head/barrel	Light alloy
Valve configuration	Inclined overhead
Timing system	Double overhead camshafts
Ignition	Electronic
Carburettor	Four Dell'Orto SS 28 A
Lubrication	Wet sump
Clutch	Dry multiplate
Gearbox	Unit construction, six speeds
Transmission	Geared primary; final drive, chain
Frame/wheelbase	Demountable tubular duplex cradle - 1320 mm
Front suspension	Teledraulic fork
Rear suspension	Swinging arm with hydraulic dampers
Wheels	Light alloy, wire spoked/cast 18"
Tyres	Front 3.25-18"/3.50-18", rear 3.25- 18"/3.50-18"
Brakes	Front 250 mm twin discs, rear 230 mm single disc
Consumption	–
Fuel tank capacity	18 litres
Oil tank capacity	3 kg

Originally the ignition was by a traditional coil, but this was later replaced by an electronic system. The frame was demountable (note the bolts under the steering head).

250

 **Four 1973-1976**

In the 500 class the three-cylinder engine proved adequate throughout 1972, albeit with some difficulty, but a four had to be brought in for the the 1973 season. Following the usual MV practice, the first engine was undersized at 433 cm³ (56 × 44 × 4), with later versions being brought up to the full capacity. This bike was perhaps the most intensively developed of all the racing MVs: in the struggle to make it more competitive it was subjected to continuous modifications both to the frame and to the engine, which used two different bore and stroke ratios (see the technical specifications). "Monocross" rear suspension was tried with the aid of hydraulic dampers on either side of the wheel. The braking system evolved from drums to front discs and finally to an integral-disc set up with cast-alloy wheels. In 1973, however, the new four-cylinder machine managed to bring home both the Riders' (Read) and the Manufacturers' titles, whilst the following year – thanks to the way the points total was calculated – Read won the riders' title but the marque missed out on the Manufacturers' championship. 1975 was an unlucky year and 1976 was a poor one right from the outset, despite the fact that Agostini's return ensured sponsorship by Marlboro. MV's last victory in a World Championship event and the marque's last victory in the half-litre class was notched up at the Nurburgring in August; after that the final curtain fell on the most glorious motorcycling saga of all time.

Power/rpm
98 hp at 14,000 rpm
Dry weight
120 kg
Maximum speed
285 km/h

TECHNICAL SPECIFICATIONS

Model/year	500 four - 500 cm³ - 1974/76
Engine	4-stroke four 58 × 47.2 × 4 mm - 498.6 cm³
Compression ratio	11.2 : 1
Cylinder head/barrel	Light alloy
Valve configuration	Inclined overhead
Timing system	Double overhead camshafts
Ignition	Magneto
Carburettor	Four Dell'Orto E 154-32
Lubrication	Wet sump
Clutch	Dry multiplate
Gearbox	Unit construction, six speeds
Transmission	Geared primary; final drive, chain
Frame/wheelbase	Demountable tubular duplex cradle - 1360 mm
Front suspension	Teledraulic fork
Rear suspension	Swinging arm with hydraulic dampers
Wheels	Cast light alloy 18"
Tyres	Front 3.25-18"/3.50-18", rear 4.00- 18"/4.50/4.75-18"
Brakes	Front twin 250 mm discs, rear single 230 mm disc
Consumption	–
Fuel tank capacity	18 litres
Oil tank capacity	3 kg

Above and overleaf, the 500 four from 1973, with a traditional frame. Unlike the 350, this engine had magneto ignition, located at the front.

In 1974 a new frame was adopted with struts running from the steering head to the swinging arm that were arched to clear the cylinder head. Cast alloy wheels were fitted along with three hydraulic disc brakes. The swinging arm mounting was also changed.

On this example, also from 1974, note the oil cooler in front of the steering head and a new, more anatomical, fuel tank. The frame downtubes are set at a different angle.

In 1975 experiments were carried
out on a frame with the
traditional telescopic rear
suspension units mounted at an
acute – and adjustable – angle.
Note the perforations on the nose
of the fairing to allow air onto
the oil cooler.

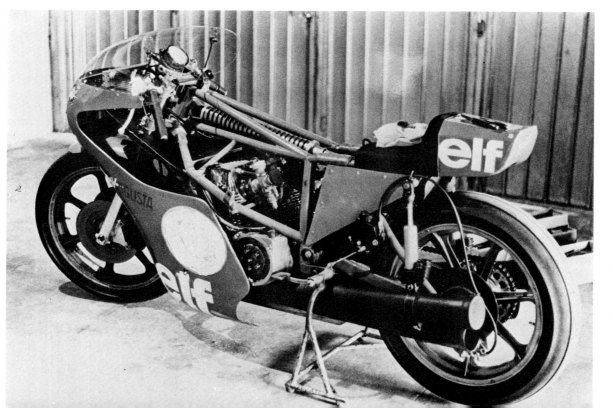

A frame with "monocross" rear
suspension was also prepared
and raced in 1975. Apart from
the triangulation of the frame,
note the small hydraulic dampers
at the sides of the rear wheel.

Thanks to sponsors Marlboro, the MV 500 appeared for a certain period in 1976 painted in a red and white colour scheme, within which the glorious Cascina Costa badge was of almost secondary importance compared with that of the cigarette company (top left). Top right and left, the last version of the MV (also dated 1976) with further frame modifications; the lateral struts had disappeared in favour of a more traditional duplex cradle structure with detachable bottom rails for easy engine removal. The fuel tank was also changed and the megaphones were upswept as high as possible. A slick tyre was mounted on the rear wheel whilst a treaded cover continued to be used at the front. And with this specification the MV 500 bowed out of the magical world of competition.

Finito di stampare
dalla Poligrafiche Bolis S.p.A.
nel mese di marzo 2000